Running Ultras

Dedication

For Josh.

Your senior photo was folded inside my bib number
during the 2006 Western States Endurance Run.

Even though you were battling an ultra of your own,
your presence provided the inspiration
I needed to get me to the finish line.

Al Barker was the only person other than me who knew about this.

Until now…

RUNNING ULTRAS

TO THE EDGE OF EXHAUSTION

BY SCOTT LUDWIG

Meyer & Meyer Sport

British Library Cataloguing in Publication Data
A catalogue record for this book is available from the British Library

Running Ultras
To the Edge of Exhaustion
Maidenhead: Meyer & Meyer Sport (UK) Ltd., 2014
ISBN: 978-1-78255-046-4

© 2014 by Meyer & Meyer Sport (UK) Ltd.
Aachen, Auckland, Beirut, Budapest, Cairo, Cape Town, Dubai, Hägendorf,
Indianapolis, Singapore, Sydney, Tehran, Wien
Member of the World Sport Publishers' Association (WSPA)
Printed by: Versa Press
ISBN: 978-1-78255-046-4
E-Mail: info@m-m-sports.com
www.m-m-sports.com

CONTENTS

CONTENTS

FOREWORD:
THE EDGE OF EXHAUSTION

There's nothing I fear more and no place I'd rather be.

I have run every day since November 30, 1978. I have run over 135,000 miles in my lifetime to this point. I've competed in 800 races, 250 of them at marathon distance or longer. I married my wife Cindy before I started running. We've raised two sons and were blessed with a grandchild in 2009. Cindy and I have both worked steadily since we graduated from the University of Florida in 1977. In addition to our day jobs, Cindy opened a retail store early in 2012; as for me, I've been writing books and articles about running as well as putting together my Darkside Running Club's newsletter for the past decade or so.

As you can imagine, sacrifices had to be made along the way. For me, the number one sacrifice has been sleep. On a good night, I'm lucky to sleep five and a half hours. It's difficult to get much more than that as I wake up every day at 3:30 a.m. to get in my daily run. On weekends, I get to sleep in until 4:00 a.m., as those are the days for either racing or getting in a long run of 20 miles or more. I calculated that over the past 35 years I have been awake the equivalent of three and a half years longer than a person who has slept a more familiar eight hours a day in those 35 years.[1]

---

1   Let me be up front with you and tell you I'm a numbers guy. My world has always revolved around numbers, at work and at play (the latter will be very evident in this book).

For many years earlier in my running career, I ran two times a day—sometimes even three or four. There was a 20-year stretch that, if I had any free time (before our sons were born, later when they were in daycare and I had time for a post-work run before I had to pick them up, and later still when Cindy and I became empty-nesters), I would go for an additional run. There was nothing I enjoyed more than finishing my last run of the day, taking a shower and savoring the well-earned rest that comes after taking full advantage of every waking minute I had.

This running regimen prepared me well for what was known at the time as the *running boom*. Thanks to people like Frank Shorter and Bill Rodgers, the general public became fascinated with running marathons, or 26.2-mile footraces. I was certainly one of those who became enamored with long-distance running; in fact, soon after my first marathon I was looking for more. It didn't take long to discover there were running events farther than the marathon: the ultramarathon.

Running allowed me to visit places and cross finish lines I would have never dreamed possible. I'm not the most physically gifted runner in the world. I didn't inherit what I would consider to be "running genes." I simply have the mental and physical conditioning made possible by my daily regimen of pushing myself to the edge of exhaustion.

I have found every run to be an adventure. I've lost track of how many crazy thoughts have crossed my mind, how many amazing people I've met, how many incredible places I've been, and how many unbelievable things have happened in my running lifetime, but I can promise you that the very best of them will be presented to you in the contents of this book. I have literally put my heart and sole (pun intended) into providing you with the inspiration, motivation, and confidence to lace 'em up and get out there and run and discover what I am writing about. I guarantee it will change your life.

Scott at Peachtree Roadrace, July 1987

Run for fitness…run for fun…run as a relief for stress and anxiety… run to clear your mind… run to get your thoughts in order… run to be free!

Run a mile. Run a 5K or a 10K. Run a half marathon. Run a marathon. There's a distance for everyone!

If you're intrigued and fascinated by the ever-growing community of runners who don't give a second thought to running 50 miles, 100 miles, or for 6 days straight, this book is for you.

If you have the desire, the willingness, the fortitude, and the *gumption* to run an ultra, this book is for you.

Believe me when I tell you that once you cross the finish line of your first ultra, you will unlock secrets only a long-distance runner can understand and appreciate.

After all, if someone like me can run an ultra, *what's stopping you*?

* * *

BEFORE YOU BEGIN READING THERE ARE A FEW THINGS YOU NEED TO KNOW:

- I don't take myself seriously.

- I do take my running seriously.

- I've loved every single minute and every single mile of my journey so far.

1

CHAPTER

BEYOND MARATHONS

I ran my first marathon in 1979. Less than three years later I ran my first ultramarathon. I had been running less than four years. I had a mere half-dozen marathons under my belt, the fastest being 3:13 at Atlanta on Thanksgiving Day 1981. Why I chose the Atlanta Track Club's 50-Mile Race at hilly Stone Mountain, Georgia as my first race longer than a marathon—well, if I said I knew why, I'd be lying. Let's just say the thought of running 50 miles was *intriguing*.

I'll spare you the details of the race other than to tell you the course consisted of 10 5-mile laps around the base of Stone Mountain that included two severe uphills on each lap. The first uphill, as I was trying my best to maintain an early eight-minute-per-mile pace, a local veteran ultramarathoner (Vaughn Crawley—I remember his name vividly because I've heard his advice over and over again in my head over the past three decades) calmly suggested to me as I was passing him by: "Walk the uphills." Yes, my friend, in an ultra, it's OK… in fact *highly recommended* to walk the uphills.

I finished on that cold winter day in 7 hours and 28 minutes and in sixth place. Ultrarunning, arguably in its infancy in the early 80's had a new advocate: ME!

Barely seven months later I was ready for the next step: 100 miles. I entered the Atlanta Track Club's 24-Hour Run and covered just over 101 miles in a little over 19 ½ hours.

My fascination with ultrarunning grew over the years, and I eventually set my sights on competing in arguably the Big Four of the sport: the JFK 50-Mile Run, the Badwater Ultramarathon, the Western States Endurance Run and the Comrades Marathon.

For a runner like me, of moderate physical abilities supplemented by healthy doses of grit, determination, and drive, the Big Four seemed like the perfect challenge. In the years ahead I would realize just how right I was.

This is the story of how I found my way to the finish line of arguably the four most prestigious ultramarathons in the world. You'll meet the people who ran with me, motivated me, and, in many cases, supported me in my running adventures. You'll experience the training and the races that offered me the experience I needed to consider competing in the Big Four. You'll gain an understanding of the psyche of an ultradistance runner; well, at least one ultradistance runner in particular.

I look forward to sharing my journey with you.

***

2 CHAPTER

FINDING MY NICHE

1954–1974

I was born in Norfolk, Virginia on December 10, 1954. Until I was almost 24 years old, I fluctuated from one sport to another, searching for my niche.

My dad was a career Navy man, which meant our family had to relocate from one place to another every three years as my dad alternated sea and shore duty: Norfolk, Virginia; Den Haag, Netherlands; Quonset Point, Rhode Island; Pearl Harbor, Hawaii; Mayport, Florida; and back to Chesapeake, Virginia. My parents were always avid bowlers, and they had me bowling as far back as I can recall. As a 12-year-old, I would consistently hold one of the highest averages (+/- 150) in the youth bowling leagues. Once I reached my teen years, my average hovered in the 170s. Ultimately, I gave up the sport entirely after my sophomore year in college, albeit at "the pinnacle of my bowling career" (more on this later).

My first attempt at organized sports was playing Little League baseball in Rhode Island. As a nine-year-old, playing a sport I wasn't particularly good at in front of people (primarily parents!) was frightening. My coach would usually put me in the safest place possible—right field—since baseballs are rarely ever hit in right field by nine- and ten-year-olds, which meant I wouldn't be afforded the opportunity to catch too many balls (or more accurately, *miss* too many balls). However, there was still the little matter of me having to *bat* several times a game. My very first time in the batter's box I struck out on three straight pitches. If I remember correctly, I think only *one* of them didn't bounce in front of home plate before I swung at it, and it was so far outside the strike zone I had to take two steps *forward* to get close to the ball. At season's end I was selected for the all-star team—simply because I was the only player on our team old enough to be eligible. They put me on third base (for the first time in my life), and I'm sorry to say there were *many* balls hit in my direction, most of them finding their way past me and out to our left fielder. That day mercifully marked the end of any thoughts of a career in baseball.

After mastering baseball, I moved on to football. As a chunky, overweight 13-year-old pushing the Pearl Harbor (Hawaii) Youth Football League weight limit of 135 pounds, I found myself in the sauna the day before our games so I'd sweat off enough to make "game weight" and therefore be eligible to play. That happened only once. No, not making game weight—actually playing in a game! My team, the Commodores, was in the process of destroying a team by an eventual final score of 56-0. Once it was obvious we were going to have no problem winning the game, the coach put me in to play middle linebacker, a position I had played in practice...gee how often? Oh yeah—*never!* I'm pretty sure the score at the time was, well, 56-0. While I didn't make any solo tackles or intercept any passes, I did manage to jump on the pile a couple of times after a tackle was made without being penalized for a late hit. That day I played the first, last, and only game of organized football in my life.

Now that I had two sports ruled out (*three* if you count bowling), I finally found one I enjoyed—basketball! Without boasting, I had the best jump shot in my high school. *I* knew it, my *best friend* knew it, and *all the guys who played at the high school gym on Tuesday and Thursday nights* knew it (many of them being on the high school team). The only one who didn't seem to know it was the high school basketball team's *coach!* During team tryouts, each player had to take 20 free throws at the end of practice. I guess the coach failed to notice that over the five days of practice, *one* of the players trying out for the team only missed one of his free throws ALL WEEK LONG! I couldn't believe it when the team was announced, and I wasn't on it. However, my best friend, who was about five inches taller than me and knew I had the best jump shot in high school (I know he knew it because he saw enough of them sail over his head when I would beat him like a drum playing one-on-one after school every day) *made* the team. OK, what's next?

How about *golf?* I had been playing golf since I was 12 years old. In fact, I won the Oahu Junior Golf Association B Division Championship in 1967 by shooting an 18-hole score of 87! (I've still got the trophy to prove it.) I tried out for the Fletcher High School (Neptune Beach, Florida) golf team as a freshman, and, by my sophomore year, I was playing in the #1 position and eventually earned All-City (Jacksonville) honors with my 37 average (for 9 holes). During my senior year, however, my golf coach (we had a new coach each of my four years in high school, usually an assistant football coach who just did it so he could play golf for free) and I disagreed over a very vital issue—the length of my hair! I had just started dating Cindy (my future wife) in January of my senior year, and there was no way I was cutting my hair in *March*, because I just knew if I did Cindy would drop me faster than I dropped any aspiration of playing professional baseball or football. I quit the team, as did the #2 and #4 players on the team to show their support for what would ultimately be a lost cause. Unfortunately, this did not matter one iota to the coach, who went on to lead our team to its worst season in the history of our school.

When I enrolled as a freshman at the University of Florida, I tried out for the golf team as a walk-on. After playing seven rounds of golf in (what I believed to be) an impressive 10 over par, I was shown the same door my high school basketball coach had shown me several years ago. For the record, the University of Florida golf team has produced some stellar golfers throughout the years. Andy Bean, who would go on to become a star on the PGA tour for many years to come, was one of the students who barely noticed my 10-over-par score in his rearview mirror.

As a sophomore, I tried out for the University of Florida bowling team, mainly because it meant I would be able to bowl 30 games (the length of the tryouts) for free. Would you believe I actually *made the team?* I averaged 188 and bowled my (still) all-time high three-game series of 670 in the process. Making the university bowling team meant I was able to bowl as many games as I wanted throughout the year absolutely free. It also meant I could bowl in matches against other college teams; however, if we did in fact bowl against other college teams, no one ever told me. Not once was I notified of any matches. And yes, I *know* I was on the team because every time I showed up to bowl, I said I was on the team and the person behind the desk would check the Gator Bowling Team roster and say, "Oh, yeah, here it is—Ludwig. No charge." It would have been nice to bowl in at least one match, though.

All and Scott at Western States 2006

Alas, I found my true love in sports when I was in graduate school at the University of Florida. Thinking back to when I was in 10th grade in high school, I should have realized *then* I had some potential as a runner. Part of our final exam in our physical education class was completing the 600-yard run. I finished in 3rd place out of my entire 10th-grade class, beaten only by two guys on the cross-country team. Both of them vomited after they finished; not me—I was officially "the fastest 600-yard runner in 10th grade that didn't throw up afterward." I built on that title to become the runner that I am today.

The point I am trying to make is that I'm not the greatest athlete who ever graced the planet. I was never one of the really athletic guys growing up. I wasn't strong. I wasn't fast. I wasn't agile. I wasn't limber.

But I was always, *always* determined and had the focus, willingness, and stick-to-it-ness (regardless of my ill-fated baseball and football careers) that a sport like ultrarunning requires. It was only a matter of time before our paths would cross.

* * *

3

CHAPTER

DANCING THROUGH
MY FIRST MARATHON

University of Florida Dance Marathon, May 1975

During my sophomore year at the University of Florida, I pledged a fraternity. Why? Let's just say most of the fraternity brothers worked at the on-campus bar, the Rathskellar. On my limited budget, it was convenient to be able to drink beer for…well, let's say at a slightly reduced cost.

My sophomore year was also Cindy's (you met Cindy earlier—my high school sweetheart who later became my wife, although to be honest she's still my high school sweetheart) first year as a Gator, as she had attended the University of North Florida her freshman year and enrolled at U of F as a sophomore. Cindy lived on campus in a dormitory with her roommate Wanda.

In the spring of 1975, the Rathskellar was hosting a 28-hour dance marathon for charity. The rules were simple:

- Couples only.
- Couples had to dance ("move your feet") the entire 28 hours.
- Couples got a 10-minute break each hour.

Even though I was not yet a runner, I knew I had a lot of endurance. I did enough all-nighters my sophomore year (you see, I needed to make amends for my poor academic showing during my freshman year) to know dancing for 28 hours would be a piece of cake. Cindy, however, thought otherwise. She knew I could do it, and she also knew if she were my partner and we failed to go the distance, I would be really, really upset with her.

She was 100 percent correct. That's why she volunteered Wanda, her roommate.

Unfortunately, Wanda's boyfriend Wayne was opposed to the idea. Fortunately, Wanda was incredibly strong willed (like me) and agreed to be my partner.

The dance marathon was to begin at 8:00 p.m. Friday night. Wanda, Cindy, Wayne, and I showed up at the Rat for our pre-marathon "dinner" at 7:00. You must understand that as a shy 20-year-old, I needed a little motivation to get out on the dance floor. I used my last hour wisely (or so I thought) by drinking the better part of two pitchers of beer. By 8:00, I was more than ready to dance. By 8:15 I had to urinate so badly…so *furiously* I thought I would pass out—and my first (bathroom) break wouldn't be until 8:50. I spent 35 minutes keeping both feet moving while holding my thighs tightly pressed together. Try it sometime—not particularly easy to do.

The disc jockey started off by playing lots of Motown and pre-disco songs, not particularly fan favorites. Thirty minutes into the evening, one of my fraternity brothers (who had an uncanny resemblance to D-Day from *Animal House*) took control of the turntable and put on *Black Dog* by Led Zeppelin. At first, all the couples on the dance floor cheered—until we collectively realized it was not a song one could easily dance to. Eventually sanity (meaning Motown and pre-disco songs) was restored, and the remaining 27 hours were filled with music you *could* dance to. (Note: I believe this was the beginning of my fondness for disco music. I am not kidding—I *love* Donna Summer and pretty much the entire Motown catalog).

At our first break at 8:50, I headed straight for the men's room. I was there so long I barely made it back to the dance floor by 9:00 to resume dancing. Within the next hour, my beer buzz had worn off. Around 10:30 that evening, I danced for the first time without any effects from "liquid encouragement." After a few hours, I began to feel comfortable with what I was doing.

Wanda and I hit a few rough spots during the marathon: When Cindy went back to the dorm to go to sleep…when Wayne (finally) gave in and went back to his car for a short nap…when the sun came up Saturday morning (my usual bedtime following an all-nighter)… when Wayne did his best to persuade Wanda to quit (fortunately, Wanda—like Cindy—knew I would be really be upset if she didn't go the distance). But we persevered, and we made it.

Much to our chagrin, four other couples made it as well. But to be totally honest, Wanda and I were the only ones still abiding by the rules. The other couples were basically leaning on one another when midnight rolled around, signifying the end of the contest.

All five couples were declared winners, but we all know which couple really made it to the finish line. In time, I would discover that standing on my feet for 28 straight hours would become something near and dear to me with one minor difference: I would be doing just a little bit more than simply standing in one place.

Wanda 1975

* * *

4

CHAPTER

THE COLLEGE YEARS

1973–1978

I enrolled at the University of Florida in the center of the universe—
Gainesville, Florida—in the fall of 1973. It was the first time since
I started dating Cindy in January of 1973 that I was away from her,
and I was miserable. When Cindy enrolled at the U of F in the fall
of 1974, I was a new man. We had a wonderful college experience
I wouldn't trade for the world. We graduated together in the spring
of 1977 with our Bachelor's degrees, were married that June, and
earned our Masters degrees before settling down and starting our
careers…and our family in Atlanta, Georgia.

I do, however, have two running-related stories from my undergraduate days (i.e., before I began running with my professor during graduate school; more on that later):

- In my first U of F physical education class, part of our final exam was to see how far we could run on a track in 12 minutes. Considering I hadn't done any running since 10th grade, I felt pretty good...for about five laps. I held on to complete what I thought to be six laps; however, my lap counter reported I ran seven which earned me an A. Granted, I may have lost count as to how many laps I ran, but seeing as I only ran for 12 minutes, I don't see how. This lap-counting discrepancy stayed with me and will have a small role in my first 100-mile adventure, as you will read about later.

- In my senior year, a fraternity brother of mine came back after running six miles. Without stopping. I was totally amazed ANYONE could run six miles without stopping. As he was telling me all about it, I honestly felt like I was talking to someone from another planet. This conversation stayed with me for a while as well but will have no role whatsoever in the rest of this book. I just mention it here to provide you with my initial perspective on long-distance running.

***

5
CHAPTER

ONCE YOU GET STARTED

Becoming a Runner, Summer 1978

"Once you get started...oh it's hard to stop."

Truer words were never spoken, even if Chaka Khan said (well, actually *sang*) them first.

I wish I could tell you who was primarily responsible for me becoming a runner, or even to pinpoint the exact moment I actually *became* a runner.

As a newlywed in graduate school in 1977, I quickly discovered eating three honest-to-goodness meals a day for the first time in four years added up quickly. From a wedding-day weight of 165, it was only one year later I discovered I had been gaining weight at a rate of 2 ½ pounds a month. Yes, I had ballooned up to 194 pounds in one short year. Cindy began a running program and encouraged me to learn all I could about "aerobic points," a phase that would be short-lived but certainly pushed me into riding my bicycle, playing tennis, and (drum roll) running to accumulate all the aerobic points I possibly could. (Do you see a compulsive behavior here? More to come.) Soon I was joining her for her afternoon jog around our married housing complex. That summer of 1978, I began running the 4/10-mile loop around my married housing complex five times in the afternoon (two miles!) all by myself (i.e., without Cindy), never straying too far from my front door in case of an emergency; you know, like passing out from exertion.

Then there was my graduate school faculty advisor, Thomas Jefferson Saine III, who repeatedly asked me to join him in the two aerobic sports he participated in: running and racquetball. I remember my first really long run (eight miles!) with Tom in October of 1978 and five months later Tom running the last eight miles of my first marathon with me at the Florida Relays Marathon in Gainesville. (History lesson: *The Florida Relays Marathon is no more; however, today there is the Five Points of Life Marathon in Gainesville, which starts and finishes a couple hundred yards away from the married housing unit Cindy and I lived in when we began running. I find this very, very cool.*)

Tom Saine was not only my professor and mentor but a friend as well.

I can't imagine what my life might have been like had I not accepted Tom's invitation to run so many years ago.

Thanks, Tom.

Here's hoping you're reading this and will call me to join you for a run.

Later that summer, I ran three miles in Piedmont Park in Atlanta with Tom (although I would alternate running and sitting out the one-mile loops Tom was running).

The Day After—Western States 2006

By the end of that summer, I had dropped down to 150 pounds and lost five inches around my waistline. I made a bet with Tom in November of 1978 that I could run 13 miles without stopping. I won. The day after, I spent most of the day in the bathroom. But I won the bet, and TO THIS DAY that day in the bathroom in our married housing apartment in Gainesville, Florida remains the last day I did not run (and there you have it—the other compulsive behavior I promised).

As I mentioned a few pages earlier, I was always determined and had the focus, willingness, and stick-to-it-ness that a sport like ultrarunning requires. As my consecutive-days-of-running streak is now into its fifth decade, I trust you'll agree.

**

LEARNING TO CRAWL

1979–1981

*In 1977, one of my college roommates
went out for a run one afternoon.
He was out the door and back again in two minutes,
saying he forgot something.
When I asked him what he had forgotten, he replied,
"I forgot I'm horribly out of shape and only able to run
for two minutes."*

My first full three years of running was (without trying to be overly dramatic) life altering. On second thought, life-modifying might be a better way to describe what I was experiencing, from a physical perspective and perhaps more importantly from a psychological perspective. Running—pushing my body more than I had ever before—each and every morning was a great way to start the day. After physically exerting myself for an hour or more before facing the daily demands required of my job and my family, I always had the peace of mind knowing that no matter what the rest of the day would bring, for the most part, it could not compare to what I had put myself through while everyone else was fast asleep.

To say that running was a *confidence* builder would be an understatement. Character builder would be more accurate.

I was gaining a confidence in my body, my social skills, my decision-making, and many other areas like never before. I could think more clearly. I began to feel more comfortable around people. My pulse dropped 20 beats per minute. I lost five inches from my waistline. I discovered running to be a great way to cure what ails you: headaches, nausea, hangovers (I drank quite a bit of beer in my 20s; I blame my fraternity brothers), and other assorted malaise.

I couldn't understand why everyone wasn't doing it. It didn't take long for running to become an ingrained part of my daily routine: wake up, use the bathroom, drink coffee, read, run, shave, brush teeth, shower, dress. Repeat daily.

It wasn't long before I was running marathons. Not long after that I was looking for something more…

* * *

7
CHAPTER

SOMETHING
I ALWAYS WANTED TO DO

Run Across Georgia #1, Fall 1982

I became fascinated with ultramarathons early in my running career. I ran my first marathon after only six months of running and moved on to my first ultra three years later. In the winter of 1982, I, along with 17 other adventurous souls, started a 50-mile race around the base of Stone Mountain (10 5-mile loops). After some sound advice from a veteran ultrarunner early in the race ("walk the uphills or pay the price later") I had no trouble completing the race, finishing in 7:28:20…good enough for 6th place. To this day I am eternally grateful for perhaps the most important piece of advice I ever received in my running career (you met Vaughn Crawley earlier, and to this day I can still see the look on his face as he saw me running hard up the first of two dramatic uphill climbs which were included in each 5-mile loop). I decided right then and there that the longer the race, the better off I was. I was, indeed, an ultrarunner (or at least I had the potential to be).

Then I made another decision: to run an ultramarathon that no one had ever run before. Inspired by the efforts of two southeastern runners who had run across not only states but entire countries as well, I decided I would run width-wise across the state of Georgia, from Columbus to Savannah (crossing the state from west to east). I knew that one of the aforementioned runners had run Georgia from north to south, but no one had ever run west to east (or east to west, for that matter). I hoped to be the first. Here was my chance to complete an ultra that had never been attempted, let alone completed.

The preparatory stage of my forthcoming journey was enjoyable. Initially, I looked on a map of Georgia to find an out-of-the-way two-lane road that ran from one side of the state to the other. Georgia Highway 280 fit the bill. I could start at the Georgia–Alabama border in Columbus, Georgia and finish along the coast in Savannah. I drove the route two months prior to the actual run, which I had scheduled to begin on Saturday, October 30 and end on Saturday, November 6. I plotted every conceivable landmark, water stop, motel/hotel, convenience store, gas station, and town on my route. If it existed on Highway 280, it was on my map. Every mile was indicated so that I would be able to monitor my progress along the way. My goal was to run between 33 and 38 miles a day, allowing me to complete the 280 miles in approximately eight days.

The week prior to my run was enjoyable as well. Getting all my supplies ready—three pairs of running shoes, numerous changes of running attire, toiletries, canteen, cash/credit cards, medical supplies, and lots of Vaseline—added fuel to my already burning fire. I couldn't wait to get started. I had it all planned: My wife Cindy would drive me to Columbus on Friday, October 29, and after a good night's sleep in a hotel near the start, I would begin my cross-state trek early Saturday morning. All systems were, as they say, go.

One small detail before I moved on to the run itself. Early in the afternoon on Friday October 29, the day before the run, Cindy asked me how many people were aware of my imminent adventure. When I told her just a few close friends and co-workers (I had to take a week's vacation for my run), she said I should let the Atlanta Track Club know what I was up to. (Very) reluctantly, I phoned their office and told someone there of my plans. When the voice on the other end of the telephone concluded our conversation by asking the inevitable 'why,' I merely said that it was something I always wanted to do. Little did I know how these words would come back to haunt me.

The evening of October 29, Cindy and I drove to a small hotel in Columbus where I would get what would prove to be my last good night's sleep for a month. (Did I say "good night's sleep?" I meant as much sleep as one would expect staying in a room adjacent to a room that apparently the local military personnel were renting by the hour…if you know what I mean). The plan was falling into place nicely. Cindy would lead and follow me in our van the first two days of the run, allowing me to move along without having to carry a 20-pound pack on my back.

The first thing I did on **DAY ONE** (Saturday, October 30) was decide to run 50-plus miles each of the first two days, taking full advantage of not having to carry the backpack. I awoke around 5:00 a.m. and decided to get started right away. As the hotel was merely a half-mile from the Alabama–Georgia border, I walked to my starting line. My trek officially began at 7:10 a.m. Cindy met me around the 22-mile mark later in the morning with a dozen of the finest doughnuts I have ever had the pleasure of devouring. I ended up running 58 miles that first day, finishing slightly past the small town of Plains. Fortunately, the weather was fairly cool, and I made it through the day with few, if any, problems (*detectable* problems, anyway). I stopped running that first day at 6:30 p.m. At that point I wondered if I underestimated my ultrarunning prowess and questioned whether I could complete my run in six days, maybe less.

Awakening the morning of **DAY TWO** (Sunday, October 31), I was glad to discover I only had a few aches and pains and, lo and behold, no blisters! Immediately, I decided my goal was another 50-plus miles for the day. Beginning the second day's run at 7:30 a.m., I was pleased to find another day of cool weather awaiting me. With Cindy at my beck and call to tote my supplies and provide me with liquids at a moment's notice, I felt on top of the world. I managed 46 miles for the day, ending up in Cordele and bringing my two-day total to 104 miles. Heck, I'd be in Savannah by Thursday for sure. Maybe I should have run the *perimeter* of Georgia instead...

Sunday evening brought me closer to reality than I had been in two days. After dinner, Cindy took off with the van, heading back to Atlanta as she had to be at work the next day (apparently she didn't tell her co-workers about the adventure). I was now facing my 20-pound handicap (the backpack) for the remaining 176 miles, and food and drink were no longer available upon command. I decided to relax in the hotel that evening and enjoy the *Atlanta Journal and Constitution* before nodding off to sleep. As is my custom, I immediately flipped to the sports section and, to my dismay, found the following headline deep in the bowels of Section E:

LUDWIG TO RUN ACROSS STATE

The article went on to describe what I was doing and even quote me as to why I was doing it: because it was "something I always wanted to do." The first thought that crossed my mind was that the person *responsible* for my unwanted infamy had just deserted me less than an hour ago. My second thought was I had better complete my run or face the imminent consequences of a highly-publicized *failure*. My third thought was that my legs didn't feel nearly as peppy as they had a mere 24 hours earlier.

For the sake of argument, let's call the first two days of my adventure "the ecstasy." Logically, what would follow then would be "the agony." Well, I'm here to tell you that truer words were never spoken. I got out of the bed the morning of **DAY THREE** (Monday, November 1) with a pair of knees that felt as if the bones, tendons, and muscles inside had been fused together during the night. Being an optimist, I figured once I got out on the roads all my soreness would work its way out of my creaking joints. Stepping out of my hotel room at 6:30 a.m., I was aghast to find the temperature approaching 80 degrees on *the first day of November!* Again, the optimist in me remembered all those long training runs in July and August in temperatures approaching 100 degrees. There was no need to let little problems like stiff knees or warm weather cause me to alter my game plan at this point.

I ended up the day completing 38 more miles down Highway 280, finishing up in Abbeville around 5:00 p.m. Not only were my knees screaming at me for relief, I experienced what must have been second-degree sunburn and several blisters approximately the size of quarters on the bottoms of both feet. I checked into a hotel, took a bath, got dressed, and walked (or rather, *hobbled*) to the local convenience store in search of medical aid. I knew I was in trouble when I asked the clerk at the counter where I could find the town doctor. Her reply: "We had a town doctor once, but he died."

I needed help but didn't know where to turn. I didn't want to call Cindy for fear of hearing an "I told you so." So I turned to people who were always there for me: my parents. I called them (collect) on the store's pay phone, and, when I told them of my dilemma, (like I said earlier, not many people knew about my run before the article in the newspaper. My parents, who were living in Virginia, knew nothing about it…until I called; my mother's reply was drowned out by my father's laughter on the other line. I managed to gather "Epsom salts" from the oft-interrupted conversation and proceeded to purchase some at the convenience store. I went back to the hotel room, took an Epsom salt bath, and went to bed around 7:30 p.m., confident *(praying!)* that a good night's rest was all I needed.

> My mom and dad always worried about my running, particularly when it came to running long distances. To them, anything over three miles constituted a long run. As you can imagine, I presented my parents with lots of opportunities to worry.

I woke up around 5:00 a.m. on **DAY FOUR** (Tuesday, November 2) feeling like a heavyweight prizefighter had used my legs for punching bags during the night. I left the hotel room at 5:45, placed the backpack across my now-sunburned shoulders, and ever-so-painfully stepped off the curb and out onto the highway. The weather was still warm, and, before long, I realized I had done nothing for those water blisters on the bottoms of both feet. Being a former Boy Scout, I was prepared for an emergency of this nature. I had several sterilized needles in my backpack. I pulled off the side of the road, removed both shoes, and punctured and drained all seven blisters. *Yes, seven.*

This may come as a surprise, but 4 hours and 17 miles later, I had convinced myself that my healing prowess had been inadequate. I literally hobbled the duration of my run on day four, and after completing 159 miles filled with more agony than ecstasy, I decided that I (at least *half* of me—the lower half) had had enough. I called a friend, who just happened to be on vacation as well, and he (bless him) drove to the isolated spot where I was sprawled out along the side of Highway 280 in Milan and rescued me from myself.

For the next two weeks, it was painful to wear shoes, and my running over the next 12 weeks suffered as I was forced to a hobble after several miles each day. My knees took a long time to forgive me. I explained to them in lieu of all my training and preparation I had failed to realize what running on one side of the road for that extreme a distance would do to them. How did I know that the small slope on either side of the road would have such a drastic effect on my knees? Eventually, maybe I'll forget about it. I'll bet it would help if I got rid of my course map.

Eventually, who knows—I just might try it again…

After all, it is something I always wanted to do. And I have a hard time living with failure.

I failed to mention that Cindy was pregnant during this time. In fact, she gave birth to our first son, Justin, a mere 16 days after she left me to fend for myself in Cordele.

* * *

8 CHAPTER

THE NEED FOR SPEED

1983–1987

Virtually all of my personal bests for marathon distance or less were run in the five-year window between 1983 and 1987. This makes sense, as these were my prime years for running marathons. I was 33 years old (many experts have identified 33 as the prime year for a marathoner) in January of 1988 when I ran a personal best 2:48:41 marathon in Jacksonville, Florida. Yes, I made the experts proud.

But I noticed that my marathon times were not adhering to most predictor charts used for taking your 10K time and predicting what your marathon time would be. My marathon times were always faster than what the predictor charts called for.

Not only logic but also my gut was telling me that perhaps the longer the distance, the farther off the (predictor) chart my times would be. Which made me wonder: How would I do at 100 miles?

Our second son, Joshua, was born in 1985.

Josh's first pair of shoes?

Running shoes.

* * *

9

CHAPTER

19:31:10

National 24-Hour Championship, September 1988

8:05 a.m., Saturday, September 17, 1988. Slightly warm, a bit on the muggy side. Rain is imminent. As I stand beside 91 fellow competitors on the white strip marking the beginning and ending of the 1.01 mile track circling the Atlanta Water Reservoir, I wonder why I'm here and even *considering* what lies ahead...and ahead... and ahead.

The gun sounds, and I'm off at a brisker-than-I-had planned 7:15 minute per mile pace. I keep this pace up for a little over two hours, dropping back to a 7:45 pace for the third hour before checking in with a Georgia Tech grad student for his project: Does lung function limit performance in a 24-hour ultramarathon? The project requires me to inhale and exhale as hard as I possibly can into a plastic tube for five minutes every three hours. I would soon learn I was foolish for volunteering for this study, as this intense breathing was much more difficult than the run itself. Plus, every time I did it, I lost 15 minutes, and stopping every three hours gave my body the opportunity it needed to allow rigor mortis to set in, making it that much more difficult to get started again.

Forgive me, as I have not yet told you what I had gotten myself into. I'd entered The Athletic Congress' 24-Hour Endurance Run National Championship. Why? I simply thought it would be extremely cool to run *100 miles*.

The format for the run is to run counterclockwise for four hours, reverse direction and run clockwise for four hours, and repeat for the duration of the 24 hours. The theory is if you ran in one direction for the entire time, one leg would end up shorter than the other. Let me be the first to tell you that in the latter stages of the event (*especially* after the sun when down), changing directions was all you had to look forward to!

Aside from the research project I, like a fool, had volunteered for (well, not a complete fool, as I got a free submerge-your-body-in-a-water-tank body fat test for taking part in the study), the race went well. I was on the leader board the entire time I was competing, at one point climbing as high as 7th and usually holding steady around 11th. One other problem: Remember the imminent rain? After several rain showers, I was down to my last of three original pair of dry shoes. My wife Cindy came by around 8:00 p.m. and was kind enough to take the two pairs I wasn't wearing to a local laundromat to dry them. Sounds like a good idea, right? Maybe if they weren't dried *at two hundred degrees!* Both pairs seemed at least a full size shorter when I wore them again—it was the perfect storm of slightly shrunken shoes and slightly swollen feet. Eventually, I would lose the big toenail on my right foot—not that big a loss when you take into account all the impact my toes incurred pressing against the front of my shoes with each step. I am proud to report, however, that at least both my legs were the same length after the event (thank you, Race Director, for allowing us to change direction).

Cindy and our two sons went to sleep in my van (parked right next to the track) around midnight, at which time I had already logged 86 miles (I figured the lung experiment cost me about 7 or 8 miles already). At 2:30 a.m. Sunday morning, I caught my second wind and started back running miles at a sub-8-minute pace. I covered nine more laps between 2:30 and 3:35 a.m. before finally calling it quits after 100 laps, which equated to (officially, according to the TAC) 101 miles, 294 yards. My official race time was 19:31:10. It was an odd experience for me as (1) it was the first race I did not actually complete, (2) when I removed myself from the race, I had just caught my second (maybe third—I lost count) wind and—believe it or not—felt really strong, and (3) I had again climbed to 7th on the leader board. But at that point I could care less about being in 7th. I just wanted to *stop running!* Apparently my brain had finally talked my body out of competing any longer. I told my lap counter I was finished, packed up my gear, got in the van, and drove home (yes, I drove!). I went to bed that morning around 4:30 a.m. without benefit of a bath, a solid meal, or even (gee, I wonder why) a goodnight/congratulatory kiss from Cindy. The bath came six hours later, the meal even later sometime Sunday evening, and the kiss about 10 days later (the recovery time my body needed before I could run—or do anything else for that matter—without pain).

About two weeks later, I received a bronze medal in the mail from TAC. Apparently I had finished third in my age group (and 27th overall). The medal had the words "National Championship" embossed on it, but it failed to identify the event, although a runner is pictured beneath the TAC logo. I had achieved the goal I had set for myself: *One Hundred Miles!* As I recall, I ran one additional lap in case my lap counter missed counting any of them (you may recall my earlier erroneous lap-counting incident from my college years).

But again, this was the first race I didn't believe I truly completed, and I decided right then and there: One day I would make amends.

Make no mistake about it.

* * *

CALM BEFORE THE STORM

1989–1991

I'll be the first to admit that I had a tough time staying motivated with my running during this three-year span. In fact, I only raced 47 times (compared to 25 to 35 per year prior to that) and barely surpassed 9,000 miles. After living in Rex, Georgia for 10 years, our family moved a bit farther south to the planned community of Peachtree City, Georgia in May of 1990. As a runner, it was a welcome relief, as the city is interconnected by a system of now 90 miles of asphalt golf cart paths. You can virtually get to anywhere in town by taking the paths through the woods. That's the good news. The bad news is the paths are not marked very well. In the early days of our relocation to Peachtree City, it wasn't unusual for me to take off on a 10-mile run and return home three or four hours later after having gotten lost on the paths.

It's a good thing I took it easy for those three years; in the fall of 1993, I would begin running with Al Barker and Valerie Reynolds, and my running…and my life would never be the same.

***

BRAIN F*RT REPERCUSSIONS

Georgia Long Distance Relay, June 1992

I guess the easiest and safest answer is simply because it was there. The question is, why did I run in the 1992 Georgia Long Distance Relay?

The Georgia Long Distance Relay is a 124-mile journey through the mountains of north Georgia run predominately during the still of the night. I guess there are other answers to the question, such as, for my own personal satisfaction or to prove I have what it takes or even to share in the team goal of going the distance. Whichever one you believe, I'm sure each one of them sounds just as plausible as the next. However, all of them are lies.

I did it because I had a brain fart. Plain and simple.

A *brain fart*, also known as a *cerebral flatulation*, is when your heart is in the right place but your brain goes elsewhere. For example, you're asked to bring back a gallon of milk on your way home from work. You stop by the grocery store, proceed to pick out a nice bottle of wine to enjoy with dinner, and maybe a pint of ice cream for the kids—without *once* thinking about the gallon of milk you stopped for in the first place. Sound familiar? A brain fart!

Now that we have that established, it's easier to understand why I said yes when I was asked if I wanted to run. My heart was asking why *anyone* would want to spend the entire weekend inside a minivan full of sweaty runners, each one required to run three separate mountainous five-mile legs approximately five hours apart—which is *just enough time* for your body to become totally stiff from the prior five-mile leg while *not being enough time* to recover either physically or mentally. Naturally, while this debate was silently taking place inside my heart, my brain allowed my vocal cords to utter "yes."

A brain fart of the highest magnitude.

As most of the course was run on asphalt roads through the countryside and occasionally up and over a mountain or two, it wasn't nearly as horrific as I thought it might be when I realized I would be spending the better part of 24 hours in a small van with seven other sweaty runners and one driver who was chomping at the bit to run as well. I ran my three legs of approximately five miles each as well as one leg with each of the other seven runners. You see, the only way I could justify losing an entire 24 hours of my life would be by running at least 50 miles (which I did).

Thinking back to the weekend in the mountains, there was a whole lot more positives than negatives. It's over, the team did well, and my body (and mind) totally recovered. It provided me with a lot of fond memories, and the satisfaction of participating in a highly successful team venture of this proportion felt incredible.

Mountain Relay Team 1992

It also enlightened me to the physical effort required to *run* (and by run, I actually mean, walk as briskly as possible) up and over a mountain.

In hindsight, I'm glad I said yes, and if anyone asks me why I did it, I'm saying I did it to broaden my horizons. I would be lying, of course.

However, a short decade later I would be running in an event of an even greater distance with another team of runners with only one minor difference:

I would be doing all the running.

***

12

CHAPTER

SOMETHING
I NEVER WANT TO DO AGAIN

Run Across Georgia #2, October 1992

You may remember my attempt to run across the state of Georgia, 280 miles along Highway 280, because it was "something I always wanted to do." You may recall that my attempt ended after 159 miles in the small town of Milan simply because my knees would no longer support my bodyweight.

Ten years later I returned to the scene of the crime and am proud to report that the first run I ever failed to complete has been atoned for. That's right—I finished my self-proclaimed Run Across

Georgia, and I can say without a doubt, it is something I never want to do *again*.

It all started in the summer of 1992 when I was solicited to be a part of my company's annual United Way campaign. In those tough economic times, the United Way committee realized they would need several fundraisers to meet its corporate-mandated goal. Naturally bake sales, golf outings, and T-shirt sales were all agreed upon as being part of the campaign. I was still working for the same company as I was 10 years earlier when I first tried the Columbus-to-Savannah trek, so I casually mentioned I would be willing to once again attempt my Run Across Georgia as part of the campaign IF the company would (a) give me the week off to do it (what the heck, I figured—I still had my course map) and (b) pay for my expenses. To my amazement, the company agreed. Agreed is probably an understatement; the company was willing to consider me a loaned executive to the United Way for the week, agreed to pay all my expenses incurred during the run, gave me my choice of a fellow employee as a support crew (his expenses were included, too; PLUS he got a week off with pay as well), and printed up posters promoting the event with me in Reebok (which provided me with shoes and running attire) gear superimposed over a map of Georgia. Officially JCPenney Catalog, Reebok, and the United Way were sponsoring the event and calling it 280 on 280 (as in 280 miles on Highway 280) with the catch being for individuals to sponsor my run with a donation per mile. (By the way, when I was asked to submit a proposal for my idea, I quickly jotted down 280 on 280 as a title, and the powers-that-be *loved it*. Go figure.).

The official dates for the run were Sunday, October 18 (leave Columbus) through Saturday, October 24 (arrive in Savannah). So at precisely 7:30 a.m. (I certainly didn't want to be late for my first day of "work") on the 18th of October, not quite 10 full years after my inaugural failure, I set out in my new Reebok attire with my sights set on the east coast of Georgia.

Scott Run Across Georgia 1992

At this point, I could provide a step-by-step account of the run, but that would be too lengthy (not to mention *boring*), considering I took approximately 350,000 steps to complete my journey. Instead, I will give you a synopsis of the highlights and lowlights of the adventure. You can decide for yourself which are which:

- Total length of the run: 280.1 miles (the run finished in front of the Savannah DeSoto Hilton, an agreed-upon site for other JCPenney employees to meet at the end of the run).
- Total number of minutes actually spent running: 2,661, or 44.4 hours.
- Average pace: Exactly 10.0 minutes per mile *(honest!)*.
- Total ounces of fluid consumed during the run: 996 (62.25 pounds).
- Total weight lost during the run: *8 ounces* (my one-man crew lost 10 *pounds!*).
- Injuries incurred during the run: pulled right thigh muscle, left leg shin splint, blister on left big toe, lost toenail on right big

toe, severe sunburn/windburn of face (even with sunblock and lip balm), and cramps in arch of right foot. Not bad, considering.

- Average starting time each morning: 7:45 a.m.
- Average quitting time each evening: 5:15 p.m.
- Average length of "work day" (remember, I was receiving my regular salary): 9.5 hours
- Average bedtime each evening: 9:00 p.m.
- Total number of miles ran per day: 50, 40, 43, 45, 45, 44, and 13.1 (I could have finished the run in six days, but I had to finish on Saturday to meet a group of people from JCPenney along with Cindy and my two sons).
- Total number of uphills I walked: *all of them* (and there must have been over 150 of them. Did someone tell me south Georgia was flat?).
- Total number of downhills I walked: zero (mistake!).
- Total number of times a vehicle tried to be cute and run me off the road: three (one was successful; which reminds me—add a bad cut on my right lower calf to my list of injuries, and, yes, to this day I still have the scar to show for it).
- Best use of supplies to alleviate a pain: on the 3rd day, I took a leftover painkiller (from a previous dental surgery) with a beer to deaden the pain in my right thigh. Would you believe it *worked?*

Answer to the question, will you ever do it again? Refer back to the title of the article.

My one-man support crew, Steve Banks, summarized our adventure best when he said to me after all was said and done:

"I hate to tell you this, Scott, but you looked considerably worse each day of the run."

Imagine that.

***

## 13

CHAPTER

THE ONE I'LL ALWAYS REMEMBER

Vulcan Marathon, November 1994

I've run over 800 races to this point in my life. I have been lucky and healthy enough to run in every Peachtree Road Race since 1979. (There's yet another example of that compulsive behavior).

Two hundred of my races have been marathons. I consider myself fortunate to have run in the prestigious Boston Marathon 12 times. The Atlanta Marathon? Twenty-seven times.

Runners tend to remember their marathons. There is always something about each and every one of them that leaves a unique, indelible impression in a runner's memory. Naturally, some of the impressions are clearer and more vivid than others:

- My very first marathon in Gainesville, Florida—the 1979 Florida Relays Marathon which I ran in 3:44, a satisfying time for someone who never ran farther than 13 miles before in his life.
- My first marathon under three hours—a 2:53:29 in Jacksonville, Florida in 1986.
- My first Boston in 1987, where I lowered my personal best by 11 seconds.
- My all-time marathon personal best of 2:48:41 at the Jacksonville Marathon in 1988 (38 degrees, freezing rain, steady wind—I loved every second of it!).
- My first, last, and only New York City Marathon in 1990.
- My "other" 2:48(:45) at the St. George Marathon (Utah) in 1994, just 10 weeks shy of my 40th birthday.
- The 2003 Boston Marathon, which I ran from finish to start and then start to finish in preparation for running the Badwater Ultramarathon later in the year (it was also my 100th marathon).
- My only international marathon: Berlin in 2006. It was very, very cool running through the (Berlin) Wall!
- My 10th Shamrock Marathon (Virginia Beach, Virginia) in 2008, just five months after the loss of both my parents (they lived about 10 miles from the starting line; this race has always been very special to me).
- The 2012 Honolulu Marathon, my 200th marathon. The trip to Honolulu (a return trip for me, having lived there from 1967 until 1970) was a 35-year wedding anniversary gift to Cindy. Let's call this one a win-win.

For me, however, the memory of November 6, 1994 will always be crystal clear. That is the marathon I will—without any doubt whatsoever—remember for the rest of my life.

My son Josh (age 9) and I drove to Birmingham the afternoon of Saturday, November 5, as I was running the Vulcan Marathon the next morning. I had gotten approval from the race director for Josh to pace me on his bicycle as long as we didn't interfere with other competitors in the race. Josh assured me he was in shape to peddle 26 miles (even after I told him it would take over three hours), so we were all set for a unique father-and-son activity.

After we checked into the hotel in Birmingham Saturday night, Josh and I went looking for the expo. Unfortunately, we missed the expo by 30 minutes, so we decided to return to the room for some much-needed sleep before our big day. Before we actually went to sleep, Josh mirrored everything I did. I drank a bottle of Gatorade; Josh drank a bottle of Gatorade. I ate a PowerBar; Josh ate a PowerBar. I drank some water; Josh drank some water. I went to the bathroom; Josh went to the bathroom. You get the idea.

The next morning, Josh and I were up three hours before race time (my norm). Again, Josh followed my exact pre-race routine: He even tied and retied his shoelaces several times like I invariably do before every race. A small passenger van carried us to the starting line. Josh, his tiny bicycle, and I managed to squeeze into the back luggage compartment of the van for the (thankfully!) short ride. We arrived at the starting line a mere 10 minutes before the start of the race. I hurriedly picked up my race number and lined up behind all the runners (maybe 300 in all) near the starting line. Once the "start" command was given, Josh and I held back until all the runners had ventured out onto the course. When everyone was a good 300 yards past the starting line we began *our* marathon.

New York City Marathon 1990

The race went by quickly; *too quickly,* in fact. Josh was a fantastic pacer as he rode his bicycle in a steady, unobtrusive manner the entire time. He was sure that I didn't miss any of the sights either. After all, it isn't everyday a nine-year-old boy gets to go to Birmingham! For the longest time, Josh kept a verbal tally of how many runners we passed ("that's 34, dad"). Listening to Josh talk, he almost had me convinced it was *him* who was competing. Twice I stopped to answer nature's call, and both times Josh got *really* impatient ("Dad, we're getting *passed!*"). Josh peddled furiously with his tiny legs, successfully negotiating most of the course, although there were two lengthy uphill stretches in the final 10 miles where he needed a slight push from dear old dad.

As we crossed the finish line, Josh asked if he would get a finisher's medal. I explained to the volunteer what Josh had done, and she *wanted* to give him a medal, but an official was within earshot and quickly nixed the idea. I told Josh he had earned *my* medal; after all, I couldn't have done it without him. We went back to the hotel for a quick shower (we were in a hurry, as Josh had soccer practice back home later that afternoon), and as we were about to get into the van to leave, Josh asked if I had won an award. I told him there wasn't much chance of that, but he insisted I at least ask. I found the race director, asked if I'd won an award, and wouldn't you know I finished 2nd in my age group! Prior to that day I had *never* won an award in a marathon. As I was in a hurry to leave, the race director went ahead and gave me my trophy. I walked over to Josh to show him what we had won, and he was ecstatic. "Gee, Dad, we won a medal *and* a trophy!"

When we got home, Josh couldn't wait to show our awards to everyone—mom, brother, neighbors, family dog. Once everyone got a glimpse of them, Josh proceeded upstairs to clean off a spot on the bookcase where he placed the trophy and draped the medal over it. To this day, *OUR* awards have remained in exactly the same place Josh put them back in 1994. So has the memory of that marathon weekend.

This is the marathon I will always remember. This is the marathon I will always cherish.

Josh ran his first race when he was six years old. When he was 10, Josh ran a 76:36 10-miler on a hilly course around Stone Mountain, Georgia. Had the course been certified, it would have been a Georgia state age group record by over 9 minutes.

Josh won his first race a week after turning 15, which put him 25 years ahead of me (which you'll read about next).

Josh assures me he will run a marathon one day. When he does, count on me being there.

Lord willing, I'll be running by his side.

***

14

CHAPTER

AT LONG, LONG (LONG!) LAST

Atlanta Fat Ass 50K, January 1995

After over 350 attempts, dating all the way back to November of 1978, I finally did it.

- I don't care if there were only 30 other participants.

- It doesn't matter the weather was so cold and windy that it would chill a penguin.

- I don't even mind it went by the name Fat Ass.

Come to think of it, it doesn't even bother me that most of the 30 participants ran like penguins (a slow waddle—believe me, this one makes sense.).

Ladies, gentlemen, and fellow runners, the words you are reading are being written by the 1995 Atlanta Fat Ass 50K Champion. And I've got the trophy (well, actually it's a big rock glued to a plaque) to prove it.

The time: 7:00 a.m. The place: Stone Mountain Park near Atlanta, Georgia. The date: Sunday, January 8, 1995. The weather: low 30's, with a wind chill making it feel like the North Pole. The course: 1 mile around a parking lot, then six 5-mile loops around the base of Stone Mountain (Yes, the same 5-mile loop used for the 50-mile race in 1982).

I felt adequately trained for the event. My two foremost opponents were the weather and boredom. My two training partners, Al Barker and Valerie Reynolds, were also running the event; although, they were using it as a training run. I, however, was racing. To combat the boredom, I had two aces up my sleeve:

1. I knew that at some point I would lap Al and Valerie (which would give me the opportunity to say hello,' which, when you're running alone for almost four hours, is quite exciting), and

2. My wife Cindy was going to join me around the start of the 4th lap to pace me on her bicycle (oh boy, someone to talk to!).

I started running with Valerie Reynolds in the fall of 1993. She asked me to train her for the upcoming Atlanta Marathon. We began running 20 miles or more every Sunday for several months. Thanksgiving morning (the traditional day of the event at the time) we stayed together the entire 26.2 miles. Valerie impressed me as she caught one female runner after another the last half of the race and managed to finish in 3:30:24, thus qualifying for her first Boston Marathon.

While running the first three laps, I was looking forward to seeing Cindy around the 16-mile mark. When she wasn't there, I figured I could handle one more lap by myself...alone. At the 18-mile mark, I passed Al and Val (at *their* 13-mile mark) who, if I remember correctly, grunted as I passed by. There went my first exciting moment! After the 4th lap, still no Cindy, so I figured I could handle one *more* lap by myself...still alone...but knowing that she would be there to pull me through my 6th and final lap. After the 5th lap and 26 miles, *still* no Cindy. Well, now I knew I was on my own for the duration, and the only thing I had to look forward to was the finish line.

I haven't yet mentioned that, except for the first 10 seconds of the race when Al sprinted by me ("hey look everybody, I'm leading the race!"), I had been leading the race the entire time. As the race was run *around* the mountain, I had no idea whatsoever how close anyone was to me. I wondered if my three nature calls, which cost me a total of 75 seconds (yes, I timed them), would come back to haunt me. I had two close calls my final lap, as two runners tried their best to pass me, but after leading for 29 miles, there was no way I was going to let them pass me *now!* Although I successfully held them off, it wasn't until later I found out they weren't even participants in the race. Oh well, it was more a matter of pride, anyway. I *hate* being passed—even on training runs.

I would be remiss if I failed to mention how extremely cold I was during the race. Let me just say this: On my final three laps, I picked up two cookies each time at the aid station to get some needed calories. Of the six cookies, one made it into my mouth, and maybe half of it was eaten. My mouth and jaw were too cold to chew and my nose was so stopped up that I needed to breathe—deeply— through my mouth. Put the two together, and you can picture the cookie crumbs flying everywhere. After I crossed the finish line, one of the three race officials filled out my finish card for me. Not only could I not write, I couldn't even grip the pen.

I watched the 2nd place finisher cross the line a little over three minutes behind me. As I mentioned earlier, I had no idea how far of a lead I had. Someone could have told me three minutes or three miles, and I would have believed them. After all, we started the race in the dark, and everyone was so bundled up I never really saw any faces.

I decided to get in Al's car to warm up while I waited for him and Val to finish. Figuring I'd finish in front of him, Al had given me his car keys, and after fumbling with them with 10 frozen fingers, I managed to get the door open. I climbed inside and turned the heater on, shivering for a good 20 minutes. I changed into my warm-ups and went back to the finish line and asked about an awards ceremony. The head official, who throughout the race had been my biggest fan and supporter, told me that runners could get their awards when they finished. I asked for mine, and my biggest fan asked me innocently enough what place I finished in. Apparently I had been sitting in front of the car heater during my 15 minutes of fame.

Streaking to Comrades

Imagine running every single day since 1978. No rest days or recovery days, no chilling out on rainy days and holidays, and no niggly injuries or even a bit of flu to keep you under the covers in winter. That's 33 years, 396 months, 1 716 weeks or 12 053 days of uninterrupted running, whichever way you look at it. This is what you call a running streak, and one of the USA's top streakers, Scott Ludwig, was in South Africa recently to add a bit of African flavour to his streak as he took on the Comrades Marathon for the first time. – BY CATHARINA ROBBERTZE

ENJOYING THE ATMOSPHERE AT A LOCAL RACE

The last day that Scott Ludwig didn't run was 29 November 1978. He was still studying English at the University of Florida at the time and he went to a conference in Atlanta with one of his professors. The professor had been urging him for a long time to start running and, on the trip, on 30 November 1978, Scott finally agreed to join him for a run. He still remembers every detail about that first run and says his professor ran a one-mile loop six times. Scott ran every other loop with him until he had done 3 miles. "I was pretty proud of myself after that first run, and my professor kept me at it, eventually talking me into running a marathon in March of 1979. I was hooked and haven't stopped since."

Scott can't remember when he realised he was on a streak, but about three years later he consciously made a decision to keep the streak alive. He was in Pennsylvania in January 1982 and it was 11:30 at night, but he had not been for a run yet. "I looked out of the window and it was snowing, and I thought I can't go out in that, but I did anyway and ran three miles before midnight. Now it's second nature and I haven't really thought about ending it since then. About every six months or so I have a day where I don't feel like I want to run, but then I go anyway and I always feel better once I'm out there. The next day I'm better again and want to get out there."

33 YEARS AND COUNTING

This means that for the last 33 years Scott has been getting up at 3:30 every morning to go for a run. He has never had any injury or illness that was serious enough to keep him from running and has notched up a staggering 196 800km on about 150 pairs of running shoes. He wants to keep running until he has the longest streak in the USA and hopefully until he has run 200 000 miles (320 000km) and 200 marathons. This will probably be when he is in his late seventies.

// About every six months or so I have a day where I don't feel like I want to run, but then I go anyway and I always feel better once I'm out there. /A

So why does he do it? Ask Scott and you don't really get a concrete answer; he just loves running and wants his name next to the longest streak. "As long as I don't die and I'm not in a coma, I figure I can keep going," he explains. The United States Running Streak Association's official list of active streak runners in the country places Scott at number 35, with the runner in first place on a streak of 43 years. However, Scott says most other streak runners won't do ultramarathons and jeopardise their streak, they mostly stick to their one mile per day run and average a little less than 3 000km per year.

That is what makes Scott a little different. He has run 180 marathons and 50 ultras, and likes to do at least 5km per day in recent years. He has averaged approximately 6 400km per year but he says he is trying to cut back. "I peaked at 5 400 miles (8 640km) in 1996. Back then I ran some really good times in the ultras and over long distances, but once I turned 50 my body said I should cut back. Five years later my brain caught up with my body and now I'm trying to be sensible. This year I might not even reach 4 000 miles (6 400km), which it probably a good thing, but it's hard to let go."

JUST ANOTHER DAY AT THE OFFICE AT THE SHAMROCK MARATHON

WITH MY SUPPORT TEAM AFTER THE BADWATER MARATHON

CROSSING OVER TO THE DARKSIDE

As Scott's love for running grew he looked for people to join him on some crazy running adventures, but he couldn't find what he was looking for at his local running club. So he decided to start his own running club with long-time friend and running partner, Al Barker. In 2002 they established the Darkside Running Club with six members. "Most people think we are called the Darkside because we always run in the dark, and though this is true to some extent, it was actually because we wanted to do something a bit more adventurous than 10km runs and therefore ventured onto the Dark Side."

Today they have grown to about 200 members and the club is unique in that you only have to pay a once-off fee of $25 for lifetime membership. This fee gives you access to approximately 200 runners from all over the USA, Canada and the UK who have done almost any race you can think of. "Between our members you will find someone who has experience in just about any race in the world, and what's more, you will probably have a place to stay in a city where you've never been before. I find that runners universally are very open about offering their home to another runner, even if they don't know them from Adam." Also covered by this membership fee is the club's quarterly newsletter and three free marathon entries (all in the USA).

Like most runners the sport has not only influenced Scott's fitness and health, but also his life. It has influenced his choice of friends, given him the opportunity to travel, and even made him a writer. He's written three books and says he does most of his writing whilst running. The books are all about (you guessed it) running, and he writes his club's quarterly newsletter, but Scott says there is one thing that stands out above all. "I've always thought runners are the best people in the world. It takes a special kind of discipline and dedication to run and it has made me disciplined in everything I do. That said, I think the biggest influence running has had on my life is that I don't know what night time is anymore. Come 9:30pm my day is over, where most people get their second breath then. But I have the mornings when it's quiet and you can think. I wouldn't trade that for anything."

Comrades

He presented me—OK, he *handed* me my rock (symbolic of Stone Mountain), I ate a few frozen M&Ms, picked up my official Fat Ass T-shirt and finisher's certificate, and walked back to the car in total anonymity.

A champion at last.

My finishing time was 3:48:23. Pretty satisfying, considering it was only my third ultra.

I ran the Atlanta Fat Ass six more times, including four top-five finishes.

When I directed my first ultramarathon in November of 2002, it coincided with the 50th birthday of Paula May, one of my running partners. In her honor, the race was named Paula's Fat Ass 50K. The next year, it evolved into the Peachtree City 50K and served as the first USATF Georgia Ultra Marathon Championship; the following year it hosted the USATF National 50K Road Championship.

***

15
CHAPTER

PICKING UP THE PACE

1996–1999

Al Barker, Valerie Reynolds, and I began running 20 miles or more every Sunday—rain, shine, heat, cold, wind, snow, ice, thunder and lightning—in the fall of 1993. In the first 14 years of my running career prior to meeting them, I had run 22 marathons. In the subsequent 19 years, I would run 178 more, capping it off with lifetime marathon number 200 in Honolulu in December 2012.

In 1996, I competed in 38 races, which is still the most I've ever run in one calendar year. I also managed a personal best mile of 5:10, not bad for a 41-year-old.

In 1998, I ran my highest yearly mileage ever: 5,402 miles with 2,967 of them coming in the last six months of the year. In December, I won a 50K in Tallahassee, Florida with a personal best 3:44:58. The Tallahassee event had an accompanying 50-mile race, and on that particular day, I felt so strong that I feel pretty confident saying I could have held my 50K (31 miles) pace for 50 miles.

In 1999, I ran 46 miles on my 45th birthday (the extra mile was for good luck), repeating the tradition I set for myself on my 35th and 40th birthdays. (I would also repeat this on my 50th birthday; however, on my 55th birthday in 2009, I was content to stop at 50 miles, good enough to win the Masters title at the aforementioned Tallahassee 50-mile event).

Yes, running with Al and Valerie changed my perspective on running.

The farther the better.

***

16
CHAPTER

IT SEEMED LIKE A GOOD IDEA AT THE TIME

JFK 50-Mile Run, November 2000

The JFK 50-Mile Run was first held in the spring of 1963 as part of President John F. Kennedy's push to bring the country back to physical fitness. The initial inspiration behind the race came from then-President Kennedy challenging his military officers to meet the requirements that Teddy Roosevelt had set for his own military officers at the beginning of the 20th century: that all military officers be able to cover 50 miles on foot in 20 hours to maintain their commissions.

The race from hell has a name, and it is the 2000 JFK 50-Mile Run. I have *always*, always preferred running on roads rather than trails. After almost 24 years of running road races, it was the *first* race I vowed to *never* run again (something most runners usually say immediately after finishing a difficult race, only to change their mind when the race rolls around the following year). Well, it's 14 years later, and nothing has changed. Why? Well for starters, there's a few nasty trails along those 50 miles. Beyond that? Well, let me count the reasons why:

Reason #1

The race starts innocently enough in a small town where you run along a street (mostly uphill) for three miles. I was told you needed to make a move early, as once you entered the Appalachian Trail at the 3-mile mark, you had to run single file because the trail was so narrow; therefore, the position you were in when you *entered* the trail would be the same when you *exited* the trail at 16 miles. Boy, did I prove *that* theory wrong!

I entered the trail in 23rd place (a volunteer who was counting the runners told me so). When I exited the trail a mere 13 miles later, I was in *47th* place. Granted, if I was adept at running on mountains (say, like a mountain goat), I could have held my position. However, since I was desperately afraid of falling (I basically hopped for 13 miles from rock to rock and, fortunately, *most* of the rocks I chose to land on didn't *move!*), I repeatedly pulled to the side of the trail and allowed other runners to pass. In fact, when I left the trail, a volunteer told me my position (I dropped 24 spots on the trail) and mentioned that here was one who was *not* bleeding! It's hard to fall when you're barely moving.

Once I left the trail, I had to cross a railroad track to reach the 26-mile path along the canal. Just my luck, a train was approaching from my left and a volunteer was holding his hand up telling me to stop. Naturally, I sprinted across the track because if I *did* stop (a) I'd have to wait five minutes for the train to pass and I'd cramp up really bad and quite possibly decide to call it a day right then and there, and (b) since I was intentionally disobeying a volunteer, I thought I had a *really* good chance of getting disqualified (unfortunately, it didn't happen)!

Reason #2

So then I found myself running along the canal and bored silly. For 26 miles the scenery *never* changed. Water to the left, trees on either side of the path, and once in a while...*another runner!* There was talk from others of the prestige of (a) breaking eight hours and (b) placing in the top 50. All I wanted was for this adventure from hell to be over. I didn't give a rat's a** about top 50 *or* eight hours. I didn't stop at the numerous aid stations because I didn't want to spend any extra time on the course, even if it was for something necessary like replacing the calories I had burned. No way, just let me keep going and bring this nightmare to an end.

After a while, I was in a trance *(try looking at the exact same scene for four hours!)*, and I tried to lock on to a runner in front of me. I was so mentally disconnected from running at one point I had to focus on imitating what the other runners were doing so I could do the same...and all I'm talking about is putting one foot in front of the other. I was literally watching his feet land and trying my best to emulate his pace, his gate, and that arms-swinging-by-your-side thing he had going on.

Reason #3

After 42 miles, the course transformed into winding, hilly country blacktop. Fortunately for me, I was finishing while the sun was still shining. Others weren't so lucky. The roads were so winding and hilly that it would be really dangerous to run on them at night: no road shoulder, no traffic control, and *no lights!* I ran the final 12 miles with a female competitor from Ohio who had several ultra wins to her credit. At first she had her sights set on breaking eight hours, but as we climbed the final hill and saw that an all-out 400-yard sprint was needed to reach that goal, we settled on a quick shuffle and finished in 8 hours and 19 seconds (actually, she beat me by one second...as if that mattered). I wound up in 56th place...as if that mattered, either. All I knew was: I was done, and I *wouldn't be back.*

Flash back to 36 years earlier. I was a Cub Scout in Davisville, Rhode Island. John F. Kennedy, a proponent of 50-mile walks, had just been assassinated. My Cub Scout pack decided to go on a 50-mile hike. I can't recall how long it took a rag-tag bunch of 10-year-olds to hike 50 miles, but I'm pretty sure it was longer than eight hours because I vividly recall the sun going down. In fact, the sun may have gone down twice. (It couldn't have been three times, could it? Not sure.)

Scott and Valerie JFK 50 Miler, November 2000

KEYS TO SUCCESS

Thank goodness for youth! By no stretch of the imagination would I consider myself a trail runner, and I had no idea know what to expect on the Appalachian Trail. Ordinarily this would be a recipe for disaster, but I have to believe that my age (44) had a lot to do with making it to the finish line of the JFK 50. To say I treaded lightly for those 13 miles on the AT would be an understatement; sweating bullets would be more accurate. Once I reached the canal, I was able to put myself on autopilot and do what some refer to as a *zombie jog* before I made it to the eight-mile homestretch on the friendlier and more familiar black asphalt road.

In hindsight, 14 years later, I am rather proud of my finishing place as well as my time. But I still won't be going back; trails frighten me.

***

24:00:00

National 24-Hour Championship, September 2002

12:15 p.m., Saturday, September 14, 2002. Slightly warm, a bit on the muggy side. Rain is imminent. As I stand among 167 fellow competitors behind the starting line of the 1.091-mile path circling the lake in Olander Park in Sylvania, Ohio, I wonder why I'm here and even *considering* what lies ahead. Actually, that last part is a lie: I know *exactly* why I'm here and (for the most part) what lies ahead.

If you recall, I mentioned previously that the 24-Hour Championship in 1988 was the only race I didn't complete up until that point in my running career, as I failed—albeit intentionally—to run the entire

24 hours. This year, I intended to make amends. After all, I felt I was more than ready as

- I had averaged 90 miles per week over the past nine years (without ever taking a day off for rest);
- I had averaged 4 ½ hours of sleep (weeknights) and 5 ½ hours of sleep (weekends) per night over these same nine years;
- I had run myself to exhaustion on more days than I care to remember—or should I say more days than I'm *able* to remember;
- I had practiced my "forever' pace (you know—the one you can lock into and run so easily that you feel like you can hold it *forever*) with great success for the past three weeks; and
- I couldn't get the words of my friend Gary Griffin out of my mind, as he told me seven months earlier to run in this event and "make yourself known in the ultra world."

One other goal for this event: to pad my running résumé so that it would be more attractive to the Badwater Ultramarathon race director who would ultimately decide if I would be a part of his event the following July.

Yes, I felt more ready for this event than any athletic competition I've ever participated in. At 12:17, the horn sounded, and all 167 of us were off, each with our own goals to achieve and reasons for being here. I've told you mine.

As I'm well aware, talking about the actual *running* of an event— *any* event—has been proven to be the single most boring subject matter on the planet *(look it up!)*. So, let me offer you some of the highlights of those 24 hours:

- Kevin Setnes, a world-class ultrarunner and captain of the USATF Men's 50K National Team, was participating in the event. He, like eight other runners in the field, was a former champion of this event. As each runner is allowed to set up their own aid station along the course, I set up my cooler on a card table next to a chair I shared with a fellow runner (David Sowers, who would later become an integral part of my 2003 Badwater adventure). Directly across the asphalt from me were two large canopies, three huge beverage dispensers (one full of—are you ready for this—*bottled spring water* which was emptied into one of the dispensers one bottle at a time), enough fruit to supply the entire field for a week, six chairs, and three volunteers (groupies?). I saw Setnes beneath the canopies and figured it was headquarters for his 50K team. Well, I was half right; it was headquarters, all right. His! At one point during the race, Setnes was leading (there was a leader board which was updated every hour, although in this particular instance I knew he was leading because I asked him and he told me he was leading). Early Sunday morning, Setnes dropped out of the race because he had taken ill, and you'll never believe who wound up kicking his tail! That's right, Mister-Cooler-and-Card-Table (with a Shared Chair).

- The female winner, Ann Heaslett, didn't make it to the awards ceremony, as she was rushed to the local hospital immediately after the event and treated for dehydration. In all likelihood, I should have joined her.

- For the first several hours, my name didn't appear on the aforementioned leader board (which listed the top 10), and I just knew it should have been listed. Each time I passed the scorer's tent, I said, "check your standing; you're missing me!" Finally, my name was added (at the 9:20 p.m. update, only eight hours late!), and according to the live Internet broadcast of the event, "*unknown* Scott Ludwig continues to move up and look strong." So much for Gary's advice of making myself known in the ultra world. Coincidentally, except for my name being in the official standings each hour, I was never mentioned again in the Internet updates that accompanied the standings.

- With two hours to go, David, the runner I shared a chair with, reminded me that the race paid prize money for the top five finishers. Guess what position I was in at the time—fifth! I spent the final two hours looking beneath my name on the leader board (as I had been doing the entire race because I detest being passed, especially now that money was on the line!) and actually managed to pull into fourth place during the final 120 minutes.

- While I was officially the fourth-place finisher (as you had to be a member of the USATF to actually compete), the overall winner of the event was the greatest ultrarunner in the world, Yiannis Kouros of Greece. While I was pleased with my 129.1 miles, Kouros managed to lap me more times than I care to remember.

- Prior to the event, participants were asked to guestimate their mileage (comparable to a runner's taboo of asking prior to a race, "what time are you trying to run?"). This information was posted on the official website, and I'm proud to say I was one of 12 males who exceeded their guestimates (I had guessed 125 miles). Five females managed to exceed their guestimates.

- At 1:00 and 3:00 a.m. Sunday morning, there were two incredibly strong rainstorms (complete with thunder, lightning, high winds, and course flooding). I should have stopped (there were many runners who hid beneath some of the large trees lining the course; you can insert your own dumb runner joke here), but I kept on running only to finally change shoes around 4:00 a.m. when the rain had stopped and the course flooding had subsided. The combination of 129 miles and four hours of wet-shoe running cost me both big toenails two months later. But it was worth it! (Did I mention 4th place paid $175? Or that the cost of the trip was almost $500?)

- I ended up only nine miles out of first place. Like I said earlier, I never looked above my name on the leader board except occasionally to see how far I was behind Kouros. However, in retrospect, I don't think I lost the race—I simply ran out of time. I felt incredibly strong the last three hours, even lapping Kouros once during the final hour. (OK, he stopped to change CDs in his Walkman, but I still passed him! I promise you there are not many runners anywhere in the world who can say that. In fact, I want to mention it one more time: I lapped Kouros during the final hour!) There's no doubt in my mind that if I had another four hours, I could have made up those nine miles. No doubt whatsoever.

- Kouros lapped me for the first time as I was finishing my 6th lap (around the 10K mark). I got my revenge 22 hours later. (See previous entry. The reason? Irrelevant.)

- No, I didn't sleep during the event. In fact, I woke up race morning at 7:00 a.m. and didn't take a nap until I got back to the hotel room around 4:00 p.m. Sunday. Around 6:00 p.m,. I attempted to eat dinner. Attempted.

- I was close to dehydration after the event. In fact, the medical personnel chased me around with a bag of glucose, but they didn't know whom they were messing with (someone with an incredibly strong aversion to needles). I tried eating a hot dog, managing to force down a single bite. The awards ceremony was a blur, but I did manage to stand up through it without assistance! That's more than I can say for 3rd place finisher Steve Godale, who had to be propped up.

- I finished 29 miles ahead of the first male finisher at this year's Badwater Ultramarathon. Why was this significant? Just thinking ahead.
- I managed to beat seven of the nine aforementioned former champions in the field. I remember how intimidated I was as they were introduced at Friday night's pre-race meal. Was.
- I enjoyed running a couple laps with the editor of *Ultrarunning*, Don Allison, as he and I and another runner passed a few miles dissing (I mean, discussing) *Runner's World*. Their idea, not mine (but it sure could have been).
- Speaking of *Ultrarunning*, the editor himself wrote a three-page article on the event. No, I wasn't mentioned in the article at all, but merely listed in the results, destined to remain an "unknown."
- As I mentioned earlier, Ray Krolewicz, bless his heart, referred to me as the "South's newest phenom to the ultra ranks" in the Running Journal. Where else can you be a "phenom" at age 47? Ain't ultrarunning great?
- I almost forgot: *I won the 2002 USATF 24-Hour Male Master's Championship!*

All things considered, I have to admit I couldn't have been more pleased with my performance. I was never tired or sleepy, able to successfully lock into my forever pace when I needed to, spent the vast majority of the 24 hours passing other runners (while seldom being passed, if you factor out Kouros—did I mention, I lapped him late in the race?), and did not suffer any injuries of consequence (although it took almost three months for me to have any *zip* in my legs). I was right when I said earlier I was more than ready. After all, I'd been training for nine years.

Scott at Tybee Island Marathon 2002

The Numbers Game

- 12,535: miles run by all competitors
- 500: approximate ounces of fluid I consumed
- 175: prize money (in dollars) for my 4th place finish
- 172: most mileage for any runner *(Damn you, Kouros!)*
- 162: runners completing fewer miles than I did
- 129: miles I ran
- 118: laps I completed
- 75: average number of miles per runner
- 40: number of times I was lapped by Kouros
- 38: total runners with 100+ miles
- 24: hours I spent running
- 19: hours I needed to reach 100 miles
- 13: fewest miles by any runner
- 11:09: my average pace per mile
- 9: miles I finished behind the USATF champion
- 5: my overall place of finish
- 4: my USATF finishing place (Kouros, as an invited guest, not a member of the USATF was ineligible for awards)
- 3: pounds I lost during the event
- 1: my overall Master's ranking
- 0: times the thought of running or quitting crossed my mind

* * *

18
CHAPTER

MY 28-MILE WARM-UP

Boston Marathon, April 2003

I had already made this decision in 2001 right after I mentioned to my good friend Al Barker that the 2003 Boston Marathon would, in all likelihood, be my 100th lifetime marathon. Al innocently suggested I run the course twice, by running from Boston (at the finish line) to Hopkinton (the starting line) and then the actual marathon to commemorate the occasion. As those who know me would expect, I said I would. At that time, Al said he would do it with me.

Al suggested we make it known that we were doing a "Boston Out-and-Back" so we would get media coverage, PR, or whatever else we were due. I explained to a Boston Athletic Association official in February (two months before the race) what our intentions were, primarily to make sure we would be *allowed* to run the course in reverse prior to the noon start of the actual marathon. I was told it was acceptable, as long as we were off the course by 11:00 a.m. The next thing I know Don Makson from WCVB Channel 5 in Boston (an ABC affiliate) sends me an e-mail, asking for specifics of our upcoming adventure. Once I did, he said he'd get with me the week before the marathon to go over the details of their coverage of the event.

Sometime in March of 2003, Al hit me with some bad news: He wasn't going to do the out-and-back with me. He didn't think his back would hold up for 52-plus miles. Of course, since I already stated I was going to do it, my Darkside Running Club regulations dictated that I *had* to do it (besides, if I remember correctly, this was one of the rules I suggested). The week before the marathon, Don Makson called and advised me to find Heather Unruh on race in Hopkinton Commons for a *live* interview at 10:20 a.m. I decided I would start my journey from the finish line to the start at 6:00 a.m., as I was planning to run the first 26.2 miles in four hours.

Race morning, I left a little early: 5:45 to be exact. I wanted to allow myself a little extra time in case I got off course (I took a map with me). As I expected, Al had second thoughts about *not* joining me the instant I was about to leave our hotel room. He expressed regret about backing out but offered to take my change of clothes to the starting line for me.

I couldn't believe how the course looked without the spectators and other runners...*DIFFERENT!* So different, in fact, I had to look at the map several times. Each time I looked at the map, I was reminded of one small detail I overlooked: It was impossible for me to *read* it without my glasses, which I didn't happen to have with me. Not to worry: I could just ask someone for directions. Certainly all Bostonians knew the route, right? *Wrong!* Of the 20 people I asked if I was on the proper course, only 10 knew. Naturally, some of those that knew really didn't. In time, I could tell the difference between a definitive "yes" and an "I'll never see this nut job again so I'm *telling* him yes to *get rid of him yes*."

Fortunately, I only ran 15 minutes off course, losing the route somewhere near Beacon Street. Once I was confident I was lost, I retraced my steps until I got back on course. Thinking back, I don't know how I got lost, but I think it was because I started following the Marathon banners on the street poles and once I felt confident I *couldn't* get lost, I ran out of banners...and got lost.

Once I returned to the course, I began following the porta-johns and the ESPN (which was televising the race) towers. This worked out a lot better, as these two objects were a lot larger than the fine print on my map. The run to the start was pretty uneventful, except for these few highlights:

- 5 or 6 people along the course yelled, "hey, I heard about you on TV/the radio." No one, however, asked for my autograph or wanted to take my picture.
- One man in a car at a stoplight offered me a ride to the start, even though he was going in the opposite direction.
- Too many people to remember were kind enough to tell me I was running the wrong way.

- I passed one other runner doing what I was doing but his out distance (of *his* out-and-back) was only 12 miles. He was basically walking, taking photographs, and training for the Western States 100.
- Wellesley College is amazingly quiet at 8:00 a.m. Are there *really* students living there?
- Water is hard to find along the course prior to noon. In fact, I found that in some gas stations, when you ask for water, the attendant will give you a key to the bathroom.
- My unofficial time for the actual 26.2 miles (excluding the extra 15 minutes) was 3 hours 30 minutes—the time I was hoping to run in the actual marathon.

I arrived at the starting line around 9:30, almost an hour early for my 10:20 interview. I stretched out on the road for almost 30 minutes (still thirsty!) before I began looking for the Channel 5 tent. Once I found the tent and met Heather, she took me to their hospitality tent where I drank cranberry juice (I couldn't find any water). She then conducted a practice interview (which, in all honesty was better than the live one), which included the following exchanges:

Heather: *Boston today will be your 100th lifetime marathon. So the run out here this morning was your 99th, right?*

Scott: *No, I only count official marathons in my total.*

Heather: *What do you call the run out here then?*

Scott: *A 28-mile warm-up.*

Heather: *So where's Al?*

Scott: *He's physically exhausted after winning his age group three weeks ago at a marathon in Macon.*

Heather: *(Looking at my singlet) What is the Darkside Running Club?*

Scott: *A group of people I run with who consider what I'm doing today normal.*

Heather: *Are all runners as good-looking as you?*

Scott: *Don't count on it, sister.*

OK, so actually only her first two questions were real; the final three I imagined. But I *did* have those answers ready anyway...you know, just in case she asked!

After the interview, I made my way to the Athlete's Village to meet up with Al, Paula, and Keith Wright (who I was going to run with in the actual marathon). I was eager to put on a fresh, clean running outfit (including a BRAND NEW *Darkside* racing singlet) only to find that *someone* had accidentally spilled a bottle of Gatorade *inside* my bag, saturating my entire change of clothing. Fortunately, it was cool in the morning, so I didn't perspire much, so wearing the same outfit again wasn't too big an inconvenience (but don't tell Al...guilt is *good!*).

The marathon itself? Pretty uneventful. I waited for Keith at the two-mile mark and ran with him for eight miles. At that point, we lost contact, which I used to my advantage. For the last 16 miles, every time I needed a walk break, I looked back over my shoulder and called out Keith's name...as if I was actually *looking* for him.

To top off my day, comedian Will Ferrell passed me around the 25-mile mark, and I didn't have the legs to stay with him. Of course, for me it was actually my 53-mile mark.

***

19

CHAPTER

NO STROLLING IN THIS JIM

Strolling Jim 40-Mile Run, May 2003

I first ran the Strolling Jim 40-Mile Run (which is a misnomer, as the race is actually 41.2 miles) in May of 1998. Here's my biggest mistake: *driving* the course the day before the race, which made me think the hills weren't all that bad. *Running* these same hills, however, turned out to be pure hell. My wife Cindy was going to meet me at the 15-mile mark on her bicycle to lend her support as my one-woman crew. With the mindset that the hills weren't all that bad, I was running a 7:15-minute mile pace when I met up with her. Not bad, except for one small detail: I had already hit 'the wall'…and ironically I still had a full marathon (26.2 more miles!) remaining.

Fortunately, I had Cindy to help me through it. Unfortunately, Cindy found it impossible to negotiate the hilly terrain fast enough to keep up with me. I finished up most of the race pretty much alone, except for the occasional runner that *passed* me. OK, so there were quite a few of these occasional runners. I finished up in 5 hours and 56 minutes—not too bad for a first-timer who wasn't part mountain goat. I vowed not to return, although deep down inside I knew if I did and ran a more conservative pace, I could improve on my time.

My vow not to return ended five years later, as I selected the May 2003 edition of the Strolling Jim as the perfect course for a long and hilly training run in my preparation for the Badwater Ultramarathon two months later. I want to emphasize the word *Strolling*, as my intention was to run a slow, even pace in an effort to familiarize my legs with running long distances over hilly terrain. My **first, foremost, and** *only* **goal/priority/objective** was to **complete the distance**, no matter how long it took. As I had to make a 10-hour drive from Ponte Vedra, Florida to Wartrace, Tennessee the day before the race, this goal seemed extremely reasonable.

The race began promptly at 7:00 a.m., and a contingent of 15 or so runners took off at a pretty fast clip. I, however, was not one of them. My thighs felt as if they were asleep, thanks to yesterday's drive—more specifically, sitting on my a** for 10 hours. Of course, I was comfortable knowing my plan was to take it slow and easy. However, it wasn't three miles into the race when a **second goal** came into play. The lead female runner pulled alongside me and asked me three questions: (1) did I have a crew?, (2) did I have any fluids?, and (3) did I have anything to eat? Once I responded 'no' to all three, she verbally assaulted me with comments such as "there's no way you're going to run this race under six hours" and "you're going to cramp up in a big way before you get to the finish line."

I told her I would be fine by drinking the water along the course every three miles or so. She told me I was crazy. **Goal 2 (and 2B): Finish under six hours, and finish in front of this female runner.**

Soon afterward, a runner from Ohio, Dave Corfman, pulled up alongside me. We struck up a conversation and proceeded to run the final 36 miles of the race together. It's unusual to run that long with one person in a competitive event, but we were on the same wavelength all day long. When he felt like surging, so did I. When I thought it appropriate to walk up a hill, so did he (we began calling this practice *smart hill*, as in running the hills intelligently). We even managed to pass five other runners (while being passed by none) during this time. Eventually, we finished together tied for 8th place, but Dave got a finish card before me, so I technically was 9th (not that it mattered to me; after all, this was a training run).

Two things about my run with Dave: (1) prior to running with me he had run with the female runner who had berated me earlier. Apparently she is a nationally-ranked ultrarunner (I knew this to be true because she made that point perfectly clear) who always ran this event around 5 hours and 45 minutes, and (2) as I mentioned earlier, we passed five runners while we ran together. This second point brings me to my **third goal**, for which I can thank my friend Gary Griffin, which was to **beat (a certain runner)**. As this certain runner was in the initial lead pack early in the race (back when my legs were still asleep), I doubted I would see him again. I proved myself wrong, as he came into view with a little over a mile left in the race. He had a good half-mile lead on Dave and me, but it appeared we were slowly but surely closing the gap. As we hit the last corner, I told Dave the finish was only about 400 yards away. I asked him if he thought we could kick and catch him, but we decided it wouldn't be in our best interests. I agreed, only to change my mind 200 yards later and tell Dave I'm sorry, I just have to (kick and try to catch him). Dave went with me step for step (we were obviously still on the same wavelength), and we caught that certain runner with about 80 yards to go. The certain runner, who didn't want us to pass him this late in the race, managed a slight kick but gave up with about 40 yards to go, finishing a few seconds behind Dave and me.

Dave Corfman has become a very big part of the ultrarunning scene in the United States. Not only is he a very talented runner (about two dozen 100-mile finishes, one Badwater finish, and numerous other ultras), he is also the race director of the Stone Steps 50K Trail Run in Cincinnati, Ohio.

Seconds after I completed my place-of-finish card, I jumped in the car and headed back to my hotel room in Shelbyville (about 12 minutes away) to get a quick shower, pick up my son Justin, and check out of the room. Which reminds me of my **fourth goal**, which, if prioritized, would actually have been my *first* goal, which was to **do all of these things by 1:00 p.m.** as that was the latest checkout time I could convince the hotel manager to give me. Keep in mind the race began at 7:00 a.m., I ran it in 5:52, and it was 12 minutes back to the room.

Your math is correct: I walked into the room at 1:04, only to find Justin on the phone with the hotel manager who was calling to ask why we hadn't checked out yet. I took the phone and said I'd be out of the shower in three minutes, and fortunately I wasn't charged for another day (maybe because Justin was checking us out of the room while I was showering, which briefly distracted the manager).

Justin and I stopped back by the finish line in Wartrace to enjoy the post-race barbeque (a tradition!) before heading back to Peachtree City (another 4 ½ hours in the car). I'm glad we stopped, for three reasons:

- I was starving, and the barbeque was actually pretty good.
- The female runner approached me and said, "I can't believe you finished under six hours", and asked, "'How did you do it without any support?" To which I simply smiled and didn't say a word. I didn't find it necessary.
- That certain runner was complaining to everyone within earshot (keep in mind we had been done running for over 45 minutes at this point) that "runners just don't do that in ultras" (i.e., kick at the finish), and he didn't hear us coming up behind him. When I heard the latter, I simply said we were in stealth mode, and we were silent because "obviously we weren't even breathing hard."

Sometimes the races which you *plan* to be uneventful turn out to be the *most* eventful, not to mention rewarding. Like the 2003 edition of the Strolling Jim.

You probably noticed I didn't mention the female runner and that certain runner by name. I thought that would be inappropriate. I will, however, list the results of the first 12 finishers. I consider it my obligation to you the reader:

Runner	State	Age	Time
Tim	AL	40	5:00:04
David	TN	51	5:01:07
Stan	AR	39	5:05:30
Dink	AL	37	5:07:12
DeWayne	AL	38	5:12:37
Tom	OH	40	5:18:46
Dogman	AL	42	5:42:27
Dave Corfman	OH	40	5:52:16
Scott Ludwig	GA	48	5:52:17
Richard	GA	53	5:52:20
Carl	GA	21	5:55:40
Chrissy	AR	42	6:02:13

* * *

20

CHAPTER

THE BADWATER ULTRAMARATHON

July 2003

In 1977, Al Arnold was the first person to successfully run the route from Badwater to Mount Whitney; he did it in 80 hours. Ten years later, the crossing became an official, organized footrace known as the Badwater Ultramarathon.

Running in the 2003 Badwater 135 Ultramarathon is unquestionably the pinnacle of my running career. In fact, I originally wanted to run in the 2002 edition, but in order to ensure I reached my lifetime goal of 100 marathons (which I would not attain until the 2003 Boston Marathon), I waited until 2003 (three months after Boston). Knowing how difficult and demanding Badwater is, I feared that I might do permanent damage to my body and psyche that would preclude me from running marathon #100.

My patience paid off. It allowed me time to focus on and train for Badwater for the better part of two years. Looking back, I doubt I could have done it with anything less.

The Badwater Ultramarathon is a 135-mile invitational running race starting in Badwater in Death Valley (elevation 280 feet below sea level) and finishing at the Whitney Portals on Mount Whitney (elevation 8,360 feet).

The course runs through Death Valley—where runners could face temperatures reaching 130 degrees—and over three mountain ranges with a finish on the highest mountain in the contiguous United States.

Runners are required to make their presence known at five checkpoints along the course: Furnace Creek, Stovepipe Wells, Panamint Springs, Darwin, and Lone Pine.

Badwater is recognized as the toughest footrace on the planet.

SAND WARS: EPISODE I

Badwater Acceptance, Winter 2003
Attack of the Phantom Race Director

It took 21 long months to get to this point, but it was worth the wait. I think so, anyway. Time will certainly tell.

I became interested in running the Badwater Ultramarathon right after Father's Day in 2001 after my wife Cindy gave me a copy of the video, *Running on the Sun,* a documentary of the 1999 race. I instantly became fascinated with the event. I read everything I could find about the race, including a book written by one of the participants in the event that year. Watching the video and seeing the varying degrees of pain, anguish, and suffering the runners encountered, I realized I was extremely familiar with all of it (excluding the runners getting fluids via an IV—which, by the way, is grounds for disqualification in the event). Hell, I had been living with it in some way, shape, or form for the better part of the past two decades!

I decided once I completed my 100th marathon (projected to be Boston 2003—which wound up being accurate) I would give Badwater a shot. I had already met three Badwater qualifying standards: two 50-mile races, one 100-mile race, and one extreme event—which was my 280-mile run across Georgia in 1992, but I felt I needed to pad my resume; you know, just to make sure there was no reason for rejecting my application. After all, when I told the race director in 2001 that I had run 80 plus marathons, he told me he doesn't care how many marathons I've run. When I asked if I met the qualifying standards with two 50-milers and one 101-miler (done in a 24-hour event), he said "check the website." Pretty helpful and encouraging guy! So I entered the 24-hour National Championship in September 2002 and ran 129 miles, an achievement I felt would guarantee my acceptance into Badwater.

Let me clarify *acceptance*. First of all, I paid a non-refundable $50 just to have my application reviewed by the race director. Entries are available online on January 2 of the year of the event (2003). I began filling my entry form out at 11:00 a.m. EST that day; it took me an entire hour. Later, I found out mine was the 17th application received. As 68 applications were submitted on January 2, I didn't think it would take long to reach the race director's target of 100. Once 100 entries were received, 75 runners would be invited to compete. I figured I'd hear in the very near future whether or not I was in. I figured wrong. Dead wrong. (This won't be the first time the hint of death is used in this story.)

January 11: This was the first day I expected to receive word from the race director. My friend Paula May dropped me off after we returned from a marathon in Warner Robbins, and I asked her to wait while I checked the mail. You know, for the good karma. Nothing. Dammit Paula!

January 29: According to the Badwater website, there are 97 applications on file. The race director wants to get 100 before he makes his decisions. Damn.

February 3: 98 applications. Nothing in the mail. Damn.

February 4: One of the entrants donates $1,000 to the official charity and gets an automatic invitation. The race director advises all applicants that "you, too, can be automatically invited" by donating $1,000. There are no takers. The wait continues. Damn.

February 14: 100 applications. Finally.

February 25 (or thereabouts, I'm losing track): The race director states that the invitations will be sent out this week. Damn.

February 26: One applicant withdrew. Two were automatically invited (the second being the mayor of Badwater, Ben Jones, who was pretty much already invited as the race director asked him to attempt to become the first 70-year-old to compete in Badwater). That leaves 97 applicants for 73 spots. Damn.

March 1: I received a congratulatory phone call from Gary Griffin. His friend Jeff Bryan had gotten a rejection e-mail from the race director the day before. As I had not, Gary assumed I had received confirmation. Gary assumed wrong. But this gave me hope.

March 2: The race director sent an e-mail saying invitations were mailed out on February 28. Should be any day now. However, today is not the day. Damn.

March 3, 5:00 p.m. (Time stood still for a moment): I'm in! I notice item #7 on the Entrant Contract, which basically states that I realize I may die in the event. All that for only a $250 entry fee! Damn.

March 4, 5:44 a.m.: The check is in the mail. We're going to Death Valley! Hot damn!

2003 Badwater Application

Number of Years Running: 25
Number of Marathons and 50Ks: 102

Qualifying Standard(s):
1998 24-hour National Championship, Atlanta, GA: 101 miles (19.5 hours), 27th place
2002 24-hour National Championship, Olander Park, OH: 129 miles (24 hours), 4th place
1982 Stone Mountain 50 Miler, Stone Mountain, GA: 7:28:25, 6th place
2000 JFK 50 Miler, Boonesboro, MD—8:00:19, 56th place
1992 Run Across Georgia: 280 miles in 6 days

Previous Badwater Racing Experience: none
Previous Badwater Crewing Experience: none
Previous Badwater Clinic Experience: none

My Badwater Prediction: Under 40 hours. I base this prediction on my successes in 24-hour runs, as well as the base mileage I have (87,300 miles over 25 years, including an average of 90 miles/week over the past nine years). I have a streak of 24-plus years and am accustomed to running in the heat and humidity of Georgia and Florida. I've also run successfully in the climates of Las Vegas (3:02 marathon) and St. George, Utah (2:48 marathon). PLUS: I've got a fantastic crew lined up to assist me, and they've even got a catchy slogan: Just CREW It!

My Weirdest Experience: I attempted to run solo across the state of Georgia (from Columbus to Savannah), a distance of 280 miles, in the fall of 1982. I pulled up lame on the fourth day after 159 miles as my left shin was on the verge of a major stress fracture from running facing traffic the entire time (i.e., the nap of the road took its toll). I called a friend of mine in Atlanta to come rescue me as I lay on the side of Highway 280 for four hours until he arrived.

Note: I attempted this run again in the fall of 1992 with a support crew of ONE and MADE IT! Six days, 280 miles, and more chili dogs and onion rings than I care to remember!

My Most Challenging Race Experience: The JFK 50 Miler in 2000. I am not accustomed to running on trails (I do most of my running on the streets in my neighborhood at 3:30 a.m. in the morning), and the 13 miles on the Appalachian Trail (AT) almost did me in. I was in 23rd place ENTERING the AT, and 47th when I EXITED it. Somehow, someway I managed to hold my position until the end of the race. Not bad, considering I basically WALKED the 13 miles of the AT. I don't know how you can run on loose rocks, piles of leaves, and slippery slopes unless you're a mountain goat.

Why I Run Ultras: I've been successful at them over the years. I kind of sensed this in high school because in 10th grade, I could run the 600-yard run faster than anyone in my class and DIDN'T throw up afterward. Running 5-10 percent slower than I do in marathons makes an INCREDIBLE difference in what I'm able to accomplish over distances of 50K and up. As I'm getting older and losing my speed, ultras are more and more appealing to me.

Why I Want a Slot on the Starting Line of the 2003 Badwater Ultramarathon: I'll run my 100th marathon at Boston this year, and running Badwater this July would be the crown jewel in my running career. Plus, I've been focusing on this race ever since I received the video *Running on the Sun* for Father's Day 2001 and then read the book written by one of the participants from 1999. In fact, I gave my five crewmembers a copy of both for Christmas, and they've already watched the video (SEVERAL times!) and read the book and taken notes.

Personally, I think about Badwater every day. Some days I don't know how I can run the 135 miles across Death Valley and up Mount Whitney, and then there are days when I think I have a chance to win it. It sure would be great to find out which thought is closer to reality. I picture the finish at Mount Whitney at the end of my run each day and imagine how great it would be to complete Badwater.

My Other Ultrasport Experience: none

Media That I Will Represent or Write For: I believe the Atlanta newspaper, the Atlanta Journal-Constitution, will be interested in covering it. In the January 1 edition, they listed my hopes of running Badwater in their special "New Year's Resolutions" sections.

Media That Will Cover My Experience in This Race: I'm not sure at this time (although I doubt it). See previous answer.

The Charity That I Will Represent and Raise Funds for Is: The Alex Sudduth Memorial Fund, which benefits the children's ward of Egleston Children's Hospital in Atlanta. Alex was the seven-year-old son of my next-door neighbors (Stephanie and Anthony Sudduth) who lost their son to leukemia two years ago. Stephanie and I organized a race in Peachtree City last year, the Run for Alex 5K in his memory (held in April, Alex's birth month). We are making it an annual event.

Do I speak English? yes

Does my crew speak English? yes

Will I hike Mount Whitney after the race? (hell) no

Here is my athletic résumé:

- 87,000+ lifetime miles
- Have run every day since November 30, 1978
- Run across the state of Georgia, 280 miles
- 600 lifetime races
- Masters Champion 2002 24-hour National Championship
- Member of the Atlanta Track Club Men's Masters Competitive team
- Editor of absolutely true…Tales from the DARKSIDE (a local underground running newsletter)
- Marathon PR of 2:48:41
- 10K PR of 36:14
- 5K PR of 17:12
- 50K PR of 3:44:58

SAND WARS: EPISODE II

Badwater Training, Spring/Summer 2003
Return of the DEDI(cation)

First, let me explain about the title of Episode II. It had been a long time since I was this excited about a race—at least one in which I wanted to do well. Badwater provided me a renewed sense of dedication and purpose, something I had been missing of late.

The following recounts my preparation for the 2003 Badwater Ultramarathon. Hopefully it was enough to give me what it takes to complete the 135 miles from Badwater, California *(Death Valley!)* to the portals of Mount Whitney.

Base Mileage and Conditioning

Fortunately, the regimen I had put myself on over the past 24-plus years made this my strongest area—particularly the past 9 ½ years, as I averaged over 4,700 miles annually and survived on an average of 5 hours of sleep per night. These, along with pushing myself to the point of exhaustion more times than I care to remember, are the primary reasons I even considered tackling Badwater in the first place.

Diet and Eating Habits

Diet and eating habits are admittedly my weakest area, especially when you consider the following:

- My brown-bag lunch at work had been the same every day for 24 years: bologna and cheese sandwich, Ruffles potato chips, Little Debbie Fancy Cakes, and a Diet Coke. I call it my 87-cent lunch (I did the math).

- Five years earlier, vanilla ice cream was a daily treat, although three years ago it became a *3-times-a-week* treat. Now it had dropped down to once or twice a week (depending on my weekly mileage).

- Vanilla cake with vanilla frosting is (and remains) my biggest weakness, especially when the frosting overpowers the cake itself. Everyone I know (family, friends, workmates) is aware of this, and they all make a special effort to make it known to me when there's one around. Some —actually most—even save me extra frosting.

- I could survive on fast food and pizza if I had to. I know this for a fact, as I did it during college (not counting my freshman year when I survived on Pop Tarts and cans of spinach).

- I know what fruits and vegetables are, but I'd be hard pressed to recognize more than four or five by sight (particularly since I've been told that potato chips are not vegetables).

Fortunately for me, my Darkside Running Club teammates (most notably Paula May) designed a diet for me that I began in earnest on March 3. I began on that day as I still had not received my acceptance into Badwater, so I decided to put the cart before the horse and go ahead and start my diet anyway. As you already know, that afternoon I received my invitation in the mail. Some of the highlights (poor choice of noun) of my new and improved eating habits:

- My brown-bag lunch at work became turkey or tuna on wheat bread (no mayonnaise!), veggie crisp chips, Little Debbie Rice Treats, and a Diet Coke. Back in March, I experimented with different types of bread and chips, but I found myself continually ruling them out as most of them tasted like cardboard. I learned to enjoy—make that *tolerate*—this current menu. I forgot to mention that initially I was trying vanilla wafers as a dessert but found that I had to eat an entire box of them before my sweet tooth was satisfied.

- I consumed only three hamburgers since March 3 leading into Badwater: on Al Barker's birthday, the night of the Doobie Brother's concert (I had to grill hamburgers and hotdogs for 10 people, and it would have been a crime if I didn't have at least one of them!), and on the 4th of July. Also of note: I did not consume a single serving of anything from the fried food group after March 3.

- I ate in many fast food restaurants between March and the race but always ordered either a chicken (grilled, of course) sandwich or a salad. Prior to March 3, I had never eaten a salad—or for that matter, grilled chicken—in a fast food restaurant.

- In the early days of this new diet, I allowed myself one splurge meal per week (normally after my long run on Sunday). At some point, I began feeling too guilty to splurge. So I didn't (what's wrong with me?).

- I love sweets. This diet limited me to the following sweets: jelly beans, Rice Krispie Treats, vanilla wafers, and frozen yogurt. (I may have strayed a couple* of times in March when pieces of vanilla cake with vanilla frosting appeared on my desk at work, however.) *(by a couple, I mean 8 or 9 times. OK, 12.)

- I was actually saying sentences I had never said before in my life, such as:
  - In place of French Fries, could I have a salad with my sandwich?
  - Could you fix that without mayonnaise?
  - [At the doughnut shop drive-thru] I'll have a plain bagel, please.

- [At a Mexican restaurant] I'll have the #24—there's no meat in that, right?
- [To anyone offering me vanilla cake with vanilla frosting] No, thanks.
- [After running 40 miles] I'd like two veggie burgers, please.

However, I've got to admit that I did feel better after four months of eating right. Stomach problems were almost non-existent, and I actually found myself craving salad (sometimes, not always). And best of all, my belt was fastening one notch more to the right (so did my wristwatch for that matter). I may have only lost four or five pounds, but I lost quite a bit of my circumference.

High Mileage

I selected the eight weeks from Monday, April 21 (the date of the Boston Marathon) to Sunday, June 15 (Father's Day) for some high mileage. I targeted five ultramarathons during that time to get acclimated to running long distances, forcing my body to recover quickly and pushing myself to exhaustion (figuring I would be running a lot of Badwater in that condition). My longer runs during this period follow:

Date	Miles	Comment
Monday, April 21	54	Boston Marathon out-and-back
Saturday, April 26	20	Training run (with Kelly)
Sunday, April 27	21	Training run (with Al, Paula, Eric)
Saturday, May 3	41	Strolling Jim 40-Mile Run
Sunday, May 4	20	Training run (A, P, E, and Prince)
Sunday, May 11	23	Training run (A, P, E, P)
Saturday, May 17	31	Posey's 50K Run (with Fred and Gary)
Sunday, May 18	20	Training run (A, P, E, P)
Saturday, May 24	24	Training run (A, P, E, K)
Saturday, May 31	52	8-hour track run (A, Prince, K)
Saturday, June 7	40	Pennar 40-Mile Run (with Gary)
Sunday, June 8	20	Training run (A, Prince)
Saturday, June 14	25	Training run (A, P, K)
Sunday, Jun 15	20	Training run (A, P, E, P)

Even though I only ran 805 miles during these eight weeks, I was satisfied that I averaged just over 29 miles for the 14 days listed above (note: the other 42 days I averaged 9.4 miles—"rest" days).

As I mentioned, my goal was to push myself to exhaustion, and I managed to do just that. At approximately the 30-mile mark on my fifth (and by design, final) ultramarathon during that time (Pennar), my body was pretty much crying "uncle" (although I would have liked for it to hold out for another 10 miles!).

I used the 8-hour track run on May 31 to experiment with liquid replacements and to focus on, quite frankly, being bored for extended periods of time (like I was destined to find myself at Badwater). I learned several things with respect to hydration and energy/calorie replacement:

- My body will require (a minimum of) 40 ounces of fluid per hour. I averaged 18-20 ounces per hour (water, Gatorade, Sustained Energy, and Diet Coke) during my 8 hours on the track, and the last hour proved to me that wasn't enough. I hadn't run through Death Valley before, but figuring 8 ounces of fluid for every mile, 40 ounces an hour sounded about right.
- Why Diet Coke? This workout reminded me I use it to curtail nausea during long runs.
- Sustained Energy, which (honest-to-goodness) tasted and even smelled like swamp water, is almost palatable if you mix in Crystal Light *(thanks for the suggestion, Paula)*. By the way, the Sustained Energy drink is designed for calorie replacement during endurance events. It would be torture to drink swamp water to the tune of 300 calories every 8 ounces, otherwise.
- I detest running with a bottle in my hand. That's where I knew my support crew would come in handy (please forgive the pun—totally unintentional).

One last thing: For the 30 days leading up to Badwater, I didn't consume any beer, wine, or liquor. Fortunately, the three days *prior* to these 30 days was a guys' golfing weekend in Montgomery, Alabama. After that, I'm not sure I even *wanted* any more beer, wine, or liquor for 30 days. (With one exception: I would have loved a beer immediately after the Peachtree Road Race. It had been a tradition for 34 years and counting to polish off two or three beers before 9:00 am on the 4th of July. On the other hand, it was nice not having my usual hangover by noon that year.)

Supplemental Training During the High-Mileage Stage

A while back, noted ultrarunner Ray Krolewicz said he used long–distance driving (as in a car) as a training device for endurance events. He mentioned that oftentimes it is more difficult to stay awake and focused while driving than it is while competing in ultradistance running events. With that in mind, I approached all of my driving during those eight weeks as Badwater training, which included:

Friday, May 2: 10-hour drive to Wartrace, Tennessee (which allowed me 6 hours sleep prior to running the Strolling Jim).

Saturday, May 3: 4 ½-hour drive to Peachtree City (immediately after Strolling Jim).

Friday, May 16: 4 ½-hour drive to Tallahassee (for the Posey 50K).

Saturday, May 17: 4 ½-hour drive to Peachtree City (immediately after Posey's).

Saturday, May 24: 5 ¾-hour drive to Jacksonville Beach.

Monday, May 26: 6-hour drive to Peachtree City.

Friday, June 6: 5 ½-hour drive to Pensacola (for Pennar).

Saturday, June 7: 5 ½-hour drive to Peachtree City (immediately after Pennar).

Eight trips and the equivalent of almost two days (46 mind-numbing hours, to be exact) behind the wheel. Every little bit helps!

With this cross-training base behind me, I decided to branch out into other areas:

Swimming: I tried swimming 350 yards every day for a week. I'd tell you how long each "workout" lasted, but you'd either (a) laugh or (b) not believe me. Actually, you'd probably do both. Anyway, I noticed my legs had absolutely no life in them during my morning runs following a swim. I felt it appropriate to cease and desist immediately. The lifeguards were faced with finding some other forms of entertainment.

Weightlifting: The hardest part of my weightlifting "workouts" (I have got to quit using quotation marks around that word—it may give you the wrong idea) was removing enough weights off the barbell once my son Josh finished using them. I would take off more weight than I would leave on the barbell to work out with. Once I made the weights me-friendly, I would do three or four sets of 10 bench presses...with ample[2] rest between sets.

Walking: Eric Huguelet and I walked 12 miles the last Saturday in June. We began by walking at the track so I could get a feel for my walking pace. Walking normally, I timed a mile in 14:47. I walked another mile using my trekking poles: 14:55 (must have been the added weight!). I walked one more track mile what I thought was my fastest pace yet: 14:51. I must be getting tired. Eric and I then walked another nine miles over really hilly terrain. I learned that (a) trekking poles will be helpful going up mountains and will be a detriment on

---

2   Ample being as long as it took to read one section of the daily newspaper. I had never noticed before how fascinating the obituaries were.

flat and downhill terrain, and (b) I should wear sandals or shoes with the toes cut out when I travel downhill (as my toes were constantly striking the front of my shoes). One last thing I learned: Someone who is not used to walking should not begin a walking program by walking 12 hilly miles. If you do, your butt cheeks will be incredibly sore the next day.

I paced many a runner to a Boston Marathon qualifying time in my lifetime, but none more exciting than when I paced Eric Huguelet at the 2003 St. George Marathon. Eric, needing a 3:35 to qualify for his first Boston, was running well ahead of pace when he began fading the last three miles, stopping for several walk breaks and quickly losing the cushion we built during the first 23 miles. I pushed him the last half mile, and we managed to cross the finish line with 3:35:59 on the clock.

Eric was crushed, as he thought he didn't qualify. However, what I (intentionally) failed to mention earlier was (a) Boston (at that time) allowed an additional minute for the sake of qualifying times, and (b) Eric's chip time was faster than his gun time.

Eric officially finished in 3:35:10 and qualified for his first Boston Marathon.

I continued walking in the afternoons during July while still doing my running in the mornings but didn't count the mileage toward my weekly tapering targets. Periodically, I would do my daily run and walk in one session; I found it much easier to run first and then walk as opposed to walk first then run. Insignificant? Maybe. But in one short month, I managed to lower my walking pace per mile by more than 20 seconds.

Tapering

Although my body needed the rest, this was the toughest part for me. After running to exhaustion for the better part of the last 10 years, intentionally cutting back on my mileage was hard to do. I started my tapering phase five weeks out, hitting weekly mileage (in order) of 80, 70, 60, 50, and finally 30 while maintaining my weekly long run of 20-plus miles (except for the final week). Note: I didn't count any *walking* distance in my weekly totals.

Up until the week before Badwater (the 21-mile week), I still managed to maintain my 20-mile run every Sunday, except for the weekend in Montgomery, where I ran 22 miles on Saturday instead.

Heat Training

If there's one thing I had heard about Death Valley, it's that experiencing the heat is like sticking your head in a hot oven or blowing a hairdryer directly in your face. That being the case, my crew strongly advised that a little heat training would be in order...especially since I do most of my running in the dark *(i.e., out of the sun!)*.

I began my heat (adaptation) training four weeks before Badwater. The first day I ran seven miles in the morning wearing a T-shirt and windbreaker. While I wasn't noticeably hot, I did manage to perspire enough so that I had to wring out the T-shirt when I finished. In my mind, the key was getting the heat *index* in the ballpark of Death Valley, since I didn't think I'd see temperatures in the 120s in Georgia.

Over the next 28 days, I experimented with different combinations of attire; as long as I could work up a sweat (not too difficult in Georgia in the middle of the summer), I felt it was productive.

Kelly Murzynsky arranged for me to use the sauna at her gym for the 10 days prior to our departure to California. I maxed out at 180 degrees (the highest I could get the sauna to go—also the highest temperature I could *bear!*). I read that someone trained in a sauna at 211 degrees (one degree less than the boiling point of water). A couple times in the sauna, I put my face about 18 inches away from the rocks (the source of the heat). Considering I singed my eyebrows, I have to assume the temperature had to be close to water's boiling point.

When Kelly Murzynsky first started running 20 miles on Sunday mornings with us, I knew she had the potential to be a great ultrarunner. In time I would be proven right: Kelly won the first four 50Ks she competed in. Her strong suit was being an absolute beast running the hills. The toughest Sunday runs were the ones Kelly and I ran alone, because those were the ones Kelly would literally run me into the ground.

Physical Inventory

I'm sure it was mostly mental, but I noticed my aches and pains grew as the number of days before Badwater shrank. I even went to a doctor during the last week in June to see if he could do something about my 39-month-old numb right thigh. If you knew what little faith I have in most doctors, you would realize how desperate I was.

I figure most of my pre-Badwater aches and pains were in my mind, and once I ran the first mile in Death Valley, they would all disappear. In case they didn't, I wanted you to know what I believed to be wrong with me during my tapering stage:

* Toothache
* Cracked crown
* Sore neck, right side
* Stiff upper back and shoulders
* Numb spot in right side of chest
* Right thigh (still!) numb; possibly spreading to right knee and right shoulder
* Bone spur in ball of left foot
* Stress fracture reoccurrence in left shin
* Pain in right ankle
* Ugly toes *(perpetually ugly toes)*

Advice From the Experts

I ran into several Badwater veterans who weren't hesitant to offer some free advice, such as:

"Have different shapes of fluid bottles as you will get mentally tired of holding the same shape in your hand at some point during the event." —David Jones, former Badwater Champion

"Don't do anything stupid like running in a sauna or hooking yourself up to a dryer. You don't need to pull a tire behind you for training because you aren't doing that at Badwater." — Mark Godale (referring to the scenes shown in the 1999 Badwater documentary Running on the Sun) Note: Mark competed that year and ran 29:50.

A few more from Mark Godale:

- *Get a good crew with an ultra background.*
- *Have your crew stop each mile and give you water and ice for under your hat.*
- *Many sleep the first night. That is a mistake; it's cooler running at night than during the heat of the day.*
- *Pouring water over your head is a big mistake; it could run into your shoes and make your feet wet. Use baby powder on your feet; I didn't have a single blister.*
- *Take goggles in case of a sandstorm.*
- *Good things to eat: soup, peanut butter, mashed potatoes.*

"Running in the southeast is a big advantage as you get used to running in heat AND humidity." —Mark Henderson, Badwater Veteran

A few more from Mark Henderson:

- *In Death Valley, the heat radiates from 360 degrees—wear white and DRINK!*
- *I wore Teva Trail Sandals and a good sock. Kept my feet cooler and blister free.*
- *Demonstrate patience and discipline early to conserve your legs for the long haul.*
- *Bring a variety of things to eat and drink, maybe things you don't normally eat during races, as there's no Walmart close by.*

"Don't do it." —David Jones

"Enjoy the journey. Be happy out there. It'll be a great experience." —Mark Henderson

"The crew needs to train like the runner. The pacers will be out there quite a while, and they need to train for the conditions. The crew member who is driving the van also needs to drink frequently and stay hydrated; it's a dry heat, and you won't even notice that you're losing precious fluid." —Andy Velazco, 2002 Badwater crew member and 2003 Badwater participant (from his article "The Glamorous Life of an Athletic Supporter," Marathon and Beyond July/August 2003, as well as from a meeting he conducted with my crew and me in February).

"The runner is going to need a strong crew to make all decisions for him once the race starts. The runner's opinion of not needing something is irrelevant. The runner won't feel like eating or drinking, so just give it to him or her and make sure it's consumed." —David Sowers, veteran Badwater crew chief (from a meeting he conducted with my crew and me on April 26).

A few more from David Sowers:

- *The crew must be physically and mentally prepared for hardships as this event eats up crews as it does competitors.*
- *Water should be bought figuring 20 ounces per hour per person. The water will be used for drinking, eating, and washing.*
- *The real race doesn't begin until Stovepipe (mile 42).*
- *Buy ice and gas every chance you get.*
- *A crewmember with sunburn, blisters, or becomes dehydrated has just become a liability.*

And a personal favorite from David:

"Never say how bad Scott looks or get into a pity party with him. He is going to have some very low points and will piss and moan; just change the subject and try to figure out if it is a fuel/hydration issue or if he is just a (we'll go with) pansy."

Final Thoughts About Tapering

A thought occurred to me during my tapering phase: *I'm spending more TIME preparing for Badwater during my rest (tapering) period than I was during my high-mileage period.* How can that be, you may ask.

Consider, during the high-mileage period, running 100 miles a week took approximately 800 minutes. Add in the time for my requisite weight training, and the total grows to a whopping 806 minutes a week.

Now, during a randomly-selected tapering week (we'll go with the 50-mile week):

* 50 miles of running takes approximately 400 minutes.
* Walking three miles per day (21 miles per week) takes approximately 315 minutes.
* Spending 45 minutes in the sauna five days during the week takes 225 minutes.

Adding these up totals 940 minutes a week…*WITHOUT* weight training added in! So much for rest. I'm actually spending almost 20 percent MORE time "resting" for Badwater than I was training for Badwater.

This tapering phase not only made me feel more tired than I did during the 100-mile weeks, but I discovered I was a lot hungrier as well (my metabolism couldn't change *that fast*, could it?)!

Final Thoughts

I felt like I did my homework. I ran hard (and easy, when the schedule called for it); I (re)learned to walk; I cross trained *(Weightlifting! Swimming! Golf!)*; I improved my dietary habits; I worked on heat-acclimation; I tested all my gear (sandals, hats fuels/fluids); I obtained a wealth of advice from books, magazines, and Badwater veterans; and I tapered more than I had in the past 10 years.

But most of all, I felt ready for two very distinct reasons:

I had a very positive mental attitude about Badwater.

I had the utmost faith and confidence in (and appreciation for) my Badwater crew.

It should be memorable. I hoped my crew and I would enjoy the adventure.

SAND WARS: EPISODE III

Badwater Ultramarathon, July 2003
The Desert Strikes Back

Seven Days in July.

Badwater Week.

And what a week it was.

Friday, July 18 (4 days to go)

Paula May, our crew chief, held the final Darkside crew meeting at her house. Gary, Al, Paula, and me. Josh? Had to work. Eric? Went to the Atlanta Braves game. Priorities, you understand.

> I met Paula May at a track meet in Peachtree City in 1999. Paula is one of the finest women Masters runners in the southeast, and there is no doubt in my mind that when she is in her 60s, she will be compiling her fair share of age group records in the state of Georgia. I couldn't have chosen a better runner, organizer, and (perhaps most of all) disciplinarian to be my crew chief.

We went over our final gear check and chronological plan for the upcoming week. It appeared we had our game plan firmly in place. All that remained was the execution. Of the game plan, that is (not *me!*).

Years of training and months of planning were about to be put to the test. We believed we were ready. And willing. And yes, able. We'd find out soon enough.

Saturday, July 19 (3 days to go)

Delta takes us from Atlanta to Las Vegas (by way of Dallas). I'd like to say an uneventful airplane flight, but that would be a lie. As I had been heavily hydrating the past several days, I finished off a 20-ounce bottle of water just before boarding the plane. After sitting on the plane for 30 minutes (we still had not left the gate), I realized I had to urinate. Desperately. Just as I was about to visit the restroom, the pilot announced we were ready to take off and to please be seated. OK, I could wait until we were in the air.

However, we crept along the runway, making my particular condition magnify in urgency. When the pilot announced that we were "fourth in line for takeoff", that was it for me. I jumped out of my seat (figuring I had time, since planes take off at two-minute intervals) and headed to the restroom, despite the flight attendant reminding me that the pilot asked that we be seated. I told her I was sorry, but I simply couldn't wait any longer.

While I was inside the restroom I heard the flight attendant (obviously on the phone to the pilot) saying "I'm sorry, sir, he said he couldn't wait any longer and ignored me." Terrific; two years of dedicated Badwater training down the drain because I know once I exit the restroom I'll be escorted off the plane. The pressure was so intense that I wasn't even able to urinate. Upon exiting the restroom, I was relieved (figuratively, not literally) that the flight attendant merely assaulted me verbally (as if I were an eight-year-old) about disregarding the pilot's instructions. I apologized and told her it wouldn't happen again. Once we were in the air I returned to the restroom, where I was finally relieved (literally, not figuratively).

Once we landed in Las Vegas, we rented our 14-passenger van, dropped off two of the removable seats (we needed storage space!) at the house of a friend of Paula's and made a final shopping trip (cooler, meals, water, miscellaneous items) to Walmart. Finally, we checked into our hotel for some much needed rest (I slept for 12 hours—something I haven't done since college).

Sunday, July 20 (2 days to go)

Gary, Eric, Paula, and I went for a short run in Las Vegas. We noticed we were perspiring—something we weren't expecting, considering (a) we were running a 9-minute per mile pace, and (b) there's no humidity in Vegas. What implications did this hold for Badwater?

We loaded up the van and made the 2 ½-hour drive to Furnace Creek, where we were welcomed by temperatures hovering around 120 degrees. **Welcome to hell.** Once we settled into our rooms, we drove out to the starting line in Badwater, where it was even warmer. Driving back to the hotel, we let Josh out of the van two miles out so he could test the conditions.

Gary and I waited for Josh, anxious to hear his report. However, he didn't need to say a thing: the color of his cheeks said it all. They were BRIGHT RED, approximately the color of a ripe tomato. Later that night, Josh and I went to the pool to cool off. Or so we thought. The water temperature had to have been in the 90s, and the air temperature was still close to 110. Surely the conditions would improve by Tuesday (race day).

The rest of the evening was spent raiding the hotel's ice machines and wondering whether or not Al (he was flying to Las Vegas that evening and renting a car) would be able to find us in Furnace Creek. He did. A good omen, perhaps?

It's about time I formally introduced you to Al Barker. As Al will be quick to tell you, he and I have run about a zillion miles together. He's not far from the truth. We met at the finish line of the 1993 Atlanta Marathon, and since then we have trained together every weekend and collectively run over 350 marathons or ultramarathons and a healthy dose of shorter races while accumulating our fair share of frequent flyer miles.

Monday, July 21 (1 day to go)

A short run to start the day followed by a visit to the hotel's breakfast bar. Actually, breakfast *buffet* is more like it. Fresh fruit, cereal, breakfast burritos, eggs, bacon, sausage, hash browns, English muffins, biscuits and gravy, pancakes, apple fritters, juices, coffee, soda, water...good timing, as the crew and I were able to load up on some much-needed calories. After all, we anticipated surviving on Fig Newtons and pretzels for the next two days.

We made a trip to the Furnace Creek Visitor's center at noon to pick up my race number. We met Jay Birmingham, the first man to officially race from Badwater to Mount Whitney over 20 years ago. He autographed a copy of his book about his accomplishment, The *Longest Hill*, for me. I met Chris Kostman, the race director, and had my pre-race mug shot photo taken. Three hours later, my crew and I would return for the pre-race clinic.

Imagine 300 people in a room...for almost three hours...with barely-functioning air conditioning...and temperatures outside hovering around 120 degrees. Sound like fun? Sounds like pre-race conditioning, if you ask me. I can't remember the last time I was that hot (wait—yes I can, it was the day before!). But you get the picture. We were all familiar with most of the information presented in the clinic—race rules, race history, etc. A short video of last year's event was shown, focusing on Pam Reed's historic finish (the first female winner of Badwater). Pam was back to defend her title, and she was assigned to my time group (10:00 a.m., the other two groups starting at 6:00 a.m. and 8:00 a.m.). Pam, deservedly so, was presented with a plaque in honor of her accomplishment. At the end of the clinic, all runners were invited on stage to be introduced to everyone else in the auditorium. It was so hot on stage that my knees started to perspire.

Drops of perspiration were literally saturating my shoes. More pre-race conditioning, I assume. Twenty painful minutes later, we were free. Unless, of course you opted to attend the foot clinic. Which we did. Fortunately, Paula felt comfortable that she knew how to take care of my feet should problems arise, but she and Gary attended anyway. Me? I went outside to get Marshall Ulrich's autograph for a friend of mine. I also got to see his much-publicized feet, with all ten toenails having been surgically removed. Hmmm...no black toenails for him! Plus, it was cooler outside than it was in that damn auditorium.

We ate dinner as a crew one last time before tackling the beast. The crew gave me a card wishing me well, with a personalized message from each one of them. (Josh had signed with the insightful message "Your son, Josh" which eliminated any possibility of me confusing him with all the other Joshes in my crew.) Early to bed: 9:00 p.m. The game plan was for me to sleep until 6:00 a.m., eat breakfast at 6:30, and then nap a few more hours before we headed to Badwater at 8:55. Great plan.

Tuesday, July 22 bleeding into Wednesday, July 23 (0 days to go)

Great plan, but terrible execution. I was awake at 1:05 a.m. and absolutely could NOT get back to sleep. I was, however, ready to eat at 6:30 a.m. (although it killed me to make another pass through the breakfast bar and only eat two pieces of French toast, some eggs, and a few pieces of melon). Such a deal for $8.50. Next on the schedule? A short nap. If a short nap means lying on the bed staring at the ceiling for 90 minutes, then my nap was a success. At 8:55 a.m., I was *more* than ready to go. It was time to get this show on the road, or as one of the support vans had written on both sides, to "shut up and run." My crew and I boarded the van at precisely 8:55 a.m. and headed over to Badwater, semi-oblivious to what was in store for us. Soon enough I would be *totally* oblivious to just about everything.

We arrived at the starting area on schedule, just in time for the race director to call all runners to the Badwater sign for pre-race photos. If standing directly in the hot sun for 20 minutes *(hold the banner up a little bit higher...now lower...just a bit higher...now hold it... and smile!)* just before the race is about to begin is a good idea, then this was certainly a good idea. However, if sitting in the shade and hydrating for those final minutes before the starter's pistol goes off at 10:00 seems like a better idea, then this was a bad idea. You decide.

We assembled at the starting line around 9:58, listened to the starter's instructions, stood silently for the National Anthem, and shook off any remaining pre-race jitters. At precisely 10:00 a.m., we were on our way to a destination some 135 miles away.

First Checkpoint—Furnace Creek (18 miles)

Pacing was prohibited in this segment, so my crew provided pit stops every mile or two (depending on how I felt). At first, the entire crew would tend to me at once. Imagine being mugged by five people armed with spray bottles, water bottles, wet towels, and sunblock; it's the best description I can offer. Soon enough, they would develop an assembly-line rhythm that was much more efficient and effective. I ran with Pam Reed, the defending champion, for...oh, let's call it four miles...before she pulled away. I was content to run alone, not wanting to expend valuable oxygen by making small talk with any of the competitors. My sole focus was to move forward at all costs. I reached Furnace Creek in 3:02, an average pace of 10:06 per mile. I changed shorts, shoes, and socks, as they were totally soaked with perspiration and water.

Several members of my crew spent a lot of time talking to Pam Reed both before and after the race. Her amazing talent is overshadowed only by her incredible modesty. Her 2003 Badwater memories can be found in chapter 1 of my book *A Few Degrees from Hell.*

Second Checkpoint—Stovepipe Wells (42 miles)

Gary was my first pacer, and he opted to run this entire 24-mile stretch so he could develop a *feel* for this event. As we got close to Stovepipe Wells, Gary and I both got to experience what 130 degrees *feels* like. For weeks leading up to this event, we had heard the analogy that the heat feels like putting your head inside a hot oven or is like blasting a hairdryer directly in your face. Gary and I and the rest of the crew can now testify that is *exactly* what 130 degrees feels like! It was so hot, the palms of my hands felt like they were on fire (due to the heat radiating off the road surface). I continually asked Gary to splash water on my hands to cool them off. A crewmember for another runner said they put a thermometer on the blacktop road, and it read 141 degrees. The soles on Gary's (brand new!) shoes began to separate, as the heat was melting the glue holding them together.

Gary Griffin will be telling you how he and I came to know one another soon. Until then, just know that Gary is one of the finest people I've ever met as well as one OUTSTANDING ultrarunner. If you're looking for a great 50K or 50-miler, please allow me to recommend the Tallahassee Ultra Distance Classic in Wakulla Springs (near Tallahassee), Florida held annually on the second Saturday in December. Gary and his lovely wife Peg are the co-race directors. Please be sure to tell them I sent you!

Occasionally a desert wind would blow across the highway. If you're thinking this served to cool us off, you would be mistaken; those desert winds felt like blasts from a roaring fire, and the best thing I can say about them is that they didn't singe my eyebrows — even if it felt like they did. We completed our second leg in 6:28, an underwhelming pace of 16:10 per mile. At least we were getting ready to cool off by heading up to Towne's Pass.

Third Checkpoint—Panamint Springs (72 miles)

OK, so maybe heading up to Towne's Pass isn't such a great thing after all. It's a seemingly endless (18-mile) climb to 5,000 feet. Eric accompanied me for this portion of the course, and the only analogy I can make is that it was similar to walking up flights of stairs for the better part of five hours. Now's probably not the best time to mention that I detest walking up stairs. I experimented with trekking poles, but it was difficult to say if they were more help or hindrance. Once we reached the summit, I changed into my running sandals (actually, the crew changed them for me) so my toes would not bang the front of my shoes on the downhills. (I would repeat this for the duration of the event on the downhills.) The rest of the crew alternated pacing me once we reached the summit before Paula took the final stretch right before the checkpoint to allow the other crew members to use our hotel room at Panamint Springs to shower and take a quick nap. I mentioned to Paula that I was debating whether or not I should stop at the room and finally decided that I wanted to take a quick shower and a short nap so that I could psychologically divide the remaining 63 miles into a different day from that of the first 72 miles. We completed the third leg in 9:04, a robust 18:08 per mile pace.

Intermission

Somewhere around 4:30 a.m., Paula and I entered our room at the Panamint Springs Resort. If *resort* meant *Norman Bates Motel*, then yeah, this was a resort. I took a quick shower (I forgot to remove my watch, so once it got wet the face got all fogged up and was of no use for the remainder of the event). I stretched across the bed and managed to fall asleep, and the next thing I knew, Paula was out of the shower. She lay down on the other bed and said she was going to sleep for five minutes. As we had no alarm clock, I was afraid to fall back asleep for fear that we would not wake up in five minutes and sleep away valuable time. In approximately 90 seconds, Paula bounced up and said "Let's go!" She never fell asleep. I found out later my sleep had consumed a whole 60 seconds. Fortunately, in my mind I *did* fall asleep, and I could now mentally divide the race into two different days. (To this day, I am the absolute *master* of catnapping! What can I say? It's a gift.)

Fourth Checkpoint—Darwin Turnoff (90 miles)

Eric was called back to active duty, as the next 18 miles were uphill—*all of them!* There was very little terrain that was even remotely runnable. Eric did a superb job keeping me motivated, focused, and hydrated during this period. We even managed to pass a few other runners (climbers?) during this portion of the course. Eric (rightfully so) reprimanded me when I broke one of my racing guidelines (no wasted motion) by taking a few steps backward to see a wounded bat on the side of the road. The fourth leg took 6:22, an it-could-have-been-worse 21:13 per mile pace.

It was during this stretch that my crew and I realized just how difficult it could be to consume 300 calories per hour during an ultra event such as Badwater. Up until now, I was taking my Sustained Energy (SE) drink (flavored with Crystal Lite lemonade) for the bulk of my calories, occasionally eating pretzels, jellybeans, or peanut butter to round out my 300 calories per hour. But at this point, I was starting to gag at the thought of drinking any more SE. Paula asked me what I would like to eat, and I replied popsicles. Al made a quick trip in his "spare" car to find some. When he returned, we were disheartened to find that after eating two popsicles I had consumed a whopping 30 calories! At that point, I began eating small portions: three pretzels, four jellybeans *("how many calories now?")*, two bites of peach Jell-O *("how many NOW?")*. Unfortunately, I kept needing to take a swig of SE to round out my 300 calories. Gag.

Fifth Checkpoint—Lone Pine (122 miles)

I don't know who was looking forward to this 32-mile stretch more: my crew or me. After seeing me walk for the better part of 30 of the last 48 miles, they were ready to run (*run* in this case meaning get this thing over *with*). Paula (our downhill specialist) took the first pacing assignment, and before I knew it, we were off at an 8:00-minute pace. I would pick out targets from which to run from and to and would continue this practice over the next 32 miles. With the exception of Eric, who we were saving for the final 13-mile climb up Mount Whitney, Paula, Gary, and Josh got excited and broke a pre-race request of mine (don't tell me how my fellow competitors are doing) by mentioning I was in 8th place. To this day, I refer to this part of the race as my 32-mile fartlek.

Being this late in the race, knowing where I stood wasn't such a bad thing, as holding my place and finishing in the top ten at Badwater was certainly a realistic expectation at this point. An expectation I was fairly comfortable with, until Eric told me around mile 115 that there was a runner up ahead, and I should be able to catch him in four or five miles at our current pace. Josh was my next pacer, and I asked him if he wanted to catch the other runner NOW. He did, and so did I. We sprinted approximately a mile where we caught and passed the runner, one who I had last seen over 100 miles ago (none other than *Running the Sahara* man himself, Charlie Engle). Eric unofficially timed our mile in 8:15, but it felt like a sub-6:00. Gary took the next leg, and Eric mentioned there was yet another runner about a mile ahead who I could catch in four or five miles. Gary and I shuffled along until we spotted this runner in the distance. As I did with Josh, I asked him if he wanted to catch the other runner now. He did, and so did I. We took off at a 6:0-minute pace (or 8:15 if you believe Eric) and caught him within a mile. Adding insult to injury, we caught him on an uphill. At mile 120. Ouch. (We found out later this particular runner finished an incredible *nine hours* behind us.) Josh took the final two-mile stretch into the checkpoint in Lone Pine, where we found out we were now in 6th place.

I had the pleasure of running and talking with Charlie Engle for five miles or so during the early miles of the race. In that short amount of time, he relayed his entire life story to me. Please: do yourself a favor and see *Running the Sahara*. What Charlie and his two partners accomplished is equal parts inspiring and unbelievable.

Paula had prepared some Raman noodles for me, the first food I had in 36 hours that remotely resembled an actual meal. It was heavenly, all five bites. Even if they were cooked on the radiator of our team van.

Sixth Checkpoint—Mount Whitney (135 miles)

As Josh will be quick to tell you, I was absolutely dreading the final 13-mile leg to the portals of Mount Whitney. And rightfully so: After 122 miles of desert and two mountain ranges, making a runner cover these final 13 miles uphill was simply the work of the devil! Eric was once again my pacer, and he did everything in his power to keep me focused, positive, and hydrated. I managed to stay focused, positive, and hydrated—for seven miles. At that point—six miles from the finish line—I fell backward, barely maintaining consciousness. I asked for some more Ramen noodles, but Paula had nothing to heat them with except for (once again) the radiator of the van. The noodles were warmed, slightly, but they were extremely crisp. Paula, Gary, and Al provided shoulders to (literally) lean on, as there were a few moments I nearly fell off the side of the mountain. Paula was force-feeding me Gatorade, and Gary was continually splashing my head and shoulders with ice-cold water. I asked one of them to slap me in the face, but they wouldn't do it. I guess they thought a slap might render me totally unconscious, which would put a serious cramp in completing the journey. I continually asked Josh who was behind me thinking that—surely—someone would be passing me in my limited condition. Unfortunately, if someone *did* make an attempt to pass me at this point, there wasn't a thing I could do about it. Fortunately, no one did.

The last two miles seemed endless, as we wound around the mountain with no end in sight. Cars were passing us in both directions, many shouting words of encouragement as we neared the finish line. At least I think we were nearing the finish line. Occasionally I would find myself walking more side-to-side than forward, a victim of fatigue, exhaustion, and (I'm convinced) oxygen deprivation (we were at altitude, remember?).

Eric drove the van ahead to take his video camera to the finish line officials, hoping they would film us as we triumphantly completed our mission. He agreed to meet us at a point one mile from the finish, where the six of us would congregate and run the rest of the race as one. When we caught a glimpse of Eric in our headlamps, it was a bittersweet feeling as *thankfully*, we only had a mile to go, but nonetheless *we still had a mile to go!*

After what seemed like another hour, we saw the lights at the finish line. It was now just after 10:30 p.m. The six of us ran (meaning, shuffled sort of fast) with our heads held high through the finish line banner, officially signifying the successful completion of our journey. Hugs all around! Chris Kostman officially told us that we finished in 6th place, and we were the 3rd place male finisher. Not bad for a bunch of Badwater rookies. The sixth leg had taken 4:10 to complete, a 19:14 per mile pace. Not too shabby when you take into account the last two miles consumed a full hour.

I sat down in the official finisher's chair, surrounded by my wonderful crew, for some final photographs for the scrapbook. I literally looked like death warmed over, but I couldn't have cared less.

We enjoyed our journey, and we were successful. We couldn't have asked for anything more.

Thursday, July 24 (2 days after)

My crew—God bless 'em—joined me for a three-mile run (gotta keep the streak alive!). Actually, Paula was banging on my hotel room door at 9:00 a.m. with a pair of my running shoes and two bottles of waters in her hand, accompanied by her gentle, reassuring voice telling me to DRINK THESE, PUT ON YOUR SHOES— WE'RE GOING FOR A RUN! Afterward, a little housekeeping on the van followed by an incredible lunch at the pizza parlor across the street from our hotel, the Dow Villa. Josh and I split a large cheese pizza, but we ate less than half of it (Josh because he ate everything on the late-night menu at the hotel's diner the night before; me because my stomach had apparently shrunk over the past two days). I spent the afternoon limping back and forth across the street to the laundromat to wash some of the dirty clothes Josh and I had generated during the week. I met the wife of a Badwater entrant (Art Webb, the 211-degree sauna guy) at the Laundromat, and she told me her husband was still on the course. We passed him on our way back to Las Vegas the next morning; he was at the half-way point of the course as he was experiencing some difficulties. He did eventually finish, however.

All Badwater participants and crewmembers were invited to a pizza dinner at a local elementary school that evening. We spent a lot of time talking with Pam Reed (who successfully defended her title, by the way) about her performance and her training. She said she had to run three times a day, as she had to manipulate her running around her demanding schedule as a mother of three. I invited her to our 50K race in November, and she said she'd run (she didn't) if I'd return the favor and run her race (I didn't either) in December.

After dinner, a short video of this year's race was shown. As my luck would have it, there was a special feature on each of the top *five* finishers (I finished 6th, remember?). Regardless, it was well made and very inspirational (up to the point that it *didn't* convince me to run it again).

Following the video, Chris Kostman hosted the awards ceremony. He asked all runners who failed to complete the course to stand, and they were given a rousing ovation for having the guts to try. Very deserved. Then, all finishers were called to the front of the room to receive their finisher's medal and, for those finishing under 48 hours, the coveted belt-buckle. We posed for photographs — I've never been in front of so many flash bulbs before — and then Pam and men's winner Dean Karnazes were asked to say a few words. Chris closed the evening by referring to all of us as part of the Badwater family.

A pretty nice honor.

Postscript: On Friday, we made the drive back to Las Vegas. Obviously, we retraced our steps along the same route we started three days ago in Badwater. If I hadn't already decided I would never run the race again, this would have done it for me. I realized that, yes, the heat was a huge factor in my performance, but the mountains were much more significant. I cursed the Running on the Sun video for not highlighting the crossing of the mountain ranges (the leaders in the film ran through the mountains at night, so the terrain wasn't very noticeable.). We stopped in Stovepipe Wells for a drink, and the heat — only slightly over 110 degrees today — still made it feel like we were sticking our heads inside a hot oven.

Friday night, we enjoyed a crew victory dinner at the Pink Taco in Las Vegas. Afterward, Paula, Eric, Al, and Gary returned to the hotel for some much needed rest before our 6:00 a.m. flight to Atlanta the following morning. Me? I had promised Josh that if I was still able to walk after the race —at this time what I was doing barely qualified as walking—I would take him to see the casinos before we returned to Atlanta. The four hours Josh and I spent at MGM Grand, New York New York, Mandalay Bay, Excalibur, and Luxor I wouldn't trade for anything. Josh was so impressed with the large casinos, the bright neon lights, and the endless eye candy the city has to offer. But for me, walking on two severely blistered feet was a true test of my pain threshold. (I'm sure I exceeded it somewhere during the night.) We finally got to bed just after midnight, allowing me two hours of sleep before I had to wake up for one last run with Gary before we all headed to the airport for our long-awaited (and triumphant) return to Atlanta.

And yes, you read the previous sentence correctly.

Badwater, July 2003: Scott and the Crew

Scott's Badwater Statistics

Total Inches Ran	8,515,584
Total Minutes Ran	2,192.77
*Total Steps Taken	193,360
*Total Calories Consumed	11,000
*Total Calories Consumed via Actual FOOD	500
*Total Calories Consumed via Sustained Energy (gag)	10,500
Total Distance Covered (in miles)	134.4
Total Distance With a Pacer (in miles)	117.4
Total Distance Without a Pacer (in miles)	17
*Total Distance RAN (in miles)	90
*Total Distance WALKED (in miles)	44
*Total Number of Pit Stops	100
*Number of Pit Stops Resembling a Chinese Fire Drill	2
Number of **Incredibly Efficient Pit Stops (**if you don't factor in my lingering)	98
*Total Pounds of Fluids Consumed	100
Total Time (in hours)	36:32:46
Bib #	20
Average Pace per Mile	16:19
Total Pounds of Weight Lost During the Race	10
Overall Place of Finish	6
Number of Women Ahead of Me	3
Number of Men Ahead of Me	2
Total Number of Shoes/Sandals/Socks Worn	3/2/10

Number of Blisters on My Feet	4
Number of Blisters on My Feet That HURT	3
% Slower Than Pam Reed, Overall Winner	28%
Quickest Leg in Relation to Pam (Furnace Creek)	16% slower
Slowest Leg in Relation to Pam (Stovepipe Wells)	44% slower
From 2002 Backward, Place of Finish My Time Would Have Placed Me in 13 Previous Badwaters	6, 7, 9, 8, 4, 3, 2, 2, 3, 3, 3, 4, 4 (1990)
Number of Times I Thought About Quitting	0
Number of Times the Crew Thought About Quitting	0 (tough bunch!)
Number of Badwaters in My Future	0
Number of Hallucinations	0
Number of Hallucinations I Expected	3 (at least!)
Highest Temperature Reported on the Course (in degrees F)	133
Highest Recorded Temperature on Earth...ever!	134
# of Runners in the Race	73
# of Runners Who Completed the Race	46
% of Starters Who Completed the Race	63%
% of People Receiving Medical Aid Who Were Crew Members	40%
% of Darkside Crew Members Who Received Medical Aid	0
Youngest Starter's Age	31
Oldest Starter's Age	70
# of Men Who Started the Race	57
# of Women Who Started the Race	16
# of Men Who Completed the Race	31
# of Women Who Completed the Race	15

% of Men Who Completed the Race	54%
% of Women Who Completed the Race	94%
*Distance I Covered When Pam Crossed the Finish Line (in miles)	105
*Distance I Had Remaining When Pam Finished (in miles)	29.4
Number of Significant Items in This List	0

Badwater Elevation Profile

Checkpoint	Distance	Elapsed Time	Pace per Mile
Furnace Creek	18	3:02	10:06
Stovepipe Wells	42	6:28	16:10
Panamint Spring	72	9:04	18:08
Darwin Turnoff	90	6:22	21:13
Lone Pine	122	7:27	13:58
Mount Whitney	135	4:10	19:14

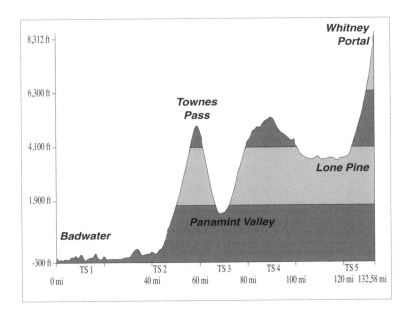

KEYS TO SUCCESS

Outside of tinkering with speed work in the earlier part of my running career, I have never trained harder or more diligently for a race than I did for Badwater. Beyond that, I have never been more intrigued, more focused, or more intent on crossing a finish line than I was when I made my way out to Death Valley. From the moment I first saw the Badwater Ultramarathon captured on film, I had no doubt that one day I would compete in the toughest footrace on the planet. If positive thinking ever got a runner to a finish line, this was that time. The support of my well-trained, always-attentive, and positive-thinking crew was the rest of the equation that resulted in our collective success.

***

21
CHAPTER

CONGRATS TO THE CREW

By Paula May

Hello, Darkside Crew:

Skinny Bitch here with the last word.

I'm very proud of everyone's contribution to the Badwater mission. An awesome job for a bunch of rookies (or even veterans, for that matter). We may have started out a little rocky with a few squirts of sunblock in Scott's eyes and looking like the Keystone Kops for those first 17 miles, but we caught on and had the pit stops down to a science by the time we were on the home stretch.

We got Scott through it with minor damage: a few (huge!) blisters and battered muscles, but no gastric upsets or injuries which would have ended our Badwater quest quickly.

Sorry about all that barking…but you guys sucked it up and responded in true soldier fashion in order to help Scott accomplish the feat he had before him. Everyone performed critical, necessary tasks that resulted in a successful race for Scott and a satisfying experience for the crew.

Josh—I know your dad is as proud of you as I am for being a great team player, always having a positive attitude, being available to run, pacing your dad through some of those difficult hot miles before Lone Pine, and being my go-fer. There were so many tedious tasks that I needed done, and you were always there to handle them. I'm so glad you were part of the crew.

Al—You were my main "go get me" guy. Smart idea to get the back-up vehicle and; to make those runs to the closest town to get me ice, popsicles, and fig newtons. And of course, being available to Scott as a pacer was invaluable. And you get the prize for comic relief with "put me down for a turd."[3]

Gary—Where you got the energy and stamina for pacing Scott through some of the most difficult, hot, early miles, I will never know. I know Scott and the entire crew appreciates that you hung with him to brave those 133-degree temperatures before Stovepipe Wells and then again when the temperature rose on the second day

---

3   Paula and the crew maintained tedious, detailed records of everyone's intake and output throughout the event. At one point Al walked out into the desert, and when he returned to the crew he—in his best John Wayne hitching-up-his-pants impersonation—proudly delivered his classic (and oft-repeated) line.

on the road to Lone Pine. Those 60 miles you ran would have left me wilted and worn out to the point I wouldn't have had much left for everything else my role as Skinny Bitch required. Your eternal optimism and support for Scott was uplifting to us all.

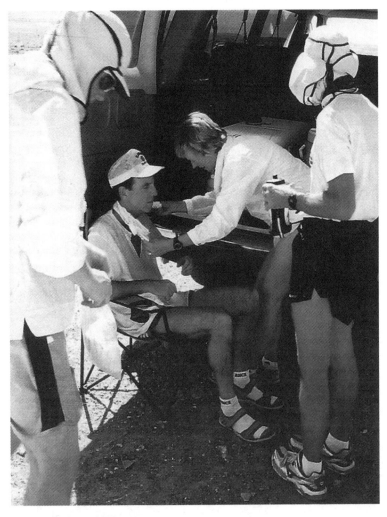

Pitstop at Badwater 2003

Eric—The number two pacer in terms of mileage! Your energy on the uphills leading out of Stovepipe and again out of Panamint and yet again on the Whitney Portal Road was a blessing, coming at a time when Scott needed your sense of humor and encouragement. I was very proud of you for stepping up to take on this difficult part of pacing. And early on, you remembered to say "yes, dear."

Everyone worked together to get the job done well, and I know Scott as well as I appreciate the hard work and sacrifices made by the Darkside Crew. Thanks for letting me be the chief; you were all excellent Indians.

Fondly,
Skinny Bitch **(Paula)**

* * *

22 CHAPTER

THE BADWATER ULTRAMARATHON EXPERIENCE

July 2003

"Yeah…but it's a dry heat."

By Gary Griffin

The Badwater Ultramarathon bills itself as the most prestigious and most difficult of all ultrarunning events, and it can make a pretty good argument for such status. It begins at the lowest point in North America, Badwater, in Death Valley National Park, some 280 feet below sea level and proceeds through some 40 miles of harsh desert, over two mountain ranges, across another 25 miles of desert valley, and finally up Mt. Whitney, the highest point in the continental U.S. that encompasses nearly 13,000 feet of climbing before finishing at the Whitney Trailhead at 8,360 feet. To make it even more fun, the race is run in July, which is statistically the hottest month of the year in Death Valley, where the average daily high temperature is 115 degrees. "Yeah," you say, "but it's a dry heat." That's what I thought, too. No problem. I'm from Tallahassee, Florida where the act of walking from one's carport to the back door in the summertime requires one to carry a water bottle for hydration, and thrice-a-day showers to stay fresh are commonplace among those of us who don't hole ourselves up in an air-conditioned, hibernating state until the first signs of fall on Columbus Day. Besides, a Florida ultrarunner won the Badwater race twice in the mid-90s, and I took that as a sure indicator that training in the southeastern U.S. prepared one for whatever some arid desert could offer up in the way of a hostile environment. Oh, you silly, silly boy...

So, why am I telling you all of this? Because by an odd twist of fate, I found myself involved in the 2003 edition of Badwater, and it was an experience I will never forget. Relating it to you all will be difficult, as such experiences always are when we have traversed the normal bounds of activity and found ourselves at some point where few have had the opportunity to go before. My opportunity began with that aforementioned twist of fate that involved a determined and talented runner with a dream...

The Runner

While on a teaching assignment in Atlanta in the winter of 2002, I ventured over to run in the Callaway Gardens Marathon one fine Sunday. Along about mile two, I found myself running next to a congenial fellow who was easy to talk to and humble. He had run a 3:08 marathon the day before over at Tybee Island and had no trouble running alongside me that day at Callaway for some 23 miles as I ran my fastest marathon in many years. At mile 23, he sprinted on in, but before that we had engaged in a non-stop review of races we had been part of and our hopes for the future. It just so happened that this fellow had won our Tallahassee 50K at Wakulla in 1998, had run our Tallahassee Marathon, and, most strikingly, was a streak runner. Now I generally am not overly impressed with streak runners, for I don't think that the act of running every day for an extended period is a particularly healthy thing and may even hint at obsessiveness and a lack of attention to other aspects of life that are important to me when I pick my friends. This guy was different, though. He was nonchalant about his streak, which began in November 1978, and which had averaged nearly 10 miles a day. He maintained a serious job as a JC Penney manager in Atlanta, was a family man, and was active in organizing local races that benefited charitable causes. I liked that. Besides, he ran alongside me that day when he could have run off and left me and encouraged me to my best marathon in years. It was when he donned a pair of Zubaz athletic pants after the run that I knew I had a lot in common with this guy, for I thought that the pair I owned were the only ones still in existence. (For those not in the know, Zubaz were a very fleeting fashion statement in the late 1980s, seen only on college sidelines during football season, and were a crazy concoction of swirling stripes on baggy pants with elastic bands at the ankles.) Well, this guy had a pair from his alma mater, the University of

Florida (a hated rival of my University of Miami Hurricanes), but the Zubaz connection helped us overcome that obstacle. In the course of sharing our dreams that day, this fellow mentioned that he was approaching 50 and that before he reached that milestone he wanted to run a little race called Badwater. The fellow's name was Scott Ludwig.

We kept in touch, as he lived in nearby Peachtree City, and maintained a tie to Tallahassee as a member of the Gulf Winds Track Club. Besides, he was turning his running career more and more toward ultrarunning. He entered the U.S. 24-Hour Championship in Olander Park, Ohio in September 2002, and I told him to "make his mark in the ultrarunning community." He did so by finishing 4th overall and was the first master with a total of 129 miles. Shortly after that, he applied for the 2003 Badwater Ultramarathon and asked me to be a part of his crew and to assume the role of "spiritual advisor." When my wife Peg and I went to Death Valley the next month, I brought him back a block of salt that makes up the ground at Badwater and a photo of the small white stripe at the end of the road at Mt. Whitney that signifies the finish line. There was never a doubt in my mind that his footprints would find their way to both of them.

The Course

Like Scott, Badwater had been a dream of mine as well. Every ultrarunner has thoughts of Badwater, for it truly offers as foreboding a challenge as any footrace on earth. Even the most talented of racers will dismiss it, for it is truly a fringe event. Many will argue that it is more adventure racing than a road race. In 2002, Badwater was won by 40-year-old Pam Reed, a mother of three, who trounced her nearest rival by five hours. A gentleman at the Mt. Whitney store told me last October that from that point forward, Badwater would be a race. Pam Reed's victory brought never-before seen publicity to the event, and several U.S. newspapers and CNN were covering the 2003 edition. A video of the 1999 race entitled *Running on the Sun* was gaining popular acclaim as more and more people were learning about this race across the burning California desert to Mt. Whitney. As a member of Scott's team for 2003, I had listened to advice from seasoned Badwater participants, read an abundance of instructional material, had seen the video, and had driven the course. I thought I knew what I (and the rest of the team) was in for. Friends, I had no clue. Until you experience Death Valley in the summer, you have no idea. It is like no other place I have ever seen. It resembles what I would expect on the surface of the moon—barren and appearing lifeless for mile upon mile upon mile. And oh, the heat. Our trip last fall found us basking in 90-degree highs that were tolerable enough that we hiked and ran and lived to tell about it. But Badwater is in July, and this is the place that has the highest temperature ever recorded in the U.S.—134 degrees—and has an annual rainfall of less than 2 inches. This is truly one of the most hostile environments on earth, and it was here that Scott had chosen to run 135 miles. For anyone that is counting, that is five marathons and a 5K cool-down.

The Crew

No one runs Badwater alone. Well, almost no one. A fellow by the name of Marshall Ulrich from Colorado has run the event several times and traveled the route one time towing a rickshaw-like cart with all of his supplies. Scott opted instead to assemble a team of friends of varying talents and to rent a large van in which to keep all of us and his mountain of supplies. I was proud to be a part of this team, as it included another current Gulf Winds Track Club member and a former Tallahassee resident named Al Barker. Besides being a very talented marathoner (he has run near 3:10 at age 58 and has several sub-3 hour marathons at Boston), Al is an optometrist and a regular training partner of Scott's. Our Crew Chief was Paula May, the 50-54 Georgia age group record holder at the 10K and a talented marathoner, as well. Besides her strong organizational and leadership skills, she brought a wealth of medical knowledge to the team as an experienced physician's assistant in anesthesia. Her husband, Eric Huguelet, was not only our filmmaker (someone had to record this for posterity!) but also a strong runner and an even stronger walker who would lead Scott up the wicked inclines from the valley floor and finally up the 13 tortuous miles of Mt. Whitney. Paula and Eric also are regular training partners of Scott's and make up the core of the growing Darkside Running Club under whose banner Scott would run the race. Finally, there was Scott's 17-year-old son, Josh. Josh must have been having an extremely boring summer back home or just really wanted something out on the far edge to write about in his "How I Spent My Summer Vacation" essay.

The Race

Badwater racers are selected based on their credentials. One makes an application to Badwater, stating why they want to run and what it is that they have done that qualifies them to be a potential finisher. Interestingly, a wealth of ultramarathoning experience is not required, as one entrant this year was participating in his first ultra. He was, however, a five-time leading finisher in the Hawaiian Ironman and a recent finisher in a triple Ironman. Such insanity gave him a slight edge over individuals that peppered their applications with tales of 100-mile runs and stories of nights spent sleeping inside saunas to build up their heat readiness. Ultimately, 75 were chosen to toe the starting line at Badwater one fine Tuesday in July, with three evenly divided waves going off at 6 a.m., 8 a.m., and 10 a.m. Those that finished in less than 30 hours had a legitimate chance to win, while those finishing in less than 48 hours won the coveted Badwater belt buckle. The official cutoff time was 60 hours, which is a long, long time to be out in Death Valley.

Scott went off at 10 a.m. with the other elite runners that included last year's winner Pam Reed, the veteran Ulrich, 10-time finisher Scott Weber, former record holder and trans-America runner Jay Birmingham, and Canadian Monica Scholz, an elite finisher of over 25 100-mile runs.

Because of the potential for crowded road conditions, crews are not allowed to pace their runner for the first 17 miles between the start at Badwater and the first checkpoint at mile 17 at the Furnace Creek Ranch. Conventional wisdom and hard statistical evidence has shown that patience pays and speed kills in the early grueling stages of Badwater, and those who are still moving by the second checkpoint at Stovepipe Wells (mile 42) have an excellent chance of making it to Mt. Whitney within the cutoff time. Scott went out with last year's winner Reed and a group of several others and then settled into a comfortable sub-9:00-minute pace in the first leg. Temperatures at this time were already near 120 degrees, and the first signs of a hot desert wind were blowing across the salt basin at Badwater. Scott arrived at Furnace Creek in approximately three hours, whereupon I joined him for the 24-mile leg to Stovepipe Wells. It is the memory of these next 6-plus hours that will forever be etched in my mind when I recall this incredible event. During these 24 miles, we encountered the unceasing near-record 130-degree heat that I trust will be as close to a near-death experience as I want to get. The intensity of the heat and the wind made it virtually impossible to stay well-hydrated. While the crew tried to get Scott's core temperature down at mile intervals by wiping him with ice cold towels and by constantly giving him ready-chilled shirts to wear, I was at times carrying a water bottle in each hand and another in my pack to get us from stop to stop. One was to keep him hydrated, one was to constantly squeeze onto his head and neck, and one was getting fluid into me…if I had the presence of mind to do so. While the crew would administer to Scott at the stops, I would do what I could to assist them while at the same time realizing that I had to get my own core cooled off and hydrated. It was an interesting experience, and one that has made me question if tackling the event as an entered runner will ever be in my future. By the time we arrived at Stovepipe, it was 6:30 p.m. I was as tired and in need of a break as I have ever been. Meanwhile, Scott had been in the desert for eight and a half hours, was not a single foot above sea level, and still had 93 miles ahead of him. But, as the sun was getting low, he had reached a point that 11 of the 75 either failed to reach or would not go beyond.

The next 18 miles were all uphill, climbing to 5,000 feet at Towne's Pass, the intermediate point between Stovepipe and the third check station at Panamint Springs (mile 72). We took turns through this stretch, with Eric doing most of the uphill walking and Paula encouraging Scott to run the steep eight-mile downhill toward Panamint Valley and the final two miles to the checkpoint. I was with Scott on the uphill leg at 10:30 p.m. under the clear desert sky, and we were told that the temperature was still 110 degrees! I never thought I could be in 110-degree heat and feel comfortable, but after the mind-altering experience of the previous afternoon, it was very much the case.

Sometime after midnight, we agreed that Josh and I should go ahead to Panamint Springs and check into the room that Scott had reserved for the purpose of getting some rest and a shower before facing the long second day of heat. We would sleep for an hour or two and then relieve Eric and Paula so that they could do the same. Scott was expected to arrive around daybreak. As soon as I lied down, I realized things were not as they should have been. Not only were my legs twisted grotesquely by cramping muscles, but also I was extremely nauseous. There was no air conditioning at the so-called resort, and the room was extremely hot. Josh was so tired that he fell asleep, but my fear over what was happening to me and the nausea kept me from doing the same. We had been told that the act of a crew member going down in such a remote area can mean the demise of your runner, and all I could think of was that I needed medical help, and it was likely to take me out of action. Scott, meanwhile, had another 60-plus miles ahead and another day in the desert. After throwing up, I went immediately to the check station to see about some medical advice. I was told that all of the medics were back at Stovepipe, treating downed runners and crew there and that none were available. I described my dilemma (which included not having urinated for 16 hours) to one of the race volunteers, and he told me that I simply was in serious need of sodium and water and that if I could get some in me, I would have a chance of being able to continue. Although the symptoms clearly supported such a diagnosis, I was shocked that could have actually been the problem, as I had been eating sodium tablets every half-hour while running and drinking very heavily all day. Evidently, neither had been sufficient to deal with the brutal conditions that I had been in, and it was apparent that in my focus on keeping Scott cooled and hydrated I had not taken care of myself as I should have. I immediately ate two *Succeed!* caps and drank the last two liters of bottled water at Panamint, which were graciously given to me by a worker at the all-night outdoor bar. As a team, our problems were further compounded by the fact that Panamint and Stovepipe were both out of ice, and the only place to restock was in Lone Pine, some 50 miles away. Although I immediately felt better after the tablets and the water (I couldn't have ever felt any worse, I don't believe!), I offered to go to Lone Pine for the ice and other supplies. The two hours out of the heat and more water returned me to normal, and I was able to hook up with Scott and the team by the time they were only a few miles out of Panamint.

The dawn brought some milder temperatures as a blessed overcast sky moved in, and we rotated two-mile shifts as Scott moved towards the mile 90 checkpoint at Darwin. He had worked hard during that 18-mile stretch and, other than some bad blisters, was looking and feeling strong. Scott is a remarkably determined runner who never lets the inevitable ultrarunning bad patches affect him; furthermore, he is a strong finisher in all endurance events and seems to be at his best when his rivals are struggling. Well, his competition this day was struggling, and his focus was on relentless forward motion and the finish at Whitney. The scoreboard at Darwin had him in about 8th place when he arrived at 10:30 a.m., and it was at this point that we again set out into the 32 miles of high desert known as Owens Valley leading us to Lone Pine, the last stop before Whitney. I had been warned back at Panamint that the previous day found temperatures of 110 degrees in this area and sand storms, but I kept this from Scott so as to not discourage him. Perhaps as much as meeting your runner's physical needs, the pacer and crew need to encourage and keep nothing but positive thoughts in the head of the runner. Fortunately for us, the temperatures remained in the low 100s, and although the sun came out and the wind blew, we encountered no dust. Scott ran incredibly well, reeling in two of his fellow competitors during this stretch. He arrived at Lone Pine at 6:30 p.m. in 6th place overall and had only the 13-mile uphill trek to the Whitney Portals ahead of him. He knew going in that this portion was basically unrunnable and that even the top finishers are reduced to a leg-numbing hike at this point. Nonetheless, he worked hard all the way to the top, maintained his position, and gloriously crossed the finish line at 10:32 p.m., some 36 hours and 32 minutes since the start, some 135 miles away.

The repeat winner was the amazing Pam Reed, in 28 hours and 27 minutes. I had the chance to spend some time talking to her at the post-race dinner and her crew chief was a tremendous amount of help to me before the start, with his advice on the importance of keeping our runner as cool as possible. For those of you out there with a disdain for long training runs, Pam has managed to win this affair two years now with no training runs longer than 20 miles. By her own admission, she is just an average marathoner but manages 100 miles a week into her busy life by running as much as four times a day. Like Scott, she is methodical, patient, and has an easy stride that never changes in spite of miles and miles of tiring running.

The Lesson

The Badwater experience was a remarkable time. It showed me the incredible harshness of nature in an environment that is not conducive to any sort of life, much less that of running 135 miles. It showed me that those who put their bodies and minds to the test in this perhaps ultimate of ultrarunning events are normal, hard-working, family-oriented, caring people who simply have a desire to conquer a tremendous challenge. It also was a case study in getting along with others under the most trying of circumstances—extreme heat and discomfort, confinement in close quarters for over 36 hours, and no sleep. It all came about because of a singleness of focus and a determined effort to do everything we could to see the talented Scott Ludwig be the best that he could be and attain his Badwater goal that he had voiced to me in our first meeting 18 months prior. He finished in 6th place in a field that included on this day the very best in the world that were willing to put themselves to the test. As a crewmember, I was deeply honored to be there and am proud of him, not just as a friend but also as a member of Gulf Winds Track Club. There may be others from GWTC who leave their footprints in Death Valley—Jeff Bryan and Fred Johnson have voiced their desire to see what the fuss is all about. The night before leaving for Badwater, I had told my wife Peg that I may give it a run next year. When I called her several days later from Lone Pine following my experience in the desert and the Panamint Springs motel room, that maybe had become an emphatic no! But, as is often the case in ultrarunning, it always gets better. It got better that morning and that afternoon, and on Whitney that night. Never say never. But, never listen to anyone who tries to tell you it's a dry heat!

Scott and Al at Oak Mountain 50k 2004

The Day After

When Scott was accepted into Badwater several months ago, the real question in my mind was not whether or not he would finish, but whether or not he would then let the streak die a peaceful death. After all, he had reached the mountaintop, both literally and figuratively, and the burning question in my mind was, "How could he possibly run the day after Badwater?" Well, that was a very silly question on my part. Those on the crew who have known Scott far longer than I assured me that he would run his mandatory minimum of three miles on Thursday. Sure enough, less than 12 hours after finishing atop Whitney, we were all gathered in the motel parking lot for day number 9,000 (more or less) of what is one of the 35 or so longest running streaks in the U.S. I feel certain, however, that none of those ahead of him have ever run Badwater. Like I say, though, he's really a fairly normal individual.

* * *

CHAPTER

REFLECTIONS OF BADWATER

After 25 years of base preparation, 2 years of dedicated training, and 6 months of *deadly serious and specific fine-tuning,* my Badwater dream came true. Without a doubt, it was the single greatest accomplishment in my running career, and I'm fairly certain it will remain that way. Obviously, it could not have been done without the teamwork and determination of my crew. Paula—I couldn't have asked for a more determined and dedicated crew chief. Al—who has lived the Badwater dream as long as I have. Gary—there is no bigger cheerleader or optimist in the universe. Eric—I'll never forget how you came through on the mountains when I desperately needed the support. And Josh—I can't tell you how glad I am that you were a very integral part of our grand adventure. I will forever be indebted to all of you. And I'll never forget our week in Death Valley.

Will you do it again? I was waiting for Chris Kostman to ask me this very question as I sat in the finisher's chair at the Whitney Portals. Unfortunately, my brain was too scrambled to come up with a clever way of saying no way in hell. Fortunately I never had to, as he didn't ask. But if he did ask me, I believe I would have simply said once is enough. As I write this several weeks later, I know in my heart (and *soles!*) that this is the right decision. The training, the expense, the logistics, the time requirements, and the sacrifices of both the runner and the crewmembers toward a goal of finishing Badwater are astronomical. The chances of everything coming together are small. Doing Badwater again would be pushing my luck, as I believe our team did it damn near perfectly the first time.

However, if anyone has followed my Badwater trilogy with a hint of giving it a try somewhere down the road, here are several pieces of advice to consider before you attempt to take on Death Valley:

Train on the mountains. Running in the heat of Death Valley was nothing compared to the miles and miles of ascent after Stovepipe Wells. Whether you run or walk the mountains isn't important; what is important, *essential*, is that you acclimate yourself to *climbing!* Running the steps in a football stadium, walking up several flights of stairs, exercising on a Stairmaster—these all would serve the purpose as well. Simply put, you MUST be ready to move your body *uphill!*

Tie bandanas around your ankles. Although it is dry heat, you will still be sweating, and by no means do you want your feet to get wet. I discovered tying bandanas around my ankles helped to keep some of the perspiration away from my feet. Unfortunately, I discovered this *after* I had small blisters forming on the balls of each of my feet. Fortunately, I had a crew chief who was masterful at taping my feet so that I could continue running (or walking, as the case may have been). Between Paula's taping and the bandanas, further damage was kept to a minimum.

Attire suggestions. The white desert hat and sun-reflecting long-sleeved shirt that come so highly recommended by race officials? Not necessary. I wished I had started the race in a Cool-Max T-shirt (soaked in ice water) and a simple baseball hat (with plenty of sunblock on my face, neck, and ears). I started the race in the desert hat and long-sleeved shirt and thought I was going to suffocate during the first few miles. Interesting fact: Although my crew and I used sunblock throughout the event, we still expected to have a few spots of sunburn. Between the six of us, we had *none*.

Do a good job of protecting your lips. Some of us really had bad sores on our lips a couple of days after the race. Don't hesitate to use plenty of lip balm or chapstick throughout the event (that includes nighttime hours as well!). The arid climate will do a number on your lips if you're not careful.

Consider two support vehicles (not just one). If nothing else, this serves as insurance should one of your vehicles have to be abandoned on the side of the road. It was reassuring to know we had a back-up vehicle should a problem arise with our primary vehicle (fortunately, we never had a problem). Additionally, the extra vehicle can be used by crewmembers to run errands (popsicles, anyone?) or to seek some much-needed relief (sleep, shower, food — SOLID food).

Refresh yourself frequently during the event. My crew had an ice-cold washrag ready for me at each pit stop. I used it on my face, the back of my neck, my thighs, and my knees. It was the closest thing to a bath I could find, the cooling effect was much-needed (and appreciated), and it kept my legs as fresh as possible. Also, occasionally gargling with mouthwash (per a suggestion by Gary) worked out well, as it was both refreshing and helped get whatever taste (salt, water, *swamp!*) or feeling *(parched throat!)* I wanted to eliminate.

Wear running sandals on the descents! I can't recommend this enough. The first time Eric and I crested a mountain and began heading downhill, my toes began striking the front of my running shoes. I instantly asked my crew to get my sandals, and for the remainder of the race wore those (Nike Straprunners) for all the descents. Thankfully, I didn't have any problems with my toes throughout the event. Side note: The sandals may come in handy for several days after the event as well, as your feet — if they're anything like mine — will swell (wider, not longer), and any shoes you attempt to put on will be a little snug.

Solicit advice from an experienced crewmember. We were blessed to have the advice (and wisdom) of David Sowers, who had been Adam Bookspan's crew chief at Badwater on several occasions. His experience and recommendations proved invaluable toward our success at Badwater. You can read all about how to prepare for and compete in this event (and believe me when I say that my crew and I read *everything* in print about the race), but there's nothing like hearing it from the horse's mouth.

If you're interested, it just so happens I know a few "horses." Five of them, as a matter of fact.

***

BADWATER TAKES CENTER STAGE

If nothing else, the 2003 Badwater Ultramarathon extended the notoriety of the race originally generated by the documentary *Running on the Sun*, which chronicled the 1999 edition of the event. A 1999 Badwater rookie, Kirk Johnson, discusses his trials and tribulations in his book *To the Edge: A Man, Death Valley, and the Mystery of Endurance*.

In her autobiography, *The Extra Mile: One Woman's Personal Journey to Ultrarunning Greatness*, Pam Reed discusses her 2002 and 2003 Badwater victories. Later, Dean Karnazes writes of his first attempt at Badwater (a DNF—did not finish—in 1995) in his autobiography, *Ultramarathon Man: Confessions of an All-Night Runner* (apparently wordy book titles are common among long-distance runners).

I conducted a telephone interview with Dean Karnazes while writing *A Few Degrees from Hell* (Dean's story of his race at the 2003 Badwater Ultramarathon can be found in chapter 2 of the book). I found Dean to be very encouraging of my writing, very supportive of my book, and simply an all-around nice, unassuming man. If you're not familiar with his accomplishments, do yourself a favor and do a little research. Then reread what I said about unassuming. Dean, I know I told you this before, but it bears repeating here: Thank you.

Pam Reed appeared on Late Night with David Letterman less than a week after her 2003 Badwater triumph. Letterman did his homework, as he asked all the right questions, making the interview both interesting as well as humorous. A few examples:

(After Pam tells him the temperature reached 133 degrees)

"I was reading that they [the runners] can't have aid stations along the route because people waiting for the competitors in the sun and the heat would die."

(After Pam tells him that women may be better suited to distance running than men because they're able to have children and mentally can go through a lot of pain, and there's definitely pain involved in running the race)

"I see, but you did not give birth during the race?"

(After Pam tells him she was awarded a belt buckle for her win)

*"Good Lord, sign me up. Where do I get in this? A new belt buckle...
are you kidding me?"*

David Letterman doesn't know me from Adam. Relevant? Not at all; I just
thought you should know.

**Later, ESPN Magazine featured an article about Chris
Bergland, who finished two places ahead of me at Badwater.** The
article, "The Road to Hell" describes what Chris was experiencing
at various checkpoints along the course. Let's see how Chris did,
and for the sake of comparison, let's see how I did at similar points
during the race (mine will be presented in *italics*):

Mile 00, Elevation -282 feet

CHRIS: As he drives to the start line in Death Valley—Eminem's
"Lose Yourself" pumping on the stereo—Bergland is eerily calm.
(Considerably less so is his rookie support crew: big sister Renee,
little sis Sandy, bud Bobby, and one magazine writer.) Before the
10 a.m. gun, he rushes to perform his final rites: tying his shoes and
clearing out his bowels.

*SCOTT: As he drives to the start line in Death Valley, Scott looks
anxiously along the course for fellow Darksider Andy Velazco, who*

started his race at 8 a.m. His rookie support crew—Chief Paula, her husband Eric, buds Al and Gary, and son Josh—eventually spot Andy running toward Furnace Creek and wave and scream vigorously. They realize later that if they had opened the windows, Andy might have actually seen or heard them. Before the 10 a.m. gun, Scott performs his final rites repeatedly, specifically, "watering" various places near the starting line.

Mile 17.4, Elevation -165 feet

CHRIS: Bergland is troubled by a charley horse in his right knee (suffered on the flight to California) and a cracked rib (he collided with a bicyclist the month before). But so far, he's cool with the 128-degree heat; he trained in a sauna leading up to the race. "Is it hot?" he asks, as he tears through Furnace Creek in first place.

SCOTT: Ludwig is troubled by the white hood and long-sleeved shirt which came highly recommended for Badwater. It's obvious that the outfit is a scam, and Scott realizes he is better off running with a T-shirt and baseball hat. Once the recommended gear is removed, Scott is cool with the 128-degree heat.

Mile 41.9, Elevation 0

CHRIS: The crew keeps Bergland doused in water, helping him fight off the now 130-degree sun. Chris reports that he feels no heat inside his body, just a warm glow from how well the race is going. But at mile 51, he yaks up his apricot energy bar. A mere gag, he insists. It looks nasty either way.

SCOTT: The crew keeps Ludwig doused in water, helping him fight off the now one-hundred-and-thirty-one-degree sun. Scott reports that the hottest parts of his body are the palms of his hands, as the heat is radiating off the surface of the road. Scott hasn't thrown up (nor will he later), although the crew is taken aback by the nastiness of the blisters of his feet.

Mile 72.3, Elevation 1,970 feet

CHRIS: As night falls, Bergland, still running in first, joyfully croons "Up Where We Belong." The temperature hovers at 110 degrees. He pounds downhill, pleased with his speed. Then as he ascends his second major hill, sleep deprivation and darkness take over. The lights on the slope produce a mirage effect, teasing him into a constant "almost there" mindset. The peak is farther than his brain has anticipated. The miscalculation sinks his spirit.

SCOTT: Night has already fallen, but Ludwig is still running. Paula joins him running the downhills, and she appears to be pleased with his speed, considering Scott has spent a substantial amount of time walking the uphill stretch out of Stovepipe Wells. Scott and Paula see the peak in the distance, but the lights on the slope produce a mirage effect, making the destination appear closer than it actually was. The miscalculation... well, the miscalculation pisses Scott off, to be totally honest.

Mile 90.1, Elevation 5,050 feet

CHRIS: Bergland says he still feels lucid, but deep into the night, the switchbacks on the pitch-black road make him feel like he's in a fun house. Fallen rocks distract him; the camber of the road abuses his legs. Chris can't decide whether to walk or run. He hears that 2002 Badwater champ Pam Reed—close on his heels—is struggling, too. He slows to a walk. Elation fades. Dejection sets in.

SCOTT: *Ludwig is lucid, but early in the morning the switchbacks on the pitch-black road make it feel like he's not advancing (as he's spending more time going left-to-right and then right-to-left). Scott has no problem deciding to walk. He hears that 2002 Badwater champ Pam Reed is virtually a light year ahead. Scott could care less.*

Mile 111, Elevation 3,600 feet

CHRIS: As the sun rises, Bergland stops without warning, pulls down his shorts, as he delicately puts it later, "Everything in my intestines comes out in one explosion." After trailing for 111 miles, Reed overcomes Chris. But he continues to chug along until another accident fills his shorts with what says feels like burning acid. His sisters change him and wet-wipe him clean.

SCOTT: *Chris did WHAT???!!! Scott realizes if he encounters similar difficulty, he is on his own. He knows this to be true because his crew told him so before the race started.*

Mile 115, Elevation 3,600 feet

CHRIS: Bergland has collapsed in the back of the support SUV, his face moth white, his lips a cadaverous blue and green. The crew fears a fatal heatstroke. But his temperature vacillates from 97 to 101.3 degrees, out of serious danger. Chilled Coke cans to his groin and armpits have him chattering and covered in goose bumps. A medic tells him to relax, rest, and continue. He's back on his feet 40 minutes later.

SCOTT: Scott catches his second wind and begins the best stretch of his race, passing two other runners in the process and moving into 6th place. Unfortunately, Pam Reed has already crossed the finish line. Fortunately, Scott is in no danger of heatstroke, as the weather has been fairly pleasant with temperatures hovering between 105 and 110 degrees—out of serious danger. Chilled Diet Coke to his throat prevents nausea.

Mile 122.3, Elevation 3,610 feet

CHRIS: Thirteen miles from the finish, his spirit is broken. Resting made his leg swell. Falling behind punctured his will. The altitude has made his lungs feel "small and synthetic" and bloated his body to an old Elvis-like puffiness. But he clings to a 9/11-inspired motto: Stay Strong: We are New York. Five hours later, arms raised to the sky, he crosses the finish line in 4th place.

SCOTT: Thirteen miles from the finish, he dreads what comes next—13 miles straight up Mount Whitney. He clings to consciousness—barely—and four hours later, arms (barely) raised to the sky, he, along with his rookie crew, crosses the finish line in 6th place.

The Aftermath

CHRIS: An hour after the race, his crew helps him into his hotel bed. He is too tired to eat much. Or move. "I feel like I've been ripped in half," he says. Three weeks later, his legs are still numb, four toenails have fallen out, and he's removed a piece of skin from his blistered foot so large that it would make the JACKASS gang queasy. A month later, he has nightmares about his surreal breakdowns. Yet he dreams of competing next year and conquering hell.

SCOTT: Ten minutes after the race, the entire crew (except Josh) has downed a beer. Scott, in fact, is already on his second one. However, he is too tired to eat. That didn't stop his crew from going to the diner, where Josh ordered everything on the menu (after surviving on energy bars and Fig Newtons for over 36 hours). Meanwhile, Scott went to sleep and during the night got up to water the toilet and blacked out on his way back to bed. Falling face forward, he was lucky not to strike the desk, television, or frame of the bed. He was not so lucky as he landed face down directly on the center of his forehead. Three weeks later, two toenails have fallen out, and he has removed three pieces of skin from his blistered feet which—if patched together—could provide the sole of an entire other foot. A month later, he sleeps as well as he ever did, knowing that he would not be competing next year. After all, hell had already been conquered.

After Badwater, I had the opportunity to speak with Chris Bergland in the lobby of our hotel in Lone Pine. Chris told me he thought Badwater would be a great test for him after winning the Triple Triathlon Championship (7.2 mile swim, 336 mile bicycle ride, and 78.6 mile run) three years in a row.

No, he most definitely wasn't boasting; he could have told me he had a tuna fish sandwich for lunch with the same emotion. He was simply explaining his rationale for being in Death Valley.

Finally, the October 2003 issue of Ultrarunning featured Badwater champion Pam Reed on the cover. Inside the issue you will find an account of my Badwater adventure that I was more than happy to write for my friend Don Allison, the magazine's editor and publisher, who has done more to promote the unique sport of ultrarunning than anyone I know. I imagine as a favor to me he also featured another runner on the cover of that issue lurking over Pam's shoulder and wearing race bib #20: *me!*

The Badwater Ultramarathon, the toughest footrace on the planet, was elevated to an even higher status by the 2005 and 2006 victories by Scott Jurek, a seven-time winner of the legendary Western States Endurance Run. I imagine in the years ahead it will continue to intrigue and captivate the imagination of runners everywhere. As well it should.

* * *

25

CHAPTER

A NOTE OF THANKS

To Paula, Eric, Gary, Al, and Josh

I will never be able to tell you how much I appreciate the support, encouragement, and dedication you willingly provided to make our trip to Death Valley a successful one. I doubt I will ever be able to put into words what completing Badwater means to me, but know that whenever I think of you, a part of me will always remember that you were there for me during the toughest footrace on the planet.

You guys are the greatest.

Scott

POST-BADWATER COOL-DOWN

National 100-Mile Championship, September 2003

I had promised one of my Badwater crewmembers, Gary Griffin, that if I was still able to *walk* after completing Badwater, I would go with him to the USATF 100-Mile Championship in Olander Park, Ohio (the scene of the previous year's 24-Hour Run) as he attempted this distance for the first time. Why not? After Badwater, 100 miles on a flat surface should feel like more of a *sprint* than an endurance run. AND I would have a little over seven weeks of recovery behind me after Badwater.

The race was scheduled for 10:00 a.m. on Saturday, September 13. The month leading up to the event I had averaged 100 miles a week (so much for tapering). So on Monday, September 8, I decided to *truly* taper—but in the long run, tapering turned out to be the least of my problems.

Monday, September 8

I ran 11 miles at a slow pace. After all, following four 100-mile weeks this felt pretty easy. I'll start my true taper tomorrow.

Tuesday, September 9

I ran eight miles at a really easy pace. By Saturday, I *should* feel pretty fresh. Should being the operative word, as that was before my wife got the phone call at 9:30 p.m.

Her friend Jan had a flat tire on I-285, a busy interstate circling Atlanta. Jan, alone and frightened (rightfully so, as she was in a bad section of town, and the 18-wheelers were literally zooming past her at 70-plus miles per hour), asked for our help. By 10:15 p.m., Cindy and I found her car—warning lights flashing—near Exit 7.

I proceeded to loosen four of the lug nuts on the flat tire; unfortunately, the *fifth* lug nut needed a key that was nowhere to be found. After searching the car four or five times, we called AAA for a tow truck. As fate would have it, we found the key just after we made the call. I got the tire changed, and we drove back to the automotive tire center near home and left her car via the overnight drop box. Our mini-adventure was over by 1:30 a.m.

Actually, for *me* the adventure was just beginning. I didn't realize it at the time, but when I loosened the lug nuts (which were on REALLY tight), I pulled something in my right shoulder blade. I didn't realize it until Wednesday morning when I had a tough time getting out of bed.

Wednesday, September 10

At 3:30 a.m., my shoulder was killing me. I figured running might do it some good. Nine miles at an easy pace felt pretty good; no problems with my shoulder whatsoever. That is, until after I finished running. The moment I stopped, the pain in my shoulder blade kicked in. Apparently the only time I wasn't in pain was when I was running (don't ask—I have no explanation), which worked out well with a 100-miler coming up that weekend.

I thought perhaps a good day's rest would do my back good.

Thursday, September 11

So much for that theory. A good day's rest on Wednesday, but yet another tough time getting out of bed. Surprisingly, running 13 miles with Kelly and Eric felt pretty good, and my shoulder didn't bother me at all. After our run, I helped Eric haul off some lawn waste to the local landfill (it took about six hours), and while I was *actually* working, my shoulder felt fine. However, on the rides to and from the landfill, I felt like a knife was stuck in my shoulder blade. Not a good sign for the upcoming weekend.

Gary drove up from Tallahassee and joined us for dinner. I told him of my dilemma. He asked me the obvious question (Do you still want to run?), and I told him the thought of *not* running never crossed my mind. Gary knew me better than that, but I imagine he asked it out of courtesy to Cindy, although, in actuality, *Cindy* knows me better than that as well.

Friday, September 12

Once again, getting out of bed was tough. The four easy miles, however, weren't. The ride on the airplane, though, was *extremely* tough. I should have warned the lady next to me of my dilemma, because I spent the 90 minutes of the flight positioning and repositioning every 20 seconds or so. I never could find a position that minimized the pain in my shoulder.

When we got to Ohio, Gary and I stopped for lunch. I had two glasses of liquid painkiller (a welcome 32 ounces on draft), and later that night at the pre-race dinner, I had three more cans of the same. Now I had *two* ways of minimizing my pain: running and beer. Fortunately, tomorrow I would have plenty of time to minimize my pain (via running. Dammit.).

Saturday, September 13

Although the race was to start at 10:00 a.m., I was wide awake at 1:08. Almost nine hours before the beginning of the race. I never did get back to sleep, as I could find absolutely no position that would minimize the pain in my back. At 7:00 a.m., Gary woke up, and I told him that if I were wise, I would take a doctor's advice (I'm guessing at this point as to what he or she might say) and take two aspirin and stay in bed. If only...instead, I'm going to try and run 100 miles.

At 10:00 a.m., my journey began. I would be pain-free for the next 18 hours, 23 minutes, and 17 seconds.

Sunday, September 14

I slept in our rental car until it was time for Gary to finish. I walked over to the finish line to take a photo of Gary finishing his first 100-miler, and we returned to the hotel for a quick 90-minute nap before we needed to head to the airport.

At 11:00 a.m., we were ready to leave the hotel. I was in serious agony at this point (my back was screaming *bloody murder* and both of my big toenails were dangling after the prior night's fun). But the worst part is: between Gary and me, *I was in the best condition to drive to the airport!*

Once we returned the rental car, we struggled with our luggage and managed to make it to our gate in time for our 12:55 p.m. flight home. This time, I forewarned the gentleman sitting next to me of my condition and told him that I would be adjusting my position in my seat every 20 seconds or so. I did adjust, but it made absolutely no difference. My body was paying me back (rightfully so) for what I had just put it through. Gary was kind enough to buy me a can of liquid painkiller on our flight.

Once we landed in Atlanta, I wished Gary a safe drive back to Tallahassee. I offered him a room for the night, but he wanted to get back home as he had to work the next day.

Cindy met me at the airport and (thankfully!) drove home. Somehow I managed to unpack and throw my dirty clothes in the washer, but I wasn't able to do the other things I normally do when I return from an out-of-town race: read the newspapers, check the mail, dry my clothes, and put them away. The *only* thing I was able to do was lie on the couch (and reposition every 20 seconds) and drink a few more bottles of liquid painkiller.

Al, Susan Scott and Gary at the 24 Hour Championship 2005

Postscript

My right shoulder blade continued to plague me for several days after the event. For whatever reason, the only way I was able to make the pain stop was by running. Running with two severely sore hamstrings, I might add.

I found out later I had finished 14th overall and 2nd in my age group at the 100-Mile Championships. To be honest, I couldn't have cared less. You see, my shoulder still hurt.

* * *

WEEKEND AT WAKULLA

Tallahassee Ultra Distance Classic, December 2003

By Gordon Cherr

Gordon is a resident of Tallahassee, Florida and a long-time member of the Gulf Winds Track Club. Gordo is also a really nice guy. He offered both his home and his service to Al Barker, Prince Whatley, and me during the second weekend in December 2003 as the three of us participated in the Tallahassee Ultra Distance Festival. You will meet Gordon later as my unfortunate pacer in the 2004 Western States Endurance Run on one of the most disappointing nights of my life.

They gathered at my home after a long Friday night drive from Atlanta, drawn here for the Ultra. First my longtime friend and running buddy Al Barker. Al is a bit new to the ultrascene, having recently finished his first 50-miler and now being accepted into the field for the Western States 100 next June. Then Scott Ludwig. Scott is anything but new to the ultrascene, a veteran of more than 100 marathons and numerous ultras, he was recently 6th at the Badwater 135 (miles!) run from the furnace of the floor of Death Valley to the frozen reaches of Mount Whitney Portal at nearly 8,500 feet. Scott is also a streak runner, and if I'm not mistaken, he has not missed a day's run in more than 25 years. And their third training partner, Prince Whatley.

They came into my home, unloaded their gear, thanked me for my hospitality, and said goodnight. Wake us up at 5:30. Three totally different personalities on the verge of a great challenge...the 50 miles of the ultra! Al looks drawn and tired, and I had forgotten just how the thought of 50 miles can weigh so heavily on one's psyche even before the first step has been taken on race day. I mean, it's not sweat off my brow; I am only going to help these three meet their demons, assist with food and drink, and maybe jog the last few miles as a pacer if someone is fading hard near the end. Being a glorified cheerleader is not stressful. At least I do not expect that it will be. Goodnight, Al.

Scott was another story. We sit in the darkened kitchen, drinking decaf, and chatting the way long time runners do. Of shared friends and experiences, of aches and pains, of hopes and dreams, children and wives and jobs. Of anything BUT the relentless challenges of the next day. Ultras are so complicated. The farther the distance, the more that can and will happen. You can train diligently with great intelligence and plan and improvise, hydrate and eat, but you don't know anything until it's over. Every ultra is a learning experience, and ultrarunners are always on the learning curve, or so it seems. I do not know Scott well. In fact, I do not know him at all, but after the miles we will share tomorrow and all is said and done, I will know him well enough. It will be my gain for sure, and I will be honored to call him friend.

Prince is a total stranger and obviously blessed with the gift of gab. He is, as it turns out, a salesman by trade, and that trade fits him well. He has the bulky, well-muscled legs of a powerlifter, not the slim aerodynamic legs of a long distance runner. But, if I have learned anything about ultras, it is that good ultrarunners come in all shapes and sizes. No one is to be discounted on looks alone. And if you could peer into their chests, you would find that one shared commodity. They all have heart and plenty of it. Guts. Backbone. Drive. Determination. Heart. Prince will be breaking new ground tomorrow; he hasn't gone the distance previously, not even close. I can read uncertainty (not fear) in his eyes, but when tomorrow comes, I'm confident Prince will have a great triumph.

The day dawns early, and we are at Wakulla Springs by 6:00 a.m. for the 7:00 a.m. start. Many friends I know, other still to be met later that day—race workers, lap counters, husbands, wives, children, and dogs—all mill about in tense anticipation.

I have parked my pickup next to the start/finish line where laps will be counted. Al, Scott, and Prince know the drill and have brought provisions sufficient to feed an army of runners. You don't know what you might need, so you bring it all. Gatorade, water, Endurox, and some magic potions that I don't even ask about. Pretzels, Fig Newtons, Gu, Carboom, crackers, Cheez-Its, a mountain of clothes, sunscreen, bodyglide, Vaseline, and more shoes than you might see at a running store. The back of the truck looks like a poor man's makeshift smorgasbord, and before the day is done, most everyone who runs the race, whether 50K or 50 miles, stops by for a handout. Not that there isn't plenty of other food here. Race directors Fred and Margarite Decker know how to throw a party, and soon after the horn sounds signifying the start of the races, I find myself gorging on bananas and oranges, cookies and cakes, bread and peanut butter, and a hot cup of coffee, courtesy of the Wakulla Springs Lodge.

But the races begin, and the runners are gone, heading out into the dark on what will be a very long and painful day for most. I'm thinking Scott should do well in the 50-miler; I can only hope the best for Al and Prince. I know Al wants to run about nine hours or so. Prince, a realist today, only wants to finish upright.

Each lap at the ultra is 2.07 miles, and the start/finish line is a great place to grab a chair and watch the race, in many cases to see the gradual disintegration of runners as the day progresses. Some will be there running before first light until after the roads are completely dark and deserted. Moving, always moving ahead. That's the key. Easier said than done. One personal drama or another, usually several at the same time, are unfolding all day long and into the night. It is impossible not to cheer for someone trying so hard for so long, putting up with the grind, running and walking after the physical body shouts quit at the top of its lungs while the heart and the head say keep on.

The first 50-mile runner is completing the first lap, and it's Fred Johnson. Fred is an accomplished and experienced ultrarunner. I have the good fortune to run a bit with Fred and Dana Stetson on a few of their 5:30 a.m. jaunts on the local golf course in Killearn. We run in the dark with flashlights and headlamps, and we often find ourselves humming the theme song from *Coal Miner's Daughter* when we run on those dark mornings. Fred has talked a bit about this race. He was disappointed with his performance last year; he calls it "paralysis by analysis", and I figure he has another plan for this year. I mean, you don't finish an ultra without a plan, and Fred is big on plans, and right now Fred is cruising along at about 7:45 per mile. He keeps this up for the first few laps, and by lap three or four, I find myself yelling at Fred to calm down and slow down, too, because I think he is going out way too fast and a crash is coming—maybe in another two or three hours—but it is inevitable at this pace.

I had the pleasure of meeting Fred Johnson before the start of the inaugural Peachtree City 50K in 2002. I was the race director but took the liberty of running the event in its first year. Fred and I ran together for most of the race before he finally put it in another gear the last few miles and won the Men's Masters Championship, beating yours truly by a little over four minutes. Considering how many pit stops he made in the woods during the race made his accomplishment that much more impressive. Fred, a dedicated husband, father, runner, and officer in the United States Army is one of the finest people I've ever met. He knows a thing or two about beer as well…always a good thing!

Scott is running an easy second in the 50-miler at about an 8:30 pace. Outwardly, he looks cool and collected, but this tells me nothing because even when he is wasted, as I will later see, Scott is cool and collected. I am getting happy feet from watching the runners go by. I can't stand to watch and not join in, but I promised Al and Prince I would pace them through the last two or three loops, although that isn't going to be for maybe seven more hours. But on one lap, Scott asks me to pull out some Fig Newtons for him the next time around and then when he next appears, he asks me to join him for a while. I'm only too happy to oblige.

We run the next six miles at that easy 8:30 pace, talking about this and that. Mostly we discuss how Fred is looking. Fred is putting about a minute on Scott every loop, and he looks good. But in my opinion, Fred is going to crash after about six hours if he doesn't come to his senses quickly, and Scott knows how to go the distance. Scott makes the conscious decision to hang where he is. Experience dictates a waiting game. Actually, ultras are dominated by finishing, and real racing is mostly nonexistent. Scott confides in me, even at this relatively early stage, that physically he is fine, but he doesn't feel mentally prepared for today's effort. But he is going to hang in there and see what is what in several hours. Several hours...the perspective of an ultrarunner sure is skewed.

I notice Gary Griffin. Gary is coming off some major injuries and is not sure where he is. I mean, he signed up for the 50K, but started with the 50-milers, who start about 1,000 yards behind the 50K group. I guess he is just used to starting there and goes there out of habit. Gary is looking a bit puny when he comes by, and I ask him if he wants some company. I can see Gary is having a rough patch after about 20 miles, and I hope that a little companionship will help him see his way to the other side. Rough patches are as common in ultras as they are in almost every race and every workout. It is hard to believe you will come out of the other side when you feel so crappy and are fighting yourself to not stop and quit. But the fact is that if you make it through a rough patch, you will actually come out the other side feeling stronger than you thought possible. For a while, anyhow.

When he sees and hears me, Gary breaks into that big country boy smile of his and says "of course, with you my friend" and thoughts of walking are shelved for the time being. Off we go at his pace, talking about this and that, and after a few more miles Gary says he will go another lap, too, because that will be one lap closer to home and maybe he'll feel better and maybe, just maybe he'll get another lap done and then another and he might actually find the finish line. Indeed, when it is all over, Gary does finish on his feet—and running, not walking—in about 5:10. And then he feels so good and full of running that he runs a few more laps for good measure, cheering and encouraging the others. See, experience in knowing that you can run or walk even when your body is badgering you to stop, and that it will get better, can make all the difference. After countless miles and hours, Gary knows this, and with a little help for a few miles, he came home the winner that he is. Good effort, Grif! No, not a good effort, rather a *great* effort.

Meanwhile, the day is wearing on, and the runners are wearing out. I am watching Fred and Scott, and Fred has continued to lead, and not only lead but stretch his advantage. When Fred puts about two miles on Scott, he actually comes up behind and could lap him, and I have a sudden realization that barring absolute and utter collapse, Fred is going to win this race. All he has to do now is keep Scott in his sights, and soon the two are running together (although Scott is now an entire 2.07-mile lap behind Fred), which they continue to do until the last few miles when Scott begins to pull away but is unable to meaningfully close the gap.

Fred, I am sorry that I doubted you this day. Your race plan was executed flawlessly, and you ran with great determination and style. Fred deserved this win, he earned this win, and his indomitable spirit was apparent to everyone who watched the 50-miler. Great race, Fred.

Scott had a great race as well. He runs a PR of 7:26, and it is impossible to be sad with that effort. He has no complaints and looks as calm now as he did before and during the race. Sitting in my beach chair, he is smiling and encouraging the others who still have so many more miles and hours to go. I can't imagine why he is not sound asleep at this point, but he looks fresh, if that is possible. He and Fred are chewing the fat about something, and I'm guessing that one of them (if not both) is discussing dinner. As it turns out, I am later proven correct.

Laps are passing, and people are coming and going. Al and Prince have hung together for nearly 36 miles. I can't stand it any longer, and I jump in with them. Prince is yakking nonstop, and then he is trying to perform mathematical calculations in his head. Anything to get through the next few miles. He does not seem physically tired as much as being mentally tested, although I know that after 36 miles surely he is a bit winded. As for Al, he is too quiet, and I know my friend does not feel well at all. He complains of an upset stomach, and as I get to the smorgasbord on the rear of the pickup truck, he begins to gorge. I think this is a very bad idea on a queasy stomach after about 38 miles, but Al will have none of it. Prince grabs a Carboom and some salted pretzels and says he will wait. But it is obvious he needs to go now, at his own pace, and I tell him to go, that I will finish up with Al. As it turns out, Prince does go, and he goes strong, too, for the remainder of the race. He looks good and smiles for the next 12 miles and kicks some booty in 9:27. What a great effort, Prince. I bet you are still smiling. I know you are still talking!

As for Al, he stuffs Fig Newtons and Cheez-Its into his mouth, some double caffeine, and drinks some Endurox. Then he goes looking for some fruit and snares a banana or two and down the hatch they go. Then more handfuls of Cheez-Its and more Endurox, and soon we are walking and then running, and I am hoping to be out of range when Al finally barfs this up. He is going through a rough patch now, and I question whether he will make it. All thought of nine hours is gone; Al is on survival mode now.

We run along at about an 11-minute per mile pace, and I am trying to talk to him about anything and everything. Being a pacer is not as easy as it seems. You are relatively fresh, and your charge is not. You can't go too fast, but you need to keep him moving at all costs. Talking encouragement, talking trash, telling jokes, anything you can think of to occupy his mind and keep him from thinking about the hell he is experiencing. The miles are passing slowly for me, and I have only been out here for 16 miles. What about Al; he is on mile 41 by now. I remember that when Al is tired, really tired, his right foot slaps the pavement and makes a loud sound when he runs. Right now, both of his feet are going *slap, slap, slap,* and we both start to laugh about it, and I can't believe he is laughing after 45 miles. And I can't believe that he hasn't coughed up all the junk he ate at the last stop, but he tells me that he is actually feeling better now that his stomach has calmed down. Hey, maybe, just maybe, he is going to make it after all.

Al and I have four laps to go, about eight miles. We are trash talking about everyone we know. Under his breath, Al is cursing out everyone else on the course, hoping no one else will run him down from behind. Then we are discussing the Western States 100, which has accepted him, but as it turns out instead of questioning his sanity about thinking of running 100 miles, Al now wants to discuss his training. Soon we are down to six miles, and things begin to look manageable except that it is getting dark out and there aren't any streetlights anywhere on the course. I never thought to bring my headlamp or flashlight.

And it is getting weird, too. At the far end of the course, a motorist who is lost and wants directions to Woodville accosts us. I give him directions, and he asks what we are doing. I tell him Al is running 50 miles. His mouth just flies open and he says "Fifty miles...fifty miles...fifty miles; are you guys crazy?" Why, yes, we are, thank you! We continue on our way. Then we are down to two laps when we pass a disheveled, elderly-looking woman in the fading light of the parking area. She looks at us in the eye and says "keep your shoulders back and your head up, keep your chin off your chest and run tall" and then she disappears toward the lodge. Now, I have only been running for 20 miles, so it is a bit too early for hallucinations. I ask Al if he saw that, and he says he saw her, too. OK, we are still OK.

Just one lap to go, and Al has emerged through the far side of the funk that earlier plagued him, and we are rolling now. The beginnings of a smile of satisfaction starts to cross his lips, and the running, believe it or not, starts to feel almost effortless. We make one more obligatory stop at the tailgate smorgasbord, and soon we are running what seems now to be a 2.07-mile victory lap. Not 20 minutes ago the thought of another two miles seemed painfully insurmountable, but now I feel the beginnings of a good runner's high setting in. I remember very little of that last lap except to applaud Al when he crossed the line to the whistles and clapping of those few remaining race workers and runners who stayed to see him through to the end. Ten hours and eleven minutes. A job well done.

Dinner was at Momo's Pizza. Although we had run 222 miles among the five of us, we still could not finish one of those enormous wagon wheel pizzas, with everything on it. Several pitchers of beer didn't hurt, either (for medicinal purposes only, I assure you). Al was almost dead asleep in his chair. Prince was still talking. Scott and

Fred were quietly discussing running the Tallahassee Marathon the next day and trying to talk Prince into running it with them. For no particular reason, I feel like a proud mother hen.

Scott and Fred at the Tallahassee Ultra 2003

As it turns out, Scott ran the marathon the next day (on the very same course as the 50-miler) in 3:58. Prince ran 4:23. Fred logged a few more miles with them before coming to his senses. And Al went to the Wakulla Springs Lodge for a breakfast of eggs, sausage, grits, toast, and coffee, and he cheered them all on until he fell fast asleep in a lawn chair.

The Tallahassee Ultra Distance Classic is one of my favorite events. I have been fortunate to have participated in either the 50K or 50-miler on 10 other occasions, including an overall victory in the 50K in my first visit to Wakulla Springs in 1998.

* * *

27
CHAPTER

A NECESSARY EVIL

Oak Mountain 50K, March 2004

I approached the 2004 Oak Mountain 50K (in Pelham, Alabama) (a) with an open mind and (b) as a training run for June's Western States Endurance Run, which I would be running for the first time in less than three months. By now I trust you know I'm not the most adept trail runner on the planet, but since I would be spending at least 24 hours on them in June, I entered this race as a prelude to the big event in California.

For your consideration (and calendar planning in the future), I will review the race in the format presented in the book *The Ultimate Guide to Marathons* by Dennis Craythorn and Rich Hanna.

Course Beauty: The entire course looked exactly the same to me—dirt, leaves, roots, and rocks. If one dared to look up to see their surroundings, one could count on taking a spill, ranging from a simple fall to the ground all the way to a 500-foot drop and roll down the side of the mountain. My running partner Al Barker experienced two (fortunately, *only* two as Al may in fact be a worse trail runner than me) of the former. I was lucky enough to not eat any dirt, although I have no idea what Oak Mountain State Park looks like aside from the dirt, leaves, roots, and rocks beneath my feet I mentioned previously. Score (on a scale of 1-10): 2.

Course Difficulty: Having to navigate a right-angle drop to a waterfall and then having to climb—hand over hand—up the other side is indicative of the difficulty of the course. Someone mentioned to me that navigating the decline was better than the alternative—navigating the *incline*—but I stated that I wasn't so sure of that, as I had never seen anyone fall *uphill* before. Also, the course wasn't an accurate 50K (31 miles); in my estimation, the distance was closer to 57 kilometers or so. Score: 10.

Appropriateness for First-Timers: Al and I approached the race with no aspirations for a competitive time. Good thing, as we only finished 10 minutes under the nine-hour cutoff. While the event was not appropriate for first–timers, Al and I noticed a large number of those around us late in the race who were competing in their first ultra. Many of them were carrying backpacks, wearing cross-training shoes, and exhibiting other forms of newness to the sport that made Al and me feel humbled. (Quite honestly, I believe some of the younger boys wearing backpacks may have been Cub Scouts in the midst of a 50-mile hike.) At least they *would* have made us feel that way had we given a rat's a**. Score: 1.

Race Organization: The race started on time, and the course was fairly well marked...for a trail run. However, the volunteers seemed clueless as to what lied ahead, as Al and I would frequently ask what we could expect next. The perfect example was at the last aid station (26 miles, but probably closer to 29 miles) where volunteers informed us that the finish was "downhill and on the road to the left." Al and I turned left onto the road running downhill, only to be screamed at by a backpack-carrying rookie who informed us we needed to retrace our steps and turn RIGHT and then go UPHILL on the TRAIL. Also, there was no ice at any of the aid stations, and as the temperature was in the low 80s, the fluids were all warm and the bread in the peanut butter and jelly sandwiches was toasted (apparently Tupperware is a luxury item at Oak Mountain). To make matters worse, the aid station at 17 miles was out of fluids. Apparently, race organizers didn't expect as many runners to pass by the 17-mile aid station as the other five or six aid stations along the course. Score: 2.

Crowds: Aside from the fact that no one—NO ONE—had a clue as to the distances anywhere along the course (Al and I heard "one mile to go" from cyclists and hikers and volunteers for at least 40 minutes toward the end of the race...and yes, we were moving), the crowds were supportive. I'm sure that for the runners who did give a rat's a**, that may have mattered. For me, I couldn't have cared less if they were throwing rocks at me, because if they were, it would mean less chance of me tripping over them. I just wanted OFF the course, OFF the trails, and IN the car heading back to Atlanta where I could once again run on the safe and sound asphalt trails of Peachtree City. Score: 3.

Summary: This was the second race I've competed in that gets my Never Again stamp of disapproval (the first being the JFK 50). I had a suspicion Western States would be the third.

I lied (about the Never Again stamp of disapproval). I returned to Oak Mountain in 2006 as a prelude to (yes, for a second time—more on that later) Western States.

As for Oak Mountain, I have this to say:

If you have to use your hands to advance, it is not a foot race.

* * *

28

CHAPTER

BEAUTIFUL DISASTER

Western States Endurance Run, June 2004

In 1971 and 1972, Gordy Ainsleigh finished the 100-mile Western States Trail Ride on horseback. In 1973, Gordy's new horse pulled up lame after 29 miles. In 1974, inspired and encouraged by Drucilla Barner, the secretary of the Western States Trail Foundation, Gordy completed the Western States Trail Ride ON FOOT in 23 hours and 42 minutes. In 1977, 16 runners competed in the first official Western States Endurance Run.

How did I feel after training for (OK, maybe not *training*, but certainly *worrying about*) the 2004 Western States (WS) Endurance Run for seven months?

How did I feel after spending over $1500 for an event I didn't even complete?

How did I feel after investing five days of my life (which I'll never get back) to travel to California to run (well, mostly *walk*) only 62 miles of a 100-mile event?

Humbled...embarrassed...but mostly RELIEVED!

Relieved I can now speak of it in the past tense.

If that's the case, you're probably wondering what led me to Squaw Valley at 5:00 a.m. on a cool, crisp morning on June 26, 2004 wearing unfamiliar running garb—trail shoes, fanny pack, water bottle—and staring at a 4.7 mile climb up the side of a freakin' mountain.

Al Barker, that's what...

After competing in the Badwater Ultramarathon last summer, Al expressed an interest in doing something out of the ordinary. So he talked me into entering the WS lottery via the buddy system, and to his delight and my dismay, our names were selected.

Before I knew it Al and I, along with our support crew of Susan Lance and Gordon Cherr, were on a flight to San Francisco. Upon arrival, we rented our support vehicle (a Cadillac—only in California, folks!) and drove east to Truckee, where we stayed for two nights prior to the start of the race and got acclimated to the elevation.

When I first met Susan Lance, I knew beyond a shadow of a doubt she was going to be one exceptional ultrarunner. In time she would prove me right. A two-time finisher of the Western States Endurance Run herself, Susan has won her fair share of ultras and, with the exception of my now 20-year training partner Al Barker, has run more miles with me than anyone else. Also, as you'll find out later, Susan Lance saved my life.

The day before the race, Al and I checked in with race officials at Squaw Valley who strapped fluorescent yellow bands on our respective wrists with our name, race number, weight, and pulse (my pulse, ordinarily 52 beats a minute, registered at 64; Al, ordinarily 50, registered at a whopping 86...he was admittedly nervous). The altitude did strange things to our bodies, elevating our pulse and blood pressure and for good measure inhibiting our ability to *breathe*.

At the official pre-race meeting, instructions were given to runners and crew. The top male and female runners were introduced, as well as half of the 1,300 volunteers responsible for the event. (Well, maybe not *half*, but it seemed that way in the hot sun. Then again maybe it was, in fact, *all* of the volunteers who were introduced. That pre-race meeting lasted for-ev-er!)

Noted ultrarunner Ray Krolewicz sat next to me on a picnic table and told me I'd do well and I'd have no problem with the course. "It's runnable," he said to me. Yes, those were his exact words; they haunt me to this day. I told Ray I was terrible on trails and feared the worst. Then again, race officials did say to add four or five hours to your 100-mile time, so using that calculation I thought breaking 24 hours would be a breeze. Guess who proved to be right (hint: it wasn't a noted ultrarunner nor the race officials) in the long run—if you consider finishing 62 miles of a 100-mile event long.

I've known Ray Krolewicz for many years. He is one of the many grizzled veterans I've admired and learned so much from over the years. In his prime, he was one of the best ultrarunners in the country, at one time holding the American record by running 216 miles in 48 hours. After I ran 129+ miles in the 2002 USATF National 24-Hour Championship Ray, who writes a regular column on ultrarunning for *The Running Journal*, referred to me as 'the south's newest phenom to the ultra ranks.' I was 47 years old at the time.

I left two drop bags with the volunteers to be delivered: one to Michigan Bluff (55.7 miles) and the other to the Rucky Chucky River crossing (78.1 miles). The plan was for Gordon to pace me from the allowed checkpoint (Foresthill School, 62.0 miles) to the finish. At that time, it would be around nightfall (my calculation derived with noted ultrarunner's help), and Gordon would bring my flashlight and headlamp. We expected that I would hit 62 miles around 8:00 p.m. (although Ray thought I'd make it by 6:00). The only thing we were all right about was that when I hit 62 miles it would still be Saturday. Barely, as it turned out.

We all ate our last meal at Subway (none of us barely said a word) the night before the race and were all fast asleep by 6:30—eight hours before our 2:30 a.m. wake-up call. At 4:00 a.m. race morning, we were at Squaw Valley eager to get the show on the road. After Al and I made our final pit stops (five for Al; one for me) we were at the starting line for the countdown to the start. It took us 25 seconds after the starter's gun to get to the starting line so we could begin— WALKING for the next 4.7 miles up to the Escarpment, going from an elevation of 6,200 feet to an elevation of 8,700 feet. Al and I experienced sausage fingers (swelling caused by altitude pressure) and realized—in a field of 444 runners—there were only 20 or so runners behind us.

Once we reached the summit, we turned a corner, *ran* for the first time, and came across our next opponent—a huge patch of ice! Al went in front of me and slipped, and when I put out my hand to stop him, I did a cheerleader-quality split, hyper-extending my right knee and pulling my left groin in the process. Terrific, and only 95 miles left to go!

Next I found myself running alone (what happened to Al?) on an eight-inch wide path with razor-like shrubs attacking my legs from both sides. Am I having fun yet?

Not to worry: Things only went downhill from there (and when I say "downhill," I mean lots of *UP*hill). I felt like I was Indiana Jones, fending off five attackers only to turn the corner to face TEN attackers…then, after defeating *them*, being chased by a rolling two-ton boulder.

I saw Gordon and Susan at Robinson Flat (24.6 miles) which, as it turned out, was the brightest spot in my day. It lasted all of 12 seconds. I gave Gordon my fanny pack (thus sacrificing one of my two water bottles—I would carry the remaining one in my hand), as it was bouncing and tearing a hole in my back. I would rough it from that point with my remaining handheld water bottle which, as it turned out, was a big mistake.

The next thirty miles offered some beautiful scenery; I was actually moving so slowly on occasion that I had time to enjoy it. The view, that is…not the event.

The three canyons between Last Chance (43.3 miles) and Michigan Bluff were without a doubt the beginning of my end. The climb up Devil's Thumb (the first canyon) required a climb of 1,600 feet in only 1.7 miles and required traversing 37 switchbacks (which caused me to flashback to the hellacious switchbacks on Mount Whitney at the end of Badwater last summer). The second canyon, requiring an 1,800-foot climb in 2.8 miles (but only seven switchbacks…seven looooooong switchbacks!) led me to Michigan Bluff. I stopped to have my big toes examined and tended to, as they were both tearing apart due to my altered foot strike caused by my accident on the ice. When I took off my left shoe, the medical team was horrified by the condition of my big toe. Unfortunately, they were ooing and aahing over damage to my toe incurred at Badwater *last summer*—they didn't even notice the toenail was tearing apart from the cuticle! A video team taped the whole repair process (for an upcoming documentary, I understand); the duct tape was a nice touch. I only had to have a large blood blister on my right big toe lanced and taped. (Later Gordon would describe my feet, tightly wound in duct tape, as something "created by a crazed artisan.")

As I was feeling a lot of pain in my thighs, my calves, my back, my… well, my BODY, I also asked for a massage. The masseuse couldn't believe how stiff my legs were, but she managed to loosen them up to the point that, when I stood up, they actually felt refreshed. However, my toes (and now my right heel) were still hurting. Terribly.

Did I mention the sun had now set, and it was dark? Or that I was still seven miles away from Gordon…and my flashlight? Or that I still had one more canyon to negotiate?

I borrowed a small penlight (from Chris of Tucson—bless you, Chris) to use through the third canyon, requiring a 6.3-mile journey. When I got to the bottom of the canyon, it was pitch black. The penlight, emitting a beam of about 4 feet, was difficult to navigate by, but I managed to finally make my way to the Foresthill School checkpoint (62.0 miles).

Did I mention I noticed a runner update board in Michigan Bluff, and it indicated Al had dropped out at 43.3 miles (appropriately named Last Chance)? Or that if I knew I would be rescued, I would have dropped in my tracks and waited for the rescue team? Or that any semblance of desire to finish this damn race was now gone? After all, this was Al's dream, not mine, and the event combined two of the four things I hate (the four things being hiking, camping, hunting, and fishing—you can figure out the two I'm referring to). Or that, in an effort to move out of the way of a participant who wanted to pass me, I lost my balance, slipped on pine straw, fell backward, and struck my head on a boulder? I decided I was in hell. I couldn't wait to make it to Foresthill...to call it a day. Literally, a *day!*

I walked with Chris and his pacer (I found out later pacers were allowed after 8:00 p.m., not at mile 62 as we thought—which meant Gordon *could* have joined me at Michigan Bluff, and I would have been spared the use of the penlight) the last 1.7 miles to Foresthill. A volunteer walked with us, encouraging Chris to complete the event. She stated that the hard part is over at 62 miles and that the course was technical (the kiss of death for me) right before the river crossing. Thank goodness she wasn't aware I had no intention of continuing, or she would have directed her comments to me as well as Chris. I simply walked along in silence, acting as if the thought of quitting never entered my mind.

Upon arriving at Foresthill School, I couldn't locate Gordon, so I asked a volunteer to find him for me while I sat in a lawn chair. I told the volunteer I might drop out of the race, but I'd tell her for sure in a moment. I weighed in and realized I had lost six pounds in the last 19 miles. I also realized I had not consumed a single calorie during that time (all I had consumed was water; lots and lots of water). Then I saw Gordon running across the parking lot—attired in the appropriate gear, wearing his headlamp, holding my lights in his hands, and most disturbing of all, EAGER TO RUN! I asked Gordon if he would be disappointed if I called it a day. After all, Gordon had trained and prepared for his designated 38-mile stretch of the WS course, and he'd been waiting for several hours to take center stage. Gordon told me I looked pretty beat up, and he would understand if I dropped out (bless you, Gordon). I walked back to the volunteer and told her number 134 is dropping out of the race. With a nod from the volunteer, it was over. I was officially out of the Western States Endurance Run.

The next four or five hours was a blur, but suffice it to say, I slept in five different spots during that time: in a volunteer's vehicle for the ride from Foresthill to the finish line, on the sidewalk next to the finish area, in a volunteer's vehicle in the finish area parking lot, in our support Cadillac, and in a hotel room (note: the original plan didn't call for a hotel room, as Al and I were supposed to be running during the night).

The four of us woke up the next morning and returned to the finish line, where we witnessed many accomplishing what Al and I could now only dream of doing—finishing WS! I saw Chris from Tucson finish and was proud of him for doing so. After all, I knew volunteers had required him to gain weight before leaving two checkpoints, and at Michigan Bluff he was so cold that I left him lying on a cot underneath two blankets, certain that his race was over. Like Ray Krolewicz the day before, I was wrong.

I spoke briefly with Don Allison, the editor and publisher of *Ultrarunning*, and he seemed to have a hard time believing he was talking to the same person who finished 6th at Badwater 11 short months ago. Like I tried to tell Ray yesterday, I'm *terrible* on trails. Maybe terrible is an understatement.

Sunday afternoon, the four of us—Al, Susan, Gordon, and I—went running (although I wouldn't call what Al and I were doing *running*). After our run, Al and I spoke with the famous "Cowman," who told us he was writing a book on his life. I thanked him for getting me national exposure on ESPN during coverage of the 1987 Boston Marathon (I was running next to him, and cameras were always looking for the runner with the horns on his head). We then saw Monica Scholz, who played leapfrog with me at Badwater in 2003 (although she eventually finished in front of me). She was excited with her WS performance, as she finally finished in the top 10. She was set to return to Badwater in two weeks, and we wished her well and told her we'd follow her on the webcast (Note: Monica went on to being the first female finisher—and third overall—at Badwater in 2004).

Monica Schulz, an attorney from Canada, is an amazing woman. In 2010, she established a world record by completing 25 runs of 100 miles, the most ever in one calendar year. Her incredible talent and effervescent personality are only two of the qualities contributing to Monica's status as one of ultrarunning's brightest stars.

We saw local legend, Tim Twietmeyer, working with several young boys to clean up the field where only moments before the grand finale of the WS had taken place. He was also the only runner I saw cross the finish line during my nap on the sidewalk the night before.

After it was over, I had no regrets. Just an overwhelming sense of relief—relief that I had no intention of running another trail as long as I lived.

Al is another story, however. A mere eight days after our beautiful disaster, he told me he wanted to try WS again someday. Susan said she wanted to try it, too.

Two years later, Al Barker and I would find ourselves in Squaw Valley once again.

Why? One part Al (WS was his dream) and one part Scott (remember how I felt when I didn't run for the entire 24 hours or finish my Run Across Georgia the first time?)

Just like that—but worse. Far, far worse.

* * *

29
CHAPTER

OLANDER MEMORIES

Olander Park Ultras, September 2002, 2003, 2005

When I first heard the news that the Olander Park races in Sylvania, Ohio would no longer be held, I felt saddened by the loss. The event and its staff—both of which I had come to appreciate tremendously—treated me like a family member since the moment I took my very first step (there would be approximately 435,000 more) on the legendary 1.091-mile path around the magnificent lake in the middle of the park—a park that (deservedly so) gets more than its fair share of use by the people of Sylvania.

I had the distinct pleasure of participating in three National Championships on the course where—according to the entry form—"the participants are treated like royalty." The entry form told the truth, a direct reflection of the tremendous work of Race Director Tom Falvey and his staff. Although I only had the pleasure of participating at Olander three times, the memories will last a lifetime.

September 2002–National 24-Hour Championship

My running pal Gary Griffin told me to go to Olander to make a name for myself in the ultrarunning community. At the point in the race where I worked my way into the top 10 on the leader board, a live webcast referred to me as an "unknown." Ultimately, I ran 129 miles and finished 4th overall male and earned the title of National Masters Champion in the process.

September 2003–National 100 Mile Championship

My first attempt at a *pure* 100-mile race. I finished in 18:23:18, good for 10th overall male and 2nd in my age group. Since I ran this event a little less than two months after running Badwater, I was very satisfied with the performance. Also, seeing my friend Gary finish his first 100-miler at Olander was a treat.

September 2005–National 100 Mile Championship

My third attempt (and my first since a failure at the 2004 Western States Endurance Run) at a pure 100-mile race. I finished in 21:34:34, good for 12th overall male and 3rd in my age group. Also, seeing my friend Susan Lance finish her first 100-miler at Olander (and Gary his second) was a pleasure.

The following September, I missed flying to Toledo and driving the 15 minutes it takes to get to the town of Sylvania. I missed eating spaghetti and drinking (usually too much) beer on Friday night at the pre-race dinner. I missed talking my running friends into giving Olander a try. I missed passing out sometime Sunday morning following an exhausting day at the track. I missed talking to the many runners, volunteers, crewmembers, and spectators lining the course. Most of all, I missed seeing my good friend Tom Falvey.

When I heard the news about the discontinuation of the Olander races, I sent Tom a note, which read:

Tom—say it ain't so.

I read in the November 2005 issue of Ultrarunning magazine that Olander will be no more. I was really sad to read that the race will no longer take place on the traditional second weekend in September due to dwindling participation and financial difficulties.

But I certainly understand your predicament.

I have many fond memories of Olander, and it always brought a special smile to my face when I received your confirmation e-mail for your events with the words "I hope you win" at the end of the note.

You always managed to treat every participant as if they were the most important person on the course, and you took the time to get to know each and every one of us. For that, you will always have the respect and admiration of the many members of the Peachtree City, Georgia-based Darkside Running Club who have run in your events through the years.

Speaking for all of us who learned a lot about running, about life, and about ourselves in the Yankee Stadium of ultrarunning,

We hope you win.

–Scott Ludwig

Olander participant 2002, 2003, 2005 (representing 329 of the best miles of my life)

* * *

30
CHAPTER

RENEGADE

Strolling Jim 40-Mile Run, May 2006
Putting the "War" in "Wartrace"

*Oh, Mama, I'm in fear for my life from the long arm of the law
Law man has put an end to my running, and I'm so far from
my home*

— "Renegade" by Styx

I had every intention of making the 2006 Strolling Jim 40-Mile Run a true, relaxing run in the country. However, it turned out to be anything but.

As a prelude, here's a posting on the ultrarunning website that appeared a couple days *after* the event–I believe it was posted by the race director:

About 10 or 12 years ago we added the trek in the Strolling Jim starting out two hours before the regular race. The idea was to provide a chance for super slow runners to run the race and get done in time to party at the finish line with the other runners.

It turns out that the trek holds a fascination for those who have no business in the trek. This year—for the second time—a trekker, who HAD NO BUSINESS RUNNING THE TREK, duked it out with the actual winner over the last couple of miles, eventually nosing him out at the finish.

But that runner was not alone: About half the trek field came in among the top runners creating a major nuisance in scoring.

Next year, the trek will be restricted to runners over 60 years of age or with special approval by me. It is my intention to dole out the trek numbers personally. Needless to say, contenders will not be trekking.

I don't have any real heartache with those who entered just to beat the sun, although they were a little too fast for the trek, but the idiot who beat the winner…

My questions, for the listers out there are:

What is going through someone's mind…

First, for a six-hour runner to enter the trek AT ALL, when it is specifically requested that anyone with the least chance of breaking nine hours NOT run the trek.

Second (and this in the one I really don't get), why the hell would you race and beat the actual winner to the finish line?

If the guilty party is on the list [author's note: I'm not—a friend forwarded this message to me], *you don't have to admit it to the list (I know your name and didn't include it here), I would really like to know what you were thinking.*

What was I thinking, he asks? Read on...

Albert the Alligator and Scott, 125,000 miles, November 2011, Gainesville, Florida

31
CHAPTER

COME SAIL AWAY

Strolling Jim 40-Mile Run, May 2006

I'm sailing away, set an open course for the virgin sea
I've got to be free, free to face the life that's ahead of me

— "Come Sail Away" by Styx

Al Barker, Susan Lance, Danielle Goodgion, and I decided to enter the 2006 Strolling Jim 40-Mile Run in beautiful Wartrace, Tennessee as a training run for that year's Western States Endurance Run. Susan and Danielle had agreed to be our pacers— Susan for Al and Danielle for me. We agreed to run all 41.2 miles in Wartrace together with the same effort Al and I expected to expend later that summer as we tackled the mountains of the Sierra Nevadas. Seeing as the Jim is run on rolling country roads, we didn't expect anything noteworthy to happen. Our intent was to spend a beautiful spring Saturday morning enjoying each other's company, experimenting in eating along the course, practicing with our fuel belts, and, in my case, taking as many photographs as I could along the way.

Sometimes, however, what should have been a calm, relaxing, nonnoteworthy morning in the country turns out to be much more than that. This was one of those mornings.

The Strolling Jim offers a trekker's start time of 5:00 a.m. (the regular, competitive race begins at 7:00 a.m.) for those who need the earlier start that allows them to finish at a decent hour. Ordinarily, the slower runners and walkers opt for the earlier start. However, as the four of us had tickets for a concert in Peachtree City, Georgia—four hours away, not to mention losing an hour due to the different time zone in Georgia—later that night at 8:00 p.m. (Styx!), we opted to begin running at 5:00 a.m. Susan and I had used the trekker's start two years prior for the same reason, and the timing of it worked out very well. Our goal was to finish in 7.5 hours or less, which would give us plenty of time to get to our seats in the amphitheater to hear "Blue Collar Man" and "Come Sail Away" (the latter could have been our theme song for our run—our soothing, relaxing run through the country).

As I had been running fairly well lately, I had told Al, Susan, and Danielle that if I felt good after getting through the hilly portion of the course known as The Walls (ending at mile 34), I was going to push the pace for the final seven miles. After almost six hours of conversation, food, drink, and many summer vacation photographs (a reference to the fact that I never appear in family vacation photos as I am always the photographer), I did in fact feel good after 34 miles. My timing couldn't have been worse, as right after I informed Al and Susan I was going to gun it (Danielle had fallen slightly back a few miles earlier), I noticed the two leaders of the *real* race about 300 yards back. The two leaders happened to be (arguably) the two finest ultrarunners in Alabama, and they were bearing down on Al and me as if we were hardly moving. I decided I would try holding them off as long as possible, and when the true leader of the race was about to pass me, I would take a photograph of myself with the leader directly over my shoulder. I wanted to use it in my Darkside Running Club's newsletter with the following caption: *Scott held off the eventual winner of the race for 37 miles.*

Two miles later, I was still in the lead (remember, I had a two-hour head start on the boys from 'bama). Around mile 36, the leader's wife, who was driving a van in support of her husband, was along the side of the road and said to me, "You're running pretty fast for a trekker." I told her that I wasn't trekking, I just had to be somewhere later that night.

Then, two more miles down the road, and I still hadn't been passed. I couldn't imagine what was taking them so long; surely at least one of them should have left me in their wake by now. I encountered the wife once again, and this time she said to me (with plenty of attitude): "It ain't over 'til it's over." I thought to myself, "Here I am out for a comfortable run through the countryside on a beautiful spring morning wearing a water belt (which I never wear when I'm competing…actually which I never wear *ever* unless I'm doing some serious preparation for Western States) with a camera in my hand and this ____ is giving me a hard time. What the hell?"

At this point, I was still ahead of everyone in the race, and I decided since I was still in this position after 38 miles I was going to make it difficult for *anyone* to pass me. I picked up the pace a bit, and I found Gary Cantrell (the founder of the race) at the 5K-to-go mark, and he handed me a feather. I asked him what it was for, and he merely shrugged. I thought maybe it was a Strolling Jim tradition for the first person to reach this point— whether they are a competitor or a trekker—to be handed a feather which would in turn cross the finish line with the eventual winner. Legend also had it that a trekker had *never* crossed the finish line before a competitor in the 27-year history of the event. Two years ago when Susan and I ran together, we had noticed Gary driving by us several times late in the race, appearing a bit nervous that two trekkers were out in front of all of the actual competitors. When Susan and I were passed by the leader at the 37-mile mark, Gary looked relieved. When I passed Gary *this* year, he had a smirk on his face. I had no idea why.

At the 39-mile mark, I encountered the wife a third (and what proved to be the final) time. This time she offered this gem: "Oh, you're carrying a feather. Do you think that will make you *fly?*" It was at this point I decided that there was no way in hell her husband—or anyone else, for that matter—was going to pass me before I got to the finish line. With half a mile to go, I heard one of the 'bama boys shouting encouragement at the other in a valiant, albeit, vain, attempt to get him to catch me. However, I managed to run a 21:16 for the final 5K, which proved to be fast enough to get me to the finish line first. Almost.

As I approached the finish line, one of the volunteers jumped out on the course and met me about five feet from the finish tape. He screamed at me to stop short of the finish line. I managed to stop, although I staggered slightly as my legs were a bit shaky after running 41 miles. Imagine that. When I staggered slightly, it was my misfortune to stagger *forward*, as this caused the volunteer to shove me in the chest with both hands and scream, "You're not allowed to cross the finish line!" Then he turned to a volunteer recording finishing times and screamed at her to notate my time as *"nine hours...give him nine hours"* (the minimum time allowed a trekker in the official results). However, the way he said—no, *screamed* it—was more like he was condemning me for having the audacity to get to the finish before those actually racing the course. I threw the feather (yes, I was still holding it) to the ground in disgust (how's that for an effective gesture, throwing a feather to the ground. With attitude!) and walked past the finish line just outside the actual finish chute. The time on my watch indicated I had covered the course in 6:47:59.

About a minute later, one of the 'bama boys crossed the finish line. He was the winner of the 28th annual Strolling Jim 40-Mile Run. Eventually, everyone who crossed the finish line throughout the day was a winner. There was only one loser on this beautiful spring morning in Tennessee. As runners and trekkers alike shared in the post-race barbecued chicken, the winner's wife was in a corner eating a bird of a different feather: crow.

Come sail away.

I have competed in four Strolling Jims. I placed a self-imposed ban on myself after the fiasco in 2006.

I did receive a note from Gary Cantrell immediately after this last episode, apologizing for the actions of the gentleman at the finish line. I would have rather gotten an explanation about the feather.

* * *

32 CHAPTER

BEAUTY AND THE BEAST (PART I)

Western States Endurance Run Training, Spring 2006

As fate would have it, I once again entered the lottery for the 2006 Western States Endurance Run (so much for staying on the roads) via the buddy system with my good friend and training partner Al Barker. For the second consecutive time, we managed to beat the odds and were selected to be on the starting line in Squaw Valley at 5:00 a.m. on Saturday, June 24. (I read that all entrants had a 17% chance of being selected in the lottery. I looked at it as an 83% chance of *not* being selected. But that was just me being the optimist.) As the lottery was held in December of 2005, that meant I had a little over six months to get (trail) serious—which was exactly the same amount of time I had to get ready for Badwater three short years ago.

I decided to return to many of the things that worked for me then (why ruin a good thing?), while supplementing my training and preparation with a few variations specific to a venture on the trails (which I felt was absolutely essential, having been primarily a road runner my entire life).

Here's a capsule summary of those six months:

The Edge of Exhaustion[4]

Although I had vowed (as I do annually, usually unsuccessfully) to reduce my mileage in 2006, I realized I needed to actually *increase* my mileage—training to the virtual edge of physical exhaustion once again—if I were to stand a chance against the demands of the 100-mile route through the mountains of the Sierra Nevadas. I resumed my **95 miles per week** regimen which, when supplemented with a job that requires 50-plus hours per week as well as enough jobs around the house to make Bob Vila nervous, managed to tire me to the point of nightly blackouts around 7:30 p.m. in my recliner. Excellent—that was just what I needed.

In a 10-week span from mid-January through late March, I managed to run **six marathons** (five of which I actually put forth a substantial effort) and **three 50Ks** (two of them being on trails and a third—on concrete—in which I set a state age group record). In other

---

4   There's nothing I fear more, and no place I'd rather be

words, I wasn't merely logging miles; I was running relatively hard, something I hadn't been doing since Badwater three summers ago. The first weekend in May, my Western States pacer—Danielle Goodgion—and Al and his pacer—Susan Lance—ran the Strolling Jim 40-Mile Run together as a final long-distance tune-up. We did reasonably well, all finishing comfortably in around seven hours.

I met Danielle for the first time when she was in the midst of her solo 20-mile run on a Sunday morning. Her route? Five hilly four-mile laps around Lake Peachtree. Danielle was in the middle of her second lap, blood pouring from her left knee, down her shin and into her shoe. She had fallen during her first lap, but there was no way that was going to stop her from finishing her 20 miles. I knew the second I saw her blood-drenched shoe that we were going to be friends and running partners one day.

I also stayed the course with my regular **long training runs:** In a five-month window from January through June, I had 15 runs of 20 miles or longer, with 4 of them being 31 miles or longer. I was diligently doing my homework.

As for the training supplements I referred to earlier, I turned my attention to the trails. As I mentioned, I ran two 50Ks on trails (Kennesaw Mountain, Georgia and Oak Mountain, Alabama), two races I'm familiar with but don't particularly care for (for the simple fact that they're *not on roads*). Additionally, I ran the Bartram Trail in North Carolina (22 miles) with Al in April, and the Pine Mountain Trail (again, 22 miles) in Georgia with Gary Griffin in May. During my run with Al, we maneuvered along the route with what we called "Western States effort", advancing as if we were going to be doing

100 miles. We completed the route in a little less than six hours. Perfect. During my run with Gary, I gained some valuable insight as to how trails should be run. Two things Gary taught me that would pay off for me in June were look ahead and plan your next three steps and trust the rocks (I have always had a tendency to do everything in my power to avoid landing on a rock when I run—probably my bad experience in 2000 on the Appalachian Trail at the JFK 50-Mile Run in which most of the rocks I opted to land on wobbled, causing my ankles to periodically twist wildly from side to side). Running that day with Gary gave me a lot of newfound confidence.

My final trail run was a **nighttime** return to the Pine Mountain Trail with Al, Danielle, and Susan two weeks before Western States. We ran 10 miles on the trail after the sun went down to test our headlamps and handheld flashlights on the trails. Although we were on the trails for three hours, we considered it a success.

The other supplement? **Hills!** Plenty of them—numerous quarter-mile and 4/10-mile hill repeats and a weekly and particularly hilly 12-mile training route with Al or Danielle.

Aside From the Running...

I returned to Paula May's prescribed **pre-Badwater diet** on January 2 and stuck with it religiously for six months. This happened to coincide with a 101-day weight-loss contest at my place of employment which I won by losing 19 pounds (just over 12% of my body weight), ultimately dropping my weight to a mere 136 pounds. And as I did three years ago, I did not consume any beer the last 30 days before Western States (which was probably a personal superstition more than anything else).

The last two weeks before Western States, I incorporated a lot of **walking** into my daily running regimen, while reducing my weekly mileage to taper. I knew I would be doing a lot of walking in the mountains and wanted to get a sense of my walking motion to feel less awkward. (I've always hated to walk—it's so much easier to *run*.)

For probably the first time in my life I kept a bottle of **water** on my desk at work and would refill it many times throughout the day (usually at the end of one of my many visits to the restroom). Did I fail to mention that I even incorporated **running with a water bottle** on some of my training runs, something I'd *never* done?

My wife Cindy surprised me with an anniversary gift (our anniversary being six days before Western States) of a gift certificate for a **full-body massage**, which I took advantage of four days prior to the race. I've always read that a massage is recommended the week prior to a major athletic endeavor. If that's true, this was absolutely the time for it.

I watched Al's video *A Race for the Soul*, which chronicles an earlier edition of the Western States Endurance Run. On the third viewing (which was sometime during the first week in May), it took, and I began to actually visualize myself crossing the finish line. In contrast, the first time I saw the video *Running on the Sun* (which chronicles the 1999 edition of Badwater), I knew instantly that one day I would cross the finish line on Mount Whitney.

My final preparation, of course, was to **prepare for the event mentally.** Obviously, the first hurdle is visualizing success. After that, a game plan—which requires the utmost in patience, perseverance, and mind over matter—has to be formulated. My game plan revolved around five elements:

1. Enjoy the course and the camaraderie.
2. Don't push; take what the course gives you.
3. Patience. Patience. Patience.
4. Focus on the positives; block out the negatives.
5. Keep moving.

Al, Scott, Gordon at Western States 2004

Last-Minute Anxieties

Considering I was running well, was feeling reasonably healthy, and was at my lightest weight since I was 13 years old, I was feeling pretty good about my chances of finishing Western States, which until now had been the only major blemish on my running career (I'm referring to my failure at Western in 2004).

But just when things were going good...

Sunday night, June 18 (six days before Western States, and the evening of our 29th wedding anniversary...not to mention it also being Father's Day), I asked Cindy to take a look at the scab on the back of my left thigh, as it had been there for quite a while and I just couldn't seem to get rid of it. Cindy politely informed me my "scab" was actually a well-fed tick, who'd been feasting on my blood for at least a week (assuming I picked it up in Pine Mountain on the night training run the weekend before). As I'd been feeling achy all weekend, I figured I had Lyme disease, and that most likely my last six months of training would be for naught. I visited a doctor (which indicates how desperate I was) the following day. He calmly removed the tick and said he doubted I had Lyme disease, and my weekend jaunt through the mountains was still a go. I felt good dodging this last-minute bullet. An omen, perhaps?

Let's hope so. I was going to be in Squaw Valley in only five days.

***

33

CHAPTER

BEAUTY AND THE BEAST (PART II)

Western States Endurance Run, June 2006

Not to put any pressure on myself, but wanting to make it to the finish line of the Western States Endurance Run had become my own personal version of Captain Ahab's elusive Moby Dick... Arnold Palmer's never-achieved U.S. Open championship... Superman's Kryptonite, for that matter. Mind you, trail running does not particularly appeal to me, and I have no false aspirations of ever being proficient—hell, I'll settle for *competent* these next 100 miles—on the trails.

Up until 2004, the only race I failed to complete was my initial attempt in 1982 at running across the state of Georgia. Ten years later, I gave it a second try and was successful.

Now, two years removed from my initial failure at Western States in 2004, here I was again in Squaw Valley with two days to make my final preparations—both physically and mentally—to give it a second (and absolutely *final*) try. Al Barker, Susan Lance (Al's pacer), and I had two days to eat, rest, strategize, and rest some more. My pacer, Danielle Goodgion, as well as her husband Bill would see me Saturday morning at Robinson Flats, approximately 30 miles into the race. In fact, the two days before the race, I slept for 10 hours and 7 ½ hours, respectively—record amounts for me. Race morning, Al and I woke up at 3:00 a.m. and headed for the pre-race breakfast–bib number pick-up literally right next door to our room at the Squaw Valley Lodge. We returned to the room immediately to avoid the pre-race tension that can be found as runners, crewmembers, and race officials make last-minute preparations and adjustments before the starting gun sounded at 5:00 a.m. Me? I'm better off avoiding the mass hysteria, and besides, it was a little late to make any last-minute adjustments that may enter into your mind. Accidentally overhearing an innocent tip, reminder, or piece of advice this late in the game is never a good thing. Stick with what got you this far, and steer clear of any too-late-in-the-game suggestions or recommendations. Staying secluded in our room at the lodge saved us from this onslaught of self-doubt and second-guessing. We had our game plan, and we were prepared to execute. We had done our homework, and we felt ready.

4:55 a.m. Saturday, Race Morning, Squaw Valley

Susan escorts Al and me to the starting line and takes a few "before" photographs. Later—maybe several hours, maybe a day or more—the "after" photographs would be taken. We're hoping for the latter, as we're both aiming for running the course in 30 hours. The gun sounded promptly at 5:00 a.m., and we were on our way up the Escarpment, a tremendous 4.7-mile climb up the side of a mountain gaining over 2,250 feet in elevation.

After we crest the mountain, we found ourselves running, walking, and stumbling in snow, a good 2 feet deep in some areas. It didn't take long for us to learn the art of butt-gliding, as it was easier sliding down the slopes than it was trying to maintain your balance and footing. Later, my butt cheeks will remind me that butt-gliding may not have been such a good idea after all.

Al and I remained together for almost 12 miles. Al took a few spills, and the only casualty I incurred happened about eight miles into the race as I stopped to get a rock out of my shoe by sitting on a fallen tree. I braced myself with my right hand and quickly discovered a sharp, jagged branch puncturing my palm. It would be the only bloodshed I incurred all day, but it was painful. At least nothing bad happened to my feet. Not yet, anyway.

1:17 p.m., Robinson Flat

As I approached the 16-mile mark at Red Star Ridge, I feared that Al was having difficulty and in danger of missing an absolute cutoff (AC) soon, which meant disqualification from the race. The race officials are very strict with enforcing the various ACs along the course, which allow a little extra cushion for those trying to complete the course in the mandated 30-hour time limit. I made my way to Robinson Flat (mile 30) where I saw Susan once again and Danielle and her husband Bill for the first time. At this point I was already exhausted; the course had been altered slightly from two years ago, and the five miles leading to Robinson Flat were a never-ending series of tortuous uphill. I remember *sprinting* to Robinson Flat in 2004 and tossing my fuel belt (which was irritating the small of my back) to Gordon Cherr (my ill-fated pacer), as I thought I was running too fast to waste any time with idle conversation. Not this year.

As I said, I was already exhausted (I would feel this way many more times) and gave my friends the "shoot me in the head" sign. Just as I could tell their initial reaction was that my run may be coming to an end very soon, I could also see that their hopes of me finishing were rekindled after a few encouraging words from the three of them as I sat for a moment and drank some fluids while resting in a lawn chair. Susan informed me that Al had missed the cutoff at Duncan Canyon, and I felt sad, as I knew how much Western States meant to him.

Feeling (ever-so-slightly) refreshed, I got up from the lawn chair and resumed my journey toward Auburn. Danielle called out that she would be in Michigan Bluff to pace me. Michigan Bluff was 26 miles and almost eight hours away. It would be dark when I met up with Danielle…and would have access to my headlamp and flashlight for the first time.

5:03 p.m., Last Chance

I had been dodging ACs for the past six aid stations, and the constant pressure was beginning to take its toll on me, both physically and worse, mentally. In fact, as I approached the Last Chance aid station at mile 43, I felt I would miss the AC and actually referred to it to another runner as my mercy killing. Somehow I managed to make the AC by 12 minutes. I would live to face yet another challenge as I made my way to the checkpoint I dreaded most, Devil's Thumb, a grueling two-mile climb incorporating 37 switchbacks into a 1,600-foot climb.

As I left Last Chance, one of the volunteers offered to pour ice water on my back. I accepted, and the cold literally took my breath away. However, in the process, it gave me a renewed vigor…a second wind…a chance to actually *have a chance* to make it to the finish line in Auburn.

6:36 p.m., Devil's Thumb

Astonishingly the two-mile climb up Devil's Thumb was without a doubt my finest effort of the day. I literally power-walked the entire way—up all 37 switchbacks—without so much as having to pause to catch my breath. Two years ago I literally stopped at every butt-high rock, stump, or ledge and sat to rest. It was almost incredulous to believe I had been literally dreading this part of the course for the past seven months. I thought as I began my climb at the bottom of Devil's Thumb that this may very well be the AC I miss, thus ending my quest abruptly, having gone less than halfway toward my goal of completing the entire 100.2 miles that comprises the Western States Endurance Run.

Only eight more miles—and a brief spell of running in the dark without light—and I would be meeting up with Danielle. If I could just hold on and make one more AC at Michigan Bluff, I could ride the wave that is Danielle's enthusiasm to the finish line.

9:13 p.m., Michigan Bluff

I made the AC with 17 minutes to spare, which isn't bad considering I ran the last mile in the dark. I spent a little more time than normal at this aid station, as I needed to change my shirt and socks, drink a little concoction from my drop bag, and gather my lights. Bill provided invaluable assistance, while Danielle's motor was racing as she couldn't wait to pace me to the next checkpoint at Foresthill School, where we would meet up with Bill and Susan once again and see Al for the first time since he was removed from the race. A volunteer looked at the bottom of my feet and said the blisters on the balls of both feet looked menacing. However, I didn't have time to hear that right then. What did he expect after running in snow, slush, and streams (which were unusually high due to rapidly-melting snow in 100-degree temperatures) for over 16 hours?

11:29 p.m., Foresthill School

At Foresthill School, runners are announced as if they were royalty as they enter the checkpoint. Danielle and I were met by our three biggest fans, and I immediately asked to see a medical volunteer to see if my feet could be duct-taped. The volunteer looked at my feet and advised I should not continue. I told him that was not an option, so he took out a needle and lanced the (many? I can't tell, because I'm not looking) blisters on both feet and wrapped them in duct tape. After a couple pain-killers and a bite of cold pizza, Danielle and I were on our way for (what I had been told) the easy part of the course. I wouldn't know from prior experience, as Foresthill was where I dropped out of Western States two years ago.

Everything I would be seeing now I would be seeing for the first time. That is, if you can call maneuvering through the great, big, *dark* outdoors using artificial light *seeing*. Truth be known, the only thing I actually saw in the dark of the night was the fluorescent markings on the heels of Danielle's running shoes.

The Wee Hours of the Morning;
Saturday Turns Into Sunday

Danielle and I made our way through the dark, her spirit as bright as her incandescent headlamp. We managed to dodge AC after AC— some by as little as four minutes—and it began to wear on my psyche. For the life of me, I just couldn't seem to gain any significant cushion on the time allowance. Cutting it as close as I was on a course I wasn't familiar with was exhausting. Danielle told me later she had been using her GPS wristwatch to determine what point of each leg we were at and how fast we needed to run or walk to make it within the next AC. She would never say anything to me during the race; she simply picked up the pace. For this—and many other things she did for me during the 12 hours she ran with me—I am forever indebted.

4:30 a.m. Sunday, Rucky Chucky River Crossing

I've heard about the mystique of this part of the race so many times that once I finish this passage, I never want to see, hear, or say it again. As the river was very deep (due to the aforementioned melting snow), this year the river crossing was via boat (most years runners have to wade across the river via a guide wire), so it was virtually painless. However, jumping in and out of the boat with feet that felt like soggy sponges wasn't particularly pleasant (the balls of my feet were literally shredding apart due to the combination of their exposure to moisture and the constant pounding throughout the day and night and now day again).

Bill joined us for the crossing, and once again assisted me with a fresh pair of dry socks. I noticed him grimacing when he saw the balls of my feet...just before he grabbed his camera to get a photograph of them.

Bill Goodgion provides a great deal of support, encouragement, and inspiration to wife Danielle. Bill's forte is climbing mountains, but he's not adverse to a run here and there. He is one of the few people I know who ran an ultra before he ever attempted a marathon. Bill also provided a great deal of support, encouragement, and inspiration to me as I tackled the Sierra Nevadas...and took some pretty fantastic photographs along the way. One in particular would become especially meaningful to Danielle.

Danielle and I made up a little ground on the AC; in fact, we entered into the checkpoint precisely at the 30-hour cutoff, a full 15 minutes ahead of the AC.

8:06 a.m., Brown's Bar

Brown's Bar is the checkpoint I had been looking forward to the most, not only because it's 90 miles into the race, but because it is in fact sponsored by a bar. And bars have beer, and after 90 miles and 27 hours of water and numerous fluids of the sweet variety, an ice-cold beer would sit quite well, thank you. Danielle and I heard loud music blaring in the woods, which was a bit ominous as it was impossible to determine if the checkpoint was right around the corner or a mile or two down the trail. As we approached the aid station, the Rolling Stones' "19th Nervous Breakdown" was playing on the stereo system. Ironically, there were almost that many (17, actually) ACs I had to deal with during the race, and each one was in fact nerve wracking, so the song was more than appropriate.

As I suspected, there was a keg of a fine red beer brewed locally. I don't recall the name of the beer, but I'll forever remember the taste. Interestingly, the bartender asked Danielle if my stomach could handle a beer at this point in the race. Danielle answered in the affirmative without as much as a second thought. Good girl. Like I said earlier, forever indebted.

9:11 a.m., Highway 49

Bill and Susan waited at Highway 49, the next-to-last AC I had to face. As was the case with virtually every AC so far, this one was a challenge as well. A long uphill took Danielle and me to Highway 49, and just as we were about to reach the top of the hill, the course took a sharp left turn and took us almost another roundabout mile to get us to the checkpoint. Once again, we made the AC, this time by a mere four minutes.

I asked Danielle to run ahead with my water bottles to have them refilled while I proceeded to the next checkpoint. I figured I didn't have the luxury of time to wait for them to be filled as I had been doing up until that point. Danielle agreed, and I headed on to the next and final AC at No Hands Bridge, another 3.5 miles down the trail. If I made this AC in time, I would be guaranteed a finish, whether I crossed the finish line within the 30-hour limit or not.

I'd come too far not to finish. Danielle told me later that two runners we had been leap-frogging throughout the early morning missed the AC at Highway 49 by less than one minute. Both wept openly when they were removed from the race. I understood completely.

A couple hundred yards into this leg of the race, Susan caught up to me with my two water bottles wearing Danielle's pacer number. I found out later Danielle had a foot injury but didn't want to worry me with her problems, as she figured I had enough of my own. I felt bad that I never sensed her distress, but I admired her courage for the tough 38 miles she had endured with me—mostly in the pitch dark of a moonless night.

Although my feet were literally screaming in agony, I ran this 3.5-mile segment as hard as I possibly could. The next checkpoint was the final AC, and there was no way I was going to miss this one after dodging 16 bullets up until that point. I remembered everything Gary Griffin taught me on the trails of Pine Mountain and planned out my next three steps and threw caution to the wind with my trust of the stability of any rocks I encountered. His advice proved worthy as I made this final AC at No Hands Bridge by 20 minutes and found myself actually five minutes ahead of the 30-hour cutoff.

There would be no more cutoffs today. I was going to finish the Western States Endurance Run. I decided to enjoy myself—cutoffs be damned.

9:59 a.m., No Hands Bridge

I'm convinced the course was designed by the Marquis de Sade. After 97 miles of tortuous passage of repeated ups and downs over tough mountain trails and 17 absolute cutoffs, you expect the course might be willing give you a break for your final three miles. Not a chance. The climb to Robie Point was—for me, anyway—practically debilitating. It was all I could do to take one small step at a time, slowly making my way up to the summit. I realized when I ran the previous section as hard as I could that I would have little, if anything, left for this final segment. Susan initially had high hopes of me breaking 30 hours, as she repeatedly said I only had a little over three miles to go with an hour to do them. However, I'm not sure I could have covered these last three (primarily uphill) miles in one hour if I was starting *fresh*. They were that difficult!

After reaching Robie Point, there was one more significant climb out of the trail onto the asphalt that would lead me to the finish line at Placer High School. Al and Bill had walked out on the course to join Susan and me for the final mile or so. Danielle would be joining us later, they said, as she was waiting outside the track, nursing her injured foot. We enjoyed ourselves and made sure to smile at all of the residents of Auburn who were still lining the sidewalks, encouraging the remaining few runners who had managed to make that one last absolute cutoff at No Hands Bridge. I was damn proud to be—I found out later—the last of them.

Danielle met us about a half-mile from the finish line and gave me a big hug and apologized for not being able to pace me the final few miles. I told her she had done a terrific job, and she had nothing to apologize for. In retrospect, I couldn't have made it this far without her.

The five of us—Danielle, Susan, Bill, Al, and I—entered the track, pausing momentarily so Bill could capture the moment on film. We proudly circled the track to the applause of the many runners, crew members, officials, and Auburn locals who were on hand to pay tribute to every last one of us who had made it through the mountains.

11:16:58 a.m., Placer High School Track

For one brief moment, I'm certain time stood still. After the many anxieties, extensive training and abundance of self-doubt I experienced about this event over the past two years, it well should have. Somewhere out there in the mountains I ran my 103,000 lifetime mile. For now, the only mile that mattered...the only *quarter* mile that mattered...was right here—right now—on this track in Auburn, California. The end seemed too short...too sudden...too *final* for what had preceded it. As Danielle, Susan and I crossed the finish line, a volunteer draped a medal around my neck, symbolizing the completion of the Western States Endurance Run.

Seconds later, a large television camera was planted in my face, and I was subjected to a string of questions about the race. I'm fairly certain I answered them coherently, although I can't recall now what I was asked. I remember telling him about butt-gliding...where I was from...how tough the course and the heat had been. What I didn't tell him was that, unlike many others, I had no desire to return in the future.

On this particular day, I captured Moby Dick, won the US Open, and proved to be impervious to Kryptonite. There was no need to return.

Western States 2006

Checkpoint	Distance	Elapsed Time	Pace per Split
Lyon Ridge	10.5	3:00	17:10
Red Star Ridge	16.0	1:30	16:22
Duncan Canyon	23.8	1:54	14:37
Robinson Flat	29.7	1:53	19:09
Last Chance	43.3	3:54	17:12
Devil's Thumb	47.8	1:32	20:26
Michigan Bluff	55.7	2:42	20:30
Foresthill School	62.0	2:04	19:41
Rucky Chucky	78.0	4:01	15:04
Auburn Lakes Trail	85.2	2:25	20:08
Brown's Bar	89.9	1:21	17:14
Highway 49	93.5	1:04	17:47
Placer High School	100.2	2:07	18:58
TOTAL		**30:16:58**	**18:08**

KEYS TO SUCCESS

After my DNF in 2004 at Western States, my second attempt was more of a vendetta than anything else. I refused to let the course get the better of me again. As I made my way to the last checkpoint before Devil's Thumb and thought there was a very real chance I would be removed from the race, I believe my inherent, imbedded refusal to fail took over, and my body and mind were able to do whatever was necessary to make one cutoff after another. At least that was the case before reaching the last official cutoff, at which time both body and mind shut down and my basic instinct for survival took over for those final three, excruciating miles. The magnificent pacing efforts of both Danielle and Susan went a long way toward getting me to the track in Auburn as well.

* * *

34
CHAPTER

BEAUTY AND THE BEAST (PART III)

Virtually moments after I crossed the finish line at Western States, I was asked the inevitable question:

Which was harder: Badwater or Western States?

I imagine some who have tackled both have had to give this question some thought, while others—like myself—can answer before the second syllable in "Western" is spoken.

Consider:

- Badwater is 130 degrees of stifling heat. Western is a variety of dry temperatures ranging from 40 to 110 degrees (the latter incurred during a hot year).
- Badwater is 134.4 miles of blazing hot asphalt through the hottest desert in the country followed by the crossing of three mountain ranges. Western is 100.2 miles of soft, mostly shaded trails through a beautiful mountain range.
- Runners in a typical Badwater field have a completion rate of less than 60 percent. Western's is usually well over 70 percent.
- Badwater's starting field is usually less than 100 runners. Western's is regularly in the mid-400s.
- Badwater has a time limit of 60 (since then it has been changed to 48) hours. Western's is 30 hours.
- Badwater has no official aid stations. Western has fully-equipped, fully stocked, and fully-staffed (by some of the finest volunteers in the country) aid stations approximately every four miles along the course.

That being said, unquestionably, the more difficult of the two is... *Western States!*

While on the surface it may appear that Western States is the easier of the two, for a road-hardened runner like me, just the opposite was true.

At Badwater, you could count on the weather being consistent; that is to say, (indescribably) hot. At Western, I found myself running through snow two-feet deep while thinking I was overdressed in a sleeveless shirt and a pair of shorts. Later in the race, while I was swallowing dust being stirred from the trails in 100-degree heat, it felt as if I were suffocating.

At Badwater, I was able to follow one of the basic tenets of my running philosophy: *no thought required.* I knew that after each step my foot would land on soft, solid (albeit hot) asphalt. At Western, each step was a surprise. Will that rock move and cause me to twist my ankle if I land directly on it? Will this patch of mud be fairly firm, or will it swallow me up to my knees? Is that wet pile of leaves going to be slippery and cause me to fall off the side of the mountain? You get the idea. Give me solid, no-thought-required asphalt any day.

At Badwater, there is a 60-hour time limit; I finished with almost 23 ½ hours to spare. At Western, I missed the get-your-name-listed-in-the-results time limit of 30 hours by almost 17 minutes. If this alone is not an indicator as to which race I thought was easier, nothing is.

At Badwater, I finished a surprising 6th overall and 3rd place male. At Western, I was the absolute last runner of slightly more than 200 finishers to officially cross the finish line. At Badwater, I received a belt buckle—not for finishing 6th, but for finishing under 48 hours. At Western, I received a framed inspirational quote—for finishing last.

Sure, Western offered numerous aid stations as well as incredible volunteer support throughout the event. However, nothing beats having a support crew to provide me with virtually anything I needed whenever I needed it like I had at Badwater. Not having to carry my own water bottle, as was the case in Death Valley, made it that much easier to run (*no hands required,* another of the basic tenets of my running philosophy).

Scott, Susan, Al at Western States, June 2006

One thing both races had in common: I had the most incredibly proficient, supportive, and encouraging crews imaginable. Paula, Gary, Eric, Josh, and Al in the desert and Danielle, Susan, and Bill in the mountains. If any of you don't know how important each of you were in crossing these two finish lines, you do now.

You may be asking why this trilogy is called Beauty and the Beast.

One school of thought is that the beauty is the magnificent Western States trail running through the Sierra Nevada Mountains. Another is that the beauty is simply my primary pacer Danielle.

Some—like myself—may refer to the treacherous Western States trail as the beast. Others may consider me as the beast, their reasons known only unto themselves.

* * *

35 CHAPTER

WESTERN STATES: A PACER'S PERSPECTIVE

June 2006

By Danielle Goodgion

I was very new into the ultrarunning world in 2006, so having the opportunity to pace Scott Ludwig in the Western States Endurance Run (WS) was not only an honor but also an experience I will never forget.

I only began running ultras that year, so it was a big shock when I offered to pace Scott for the last 38 miles of WS and he accepted. Not wanting to let him down, I worked very hard to make sure I was not only physically but mentally prepared. Although I know ultrarunning is very mental, I didn't realize how much until the night Scott and I ran 38 miles together in the mountains.

Let the journey begin...

Scott, Al, and Susan all left for California the Thursday before WS. Al was also running WS and Susan would be his pacer.

Because I happen to be from Truckee, the town 10 minutes from the start line of WS, my family and I planned our annual vacation with my parents and we would begin our vacation by pacing and crewing for Scott and Al.

Our flight left on Friday and, of course, was late. We arrived into Reno after 11 p.m., gathered our luggage, and drove to my parents' house to sleep for the night and drop off the kids.

Our morning began very early. We woke at 6 a.m., showered, and were out the door. The first checkpoint to see Scott and Al was Robinson Flat. The plan was for him to be there by 11:16 a.m., and I did not want to miss seeing him. At this point, my job was to be his cheerleader, and I was taking my job very seriously. After we left my parents house, I called Susan. She informed me there was a last-minute course change, and we didn't need to be to Robinson Flat until around noon. We decided to meet in Truckee for breakfast, and then we would follow each other up to Auburn where we would drop off Susan's rental car and all drive together in one vehicle.

Susan told us they both looked strong that morning and seemed very ready for this race. She did mention she was concerned about the heat, though. We knew the heat was bad, but we didn't realize it would be one of the hottest years in the history of the race.

So off we went. The traffic at Robinson Flat was very congested, and I was really nervous we weren't going to make it. Fortunately, we found a parking spot and made it just in time for the shuttle bus to take us to the location where we could meet the runners. Although, once we got on the shuttle bus, it took forever for us to leave because the bus driver was more interested in eating her donut than driving the bus. If you hadn't gathered, I am very impatient, and the thought of missing Scott and Al made me even more impatient.

Robinson Flat

This was the first look we had at any of the runners and the time when reality set in. It was hot, and you could not only see it on all the faces of the runners but also tell by the amount of runners dropping out of the race. As we sat and waited for Scott and Al, the volunteers would call out the names of people who had dropped. Every time a name was called, my stomach would drop just hoping I wouldn't hear "Anyone from the Ludwig crew or Barker crew?" Then it happened, "Barker crew, meet your runner at Foresthill." Susan and I looked at each other in disappointment. I was actually shocked! Al had spent so much time training and was so prepared. Without actually seeing him yet, of course, we had all these things going through our minds. I think most of all we thought Al would be very upset, and we wanted to see him. Time seemed to pass so slowly, and there was little time remaining until the cutoff. I still had in my mind Scott was going to make it...and then he came.

OK, I would like to say he was looking awesome and ready to run the rest of the 73 remaining miles, but he didn't. He looked awful. He looked tired and drained. See, I must explain to you how the rest of the runners looked physically. They were built more like mountain goats: big strong legs with meat on their bodies. Scott is a road runner; he was a little leaner...and he looked BEAT! I believe he describes it as death warmed over...wearing an aluminum blanket in a microwave. Yes, that bad.

At that moment, two things went through my mind. First, he is not going to make it (which was the first time the thought crossed my mind since I knew he had made it into WS), and second, and more importantly, I wanted to take care of him. I knew he wanted to finish WS so badly, and I knew he would be so disappointed if he didn't. So I did the best I could in the few minutes we had to cheer him up, get him a new pair of socks, and let him know we were going to cross that finish line and accomplish his goal.

That next time we would see Scott would not be until Michigan Bluff (55.7 miles)...if he made it that far.

Bill, Susan, and I left Robinson Flat and went off to Foresthill School. We were still all shocked and not really certain what we would say to Al. We were all heartbroken for him. We waited forever at the school for Al. Susan searched everywhere for him. She is a good friend, and I know she just wanted to make sure he was OK. Finally we spotted him. He had the biggest smile on his face! I think we were all a bit relieved. The heat was too much for him, and he didn't make the cutoff. If I remember correctly, somewhere around 25 people dropped at that checkpoint.

Michigan Bluff

Now it was time to wait for Scott. Al was hungry, so we drove back to Auburn to get pizza. I was a ball of nerves. I didn't know what to think. I am sorry to say I almost had myself convinced that Scott wasn't going to make it this time. I knew Scott was tough, but was he tough enough? Everyone ate pizza except for me (a big mistake). I thought if there was a chance I was going to run, I didn't want my stomach full of pizza. I only ate salad and that wasn't nearly enough. After driving everyone crazy because I wanted to leave to make sure we made it to Scott on time, Al and Susan went back to find a hotel for Al to get some much-needed rest. Bill and I were off to Michigan Bluff. We made it there around 7 p.m. The first thing we did was go to the board, which listed the runners who had dropped. NO LUDWIG! That was great news, and I was so relieved. Since Scott was running behind at Robinson Flat, I thought he may not make it to this point until after 8 p.m., which meant I could begin pacing him there. Bill and I both prepared ourselves to run—except for the one thing that I forgot at the car, my Garmin (GPS). While waiting, we were able to see our good friend Prince Whatley. That was great! We also made a lot of friends at that checkpoint. One lady was waiting for her husband. She was going to share pacing him with another person. Bill and I found a spot on the trail and waited and waited and waited for Scott. We were able to see Gordy (the founder of WS); in fact, it felt like we saw everyone. As it got darker, we would head down the trail about a quarter mile looking for Scott. Bill and I actually began making plans for the night. At that point, I was almost convinced he wasn't going to make it...9:16 p.m. (absolute cutoff was 9:30 p.m.)...HERE COMES SCOTT! I couldn't believe it! He actually looked much stronger than he did at Robinson Flat. We got him to the aid station, and I asked, "Are you ready to finish this race?" I will never forget what he said: "Will you be with me from now on?" I quickly said, "Every step of the way!"

We finished getting Scott's feet taped, which looked awful at this point, and off we went. I kissed my husband (who was just wonderful the whole time) and said we would see him at Foresthill School, only about seven miles away. With all the excitement and worry of wondering if Scott was going to make it or not, I forgot to actually think about the fact that I was going to run 45 miles, not the 38 I had expected. I had never run that far, but I blew it off and thought I could do it.

The next seven miles were great! Although we had been chasing Scott the whole day, I felt fresh and excited! Scott wasn't as fresh, but now I knew he could do it. In fact, I remember saying to him, "Cindy was right—you'll finish this race because it just isn't in you to not make it." Now remember, I had forgotten my Garmin, so I didn't have a watch to go by. All I knew was I had to keep us moving forward. Scott wasn't ready to run, so for the first part of this section, we walked very fast. Then he began to feel a little better; it was cooling down, and soon we were able to run.

Foresthill School

This part of the trail wasn't really that bad, probably because it was just beginning. We arrived at Foresthill School. Bill, Al, and Susan were there to meet us. Bill had brought my GPS (I told you, he is wonderful). We had the volunteers re-tape Scott's feet. This time, I actually got him to eat some pizza. He seemed to be in good spirits, and about 11:30 p.m., we were off to finish the last 38 miles of WS.

We wouldn't see Bill again until Rucky Chucky River Crossing (78 miles). I didn't like that, but it did motivate me to know I would see him there.

As we left Foresthill School, I began to feel a pain on the top of my foot. I had never really had this pain before, so I kind of just blew it off and thought nothing a few Advil can't take care of. We were able to run the first section of the course. It was flat and on the road (this made Scott very happy). This was the last part of the course we would be on that was road for quite a while…let the hills begin!

As the hours began to go by, I kept waiting for the trail to get a bit easier. I was under the impression this was the EASY part of the run. Let me tell you, it didn't get any easier. We may have been going down in elevation, but the up and down climbs remained difficult.

Scott completely amazed me! It didn't take me long to realize how tough he is. In fact, at one point, I said to him, "I knew you were tough, but not *this* tough!" We had three checkpoints to go through before getting to Rucky Chucky where Bill would be waiting for us. Each checkpoint we made with limited time to spare. I mean only five to ten minutes ahead of the absolute cutoff! Scott didn't know this until after the race, but the Garmin he dislikes so much was the one thing that kept us on track for making the cutoff times (that and Scott's iron will). When we left each checkpoint, I would find out the exact distance and the time we needed to be there. When we were coming close to the cutoff time, I would speed up and Scott would follow. I knew how much pain he was in because his feet were in such terrible condition, but I also knew he wanted to make it. So I would just try to motivate him as much as I could and keep him moving faster.

Most of the trail at this point was along a mountainside with a very steep drop-off to the left of us. With the exception of greeting the runners that we passed or those that passed us, we didn't say much. I could just hear Scott behind me making little grunts of pain when his foot would hit a rock or when he stepped too hard. We were trying very hard not to get his feet any wetter than they already were. I don't think they could have handled any more moisture. For the most part, we were successful.

Rucky Chucky

It was quickly approaching 4 a.m., and we would soon be at the Rucky Chucky River crossing. I had no idea what to expect, but at least I knew we were going to be able to cross in a boat. About a half mile before we reached the Rucky Chucky checkpoint, we passed the lady I had met at Michigan Bluff (the one there to pace her husband). Her husband was lying on the ground, claiming he was dizzy. Of course I asked if I could help, and she said no, he would be fine. All I could think of at that time is how tough Scott was and how much I wish I could take some of his pain away from him.

As we approached the Rucky Chucky River crossing, I could see Bill. I was so excited to see him. Bill is always there to support me through all my races, and this one was no different. Not only did he support me, but he did a great job of crewing for Scott as well. Another thing Scott and I had in our favor was we finally made up some time. We were actually ahead of schedule by a half hour. This was a tremendous relief to both of us.

As soon as I saw Bill and knew Scott was out of earshot, I told Bill my foot was in a lot of pain now. I knew Scott's feet were much worse than mine, but it was my job to keep Scott motivated, which meant I needed to be healthy. My foot was so swollen by this time I had to loosen my shoelaces. Every time I took a step, I would stretch it forward to relieve it a bit. Bill and I decided four more Advil would help. So I took them, we crossed the river (this part I did not like), taped Scott's feet again, and off we went.

The next checkpoint we would see Bill was at Highway 49. This was about 15 miles. It was now around 5 a.m. The sun would be coming up soon. We had almost survived the dark. I knew we both would get a boost once we saw the sun. In fact, Scott told me this is the time he usually gets a second wind.

Here comes the sun...we had now remembered it was Sunday morning. We had about 20 miles to go, so at this point, we were just out for our normal Sunday 20-mile run. Except we were running a single-track trail, not the asphalt Scott was accustomed to running on. Oh, and 80 miles already in the bank.

At this point, my foot was getting very bad, and I knew if I wasn't careful, Scott would notice. The last thing he needed was to know I was in pain of any sort. I was also running out of energy. Remember when I said at the pizza place I had made a mistake? That mistake was not to fuel myself properly. I was paying for it now. Scott was also going through a very bad downtime. I offered to sing to cheer him up, but he declined, which is probably best. The Sharky Bites he had in his pocket did help a little, though.

The trail never got any easier; we had constant ups and downs, and we didn't go nearly as fast as I thought we would. We continued to only make the time cutoffs by minutes. All the time we had made up at Rucky Chucky we eventually lost. Scott was getting so upset and just couldn't understand why we were always so close. I knew; we simply weren't going fast enough.

Brown's Bar

Finally, we reached the Brown's Bar checkpoint. In my opinion, this is the checkpoint that saved the race for Scott. You see, the whole time we ran together, Scott only mentioned a handful of things he wished he had: Diet Coke, popsicles, and beer. I'm telling you, if I could have eaten aluminum and pooped out a can of beer, I would have. But as fate would have it, I didn't need to…you see, at Brown's Bar, they had beer. They were trying to push us through that checkpoint as fast as they could. Of course, asking Scott if he needed anything, he asked for beer. They asked me if it was OK, and the look on my face was probably good enough, but I said, "YES! GIVE IT TO HIM!"

Highway 49

That must have been great beer because Scott got the burst of energy he so desperately needed, and we ran for a long time from this checkpoint all the way to Highway 49. This is the spot I knew Bill would be…this was a very important energy spurt because he only made the next checkpoint by two minutes. Being disqualified with only six miles to go would have been devastating. This was also a very important part of the race for me because my goal here was to pace Scott, and this race was not about me. I knew I was not in shape to be pacing Scott anymore. My foot was hurting so badly and my energy was so low that I didn't have enough to give back to Scott. I had maxed myself out on Advil and was starting to limp when I walked. I wavered back and forth: Should I have Bill pace Scott for the rest of the race? Will I be letting him down? Then, we came around the corner, knowing we had very little time left to make the next cutoff, and we looked up only to see another monstrous mountain to climb. I could just feel the expression on Scott's face, and he was behind me. I told him, "Don't look up. Just follow me." I gave it everything I had to get him to the next checkpoint, and as we came down the mountain, I saw Bill, and I knew I was done. All I could think was "I'm so sorry Scott, but you need more than me now." The first thing Bill said was "Do you want me to take over?", and I shook my head. Then I looked over and saw Susan. I know how badly she wanted to run with Scott. I told Bill that Susan should finish with him. He said, "Absolutely!" I ran down and handed her my pace number. My exact words to her were "He needs YOUR energy! Get him across that finish line!" Susan gladly took the pace number, and I could see she was so happy to be able to run with him.

Now comes the emotion…as I watched Scott and Susan run up the hill, I knew Scott was going to make it. On the other side of me were three people I saw not make the time cutoff. The worst part was they missed the cutoff by 15-20 seconds! Once they found out they didn't make it, they would first scream at the volunteer and then burst into tears. It was very sad, and I just couldn't imagine that happening to Scott.

As Bill and I drove down the hill to the finish line, I was in a fog. I wasn't sure how to feel. I just wanted to see Scott cross that finish line. Honestly, I wanted to be the one to finish with him, but I knew I had made the right decision.

Bill wanted to make sure to run from the last checkpoint to the finish line with Scott. We were able to catch up with Al. After talking to Al for a minute, Bill and Al left for Robie Point, the last checkpoint of the race.

As I sat and waited for Scott, the time went by very slowly. I talked to a few people, but nothing could keep my mind off the fact that Scott wasn't here yet. It was now past 11 a.m., the official cutoff time for the race and now I felt like a failure. Scott didn't make it to the finish line on time. All that effort on his part, and he wasn't going to finish. I was an emotional wreck. At about 11:10 a.m. or so, I saw Bill come over the hill. I ran, well, *limped* over to him and just started bawling. I went on and on about how I had let Scott down and kept asking if he was mad at me. He tried to calm me down and told me Scott was in a great mood. He told me he was just happy this would soon be over…and then came Scott. I walked over to him and once again started bawling. I think at first he didn't understand why I was crying, and then it occurred to him. He managed to calm me down enough to tell me that he was going to be a finisher; he wouldn't get a belt buckle, but he would be an official finisher. He had done it!

One of the most memorable moments at this time for me was that Bill insisted on taking a picture of me with Scott. I was adamant about him not taking that picture. But, of course, he did it anyway. Now, I am so thankful for that picture. I have it hanging at my desk and in my house; it will forever bring back the best of memories.

The Finish

With all of us together—Scott, Susan, Bill, Al, and I—we walked the rest of the way and onto the track. At this moment, time almost stopped. As we walked around the track, everyone there—and I mean *everyone*—started clapping. Not only did they clap, but they also whistled and cheered. It was just such an honor to be part of that experience. When we crossed the finish line, a few thoughts went through my mind. The one that sticks in my head the most is about Scott: While he may not be built like a mountain goat, he may not have been the fastest runner out there or the strongest physically, but there is not a doubt in my mind that he was the TOUGHEST! He finished in 30 hours and 16 minutes with feet that looked like raw hamburger and never complained once. He went through checkpoint after checkpoint, knowing he only made them by a matter of minutes, and he was on a single-track trail with 30,000 feet of elevation change when the roads are the only thing he truly loves to run on. I don't know how he did it, but I will forever be impressed with how tough he was during that race.

Once the race was over, we were able to get Scott, Al, and Susan back to their car. I hugged them all goodbye and told them to call once they got some rest.

Scott and Danielle at Western States, June 2006

The next morning, I logged on to my email and found a note from Gary Griffin. He thanked me for pacing Scott and said something very interesting that made me think. He said he wasn't sure why, but Scott's successes and accomplishments in the running world mattered a great deal to him. I realized then that they meant a great deal to me also. Going through an experience like that with a friend, especially someone you really look up to and admire, and realizing you helped make his goal a reality is a feeling I will never forget. I am not only honored but also very grateful for that experience.

***

36

CHAPTER

LEANING AT LEAN HORSE

Lean Horse 100-Mile Run, August 2008

It's 1:00 a.m. on a Sunday morning somewhere along the Mickelson Trail in South Dakota. The sky is brilliant; I can literally see every star in the sky. The bison and the mule deer are running free on either side of me. The air is crystal clear. The smell is what you would expect from the great outdoors. I'm certain this is one person's definition of heaven. Not mine, however. This is pure hell.

After my relative success at the Umstead 100-Mile Run in April 2008, I felt the time was right to strike while the iron was hot and get in another 100-miler before fall's marathon season began. The Lean Horse 100-Mile Run to be held in August 2008 along the Mickelson Trail in Hot Springs, South Dakota fit the bill. So along with three other members of my Darkside Running Club, Susan Lance, Gary Griffin, and Jill Floyd, we all headed west with four similar objectives (run 100 miles) but also four entirely different goals in mind. Gary wanted to run a 100-mile PR, which meant beating a time of 21:30; Jill wanted to complete her *first* 100-mile run; Susan wanted to break 20 hours and perhaps if the cards fell correctly, defend her women's championship from last year; and I just wanted to finish—someway, somehow—my 10th race of 100 miles or longer. After battling back and leg issues caused by a bulging disk for the past two years, I knew I would have to be extremely careful not to do something stupid which might prevent me from finishing the race.

Thursday, August 21

My flight landed at the Rapid City airport just after 8:00 p.m. Susan picked me up in her rental car, and we met Jill and her husband Ken and local resident Amy Yanni and her husband Bill at a local Italian restaurant. I had run a good portion of the 2007 Museum of Aviation Marathon with Amy, a race in which she was the overall female winner. Over the past 18 months, we had kept in touch with each other through e-mail. Amy is an avid marathon runner and one of the most energetic, encouraging people I've ever met, and like Gary, Susan, Jill and me, she is ready to run a marathon at the drop of a hat. (Dean Karnazes mentions this about Amy in his book, *50-50*. Amy was the only runner who accompanied Dean as he ran his marathon along the Mickelson Trail in South Dakota in his quest to run 50 marathons in all 50 states in 50 days.)

I ran into Amy Yanni somewhere between the 19- and 20-mile mark at the 2007 Museum of Aviation Marathon in Warner Robins, Georgia. We struck up a conversation, and she told me of her involvement with the Marathon Maniacs and was glad to be in a warmer winter climate than her home in Rapid City, South Dakota offered. Adding a marathon in another state to her résumé was simply an added bonus, as was her 1st place finish among the women in the race.

Unknown to Susan, Jill, or Ken, Amy had arranged for me to speak at the Lean Horse pre-race meeting the next evening through Jerry Dunn, the race director and a close personal friend of hers. (It was Jerry who arranged for Amy to run with Dean.) During dinner, Jill mentioned that she was surprised I wasn't asked to speak at the meeting in support of my recently-published autobiography. I didn't say anything, not wanting to jinx myself in case things didn't work out. Besides, if I *was* asked to speak, I wanted to surprise my fellow club members.

In 1992, Jerry Dunn ran 104 marathons. In 1998, Jerry ran the New York City Marathon course in Central Park 28 straight days, and on the 29th day ran the 29th annual New York City Marathon. Appearing on Keith Olbermann's show afterward and being asked "What's next for America's Marathon Man?", Jerry replied (without thinking) he would try something major for the turn of the century—perhaps 200 marathons in the year 2000. True to his word, Jerry completed the marathon distance 200 times in 2000, each on a certified marathon course.

Amy gave me a copy of one of the articles she writes for the local newspaper. In this particular article, she interviewed a friend of hers, Teresa, who was attempting her first 100-miler at Lean Horse. In the article, Amy had quoted me from my book several times. (Amy brought along a copy of my book for me to autograph and said she gave her friend a copy as well.) I was flattered on all counts.

Susan and I made it to Hot Springs around midnight; however, I was still on Eastern Standard Time, and believe me, it *felt* like it was 2:00 a.m. I had been awake for almost 23 hours straight, and I was dead tired.

Friday, August 22

I finished off my pre-l00-mile taper by running three miles. (My typical taper? 7-6-5-4-3 miles on each of the five days preceding a 100-miler.) After a quick breakfast, Susan took me for a drive through Custer National Park up to Mount Rushmore and back through Needles Highway, dodging countless bison and wild donkeys along the way. (An FYI: The bison and wild donkeys roam free. Please pay attention to the signage indicating *buffalo are dangerous—do not approach*.)

Susan and I picked up our race packets, and I confirmed with Jerry that I would indeed be speaking at the pre-race meeting. We had a quick lunch and returned to race headquarters where we met up with Jill as well as Gary and his wife Peg. We took our seats in the second row of the auditorium, and after opening comments from Jerry, the mayor of Hot Springs, and a gentleman doing a story for NPR about ultrarunners, Jerry introduced me as the guest speaker.

I started by saying that my presentation would be similar to the other five talks I had given in the past to other running clubs or at other races, as I was being paid exactly the same: nothing *(rim shot #1)*. I then stated that this presentation would be different as I was not going to talk about my book, seeing as by now everyone had read it *(rim shot #2)* and that I would be talking about my next book, specifically some of the wonderful people I would be writing about that I've met through running over the past 30 years. The stories of my personal heroes—Janice Anderson, Lloyd Young, Bobbi Gibb—seemed to capture the imaginations of everyone in the auditorium. Then I spoke of my Darkside Running Club contingent who would be competing in the 100-mile race the next day:

- Gary, a truly outstanding ultrarunner and proponent of the sport and the most optimistic and positive man I have ever met. Gary was a member of my crew at Badwater and ran approximately 60 miles with me through Death Valley while carrying two water bottles: one for me to drink from and one to pour on my head and shoulders, totaling disregarding his own personal need for fluids.
- Susan, Lean Horse's defending women's champion, who five short years ago was trying her first ultra of 50K and one year later was running over 100 miles at the 24-Hour Championship in San Diego. Susan is also the current Strolling Jim 40-Mile Run women's champion.
- Jill, who three years ago won the first ultra she ever entered, the Darkside 8-Hour Run, and was now attempting to complete her first 100-miler at Lean Horse. (Jill later told me she heard a lot of encouraging words during the race from her fellow competitors after hearing of this.)

I concluded by respecting Jerry's wishes to say something motivational. I told the runners that what they would be doing over the weekend—whether it was running 50 miles or 100 miles—was something that the vast majority of the population cannot or will not ever do. In fact, the vast majority of the population can't even *comprehend* what they were about to do. I assured them they had all done the physical training needed to reach their goals; if they hadn't, they wouldn't be here. Now their success depended on their mental faculties, specifically their ability to be patient. Running 50 or 100 miles takes time, so accept the fact that you may be on the trail for 10, 20, or even 30 hours and make sure you enjoy the course; enjoy (and thank) the volunteers, enjoy your fellow runners, and enjoy what you enjoy doing most: *running!*

Afterward, Jill's husband Ken joined us, and we ate Italian for our last meal before our 6:00 a.m. start the following morning. As we left the restaurant, Susan met up with a friend from Kansas, Dann Fisher, who she had run with at Lean Horse the year before. Dann and his wife, who had just arrived in Hot Springs, asked Susan if he missed anything exciting at the pre-race meeting. Susan shook her head and said no.

I looked at her and whispered, "Thanks a lot."

It was past 8:00 p.m. (10:00 p.m. EST, though!). Time for bed. Tomorrow was shaping up to be a long day, and our 4:00 a.m. wake-up call was less than eight hours away.

Saturday, August 23

Jill, Gary, Susan, and I met up near the starting line just after 5:40 a.m. We posed for a "before" picture while Peg and Ken snapped away on their cameras. Gary, Susan, and I agreed to start together. Gary was dead set on breaking 20 hours and figured he needed to run the first 50 miles in nine hours to have a two-hour cushion for the final 50 miles. I convinced Gary that if we ran the first 50 in 9:30, we could expect to run the last 50 in 10:30 and have a legitimate shot at a sub-20 hour finish. His agreement with this plan lasted for about 60 seconds, coinciding with the firing of the starter's pistol, at which point Gary took off like a bandit.

Susan and I saw Gary take off at a pace indicative of an EIGHT-thirty first 50 miles, while we slowly built our pace to a modest 10:15 per mile pace until we were able to find our comfort zone. Susan accelerated on most of the downhill sections during the first 20 miles, while I had to run conservatively out of fear of injuring my back or legs any further. That forced me to push the pace on the uphills to catch up with her. I met up with Jill, and we (as we always do) talked Southeastern Conference football for a good 30 minutes. I wondered if I should just stay with Jill and attempt to hold the world's longest SEC football conversation in history (I'm guessing at least 20 hours or so). I catch up with Susan once again, only to lose her on the next downhill. This allowed me to engage in a conversation with "Mike" from Texas. Mike had taken up running two years ago after not having any luck with prescribed medication to combat the posttraumatic stress he was experiencing, a condition caused by being inside the Pentagon on 9/11. Running offered him a cure, and he told me he was writing a book about his recovery. I wished him well and made my way back up the hill to Susan.

Over the next several hours, I felt confident that we were maintaining a pace that would allow us to reach the 50-mile (turnaround) mark in 9:30. However, the aid stations—if they were properly measured—were telling us differently. But I insisted that we were indeed on pace, and my beliefs proved accurate when we reached 50 miles in 9:28:18. Gary, however, was definitely *not* on pace. Just before the turnaround, when Susan and I reached the 47.5 mark, Gary was already on his way back (so he was at 52.5 miles). He said he reached 50 miles in 8:21 *(wow!)* and that he was pretty much spent and he would be waiting for Susan and me to reel him in. In all honestly, Gary looked pretty depleted, and it made me wonder if we would indeed see him later in the race.

Susan and I made *our* U-turn at 50 miles and began our trek back, when all of a sudden Susan experienced a sharp pain in her foot. The pain was so severe, Susan asked if I wouldn't mind walking for a while. I noticed Susan landing gingerly on her left foot, and she said it felt like someone was sticking a knife in her heel.

We walked for a while, then attempted to run for a couple hundred yards, only to resume walking when Susan's pain became unbearable once again. We repeated this cycle for a couple miles before Susan said it was possible she would have to walk the remainder of the race. I told her I'd stay with her and that perhaps later she would get a second wind, and we could still manage to finish in 22 hours. After walking for a while, we changed our goal to 23 hours. Later, 24 hours. The pain in Susan's foot was not getting any better. Knowing Susan's propensity to withstand pain, I knew something was wrong. Terribly wrong.

The miles passed by slowly, and somewhere around mile 67, Susan wanted to give running another try. So we ran several hundred yards, but her foot wasn't up to the challenge. Worse, now *my legs* were starting to stiffen up, I'm guessing due to too much walking. The more steps we took, the less running became an option, for either of us.

At the aid station near 70 miles, which was manned by a local Boy Scout troop, I asked for a beer (my norm at this stage in an ultra). To my dismay, they didn't have any. I asked them if their motto was still "Be Prepared," half-kidding but also half-serious. The Boy Scouts only recognized the latter. A supporter for another runner promised to have a beer for me at the next aid station as he could see how much I needed one, not only to get rid of the sweet taste in my mouth from all the electrolyte replacement fluids I'd been drinking for most of the day, but also to deaden the horrific pain I was feeling in both legs as well. The next five miles took an eternity, and by *eternity* I mean a good two hours, which in our condition *felt* like an eternity. When we arrived at the aid station, the beer man appeared...*without a beer*. Yes, you read that last sentence correctly:

WITHOUT...A...BEER!

He said he was sorry, but he wasn't able to find one. My cries of anguish caught the ear of an aid station volunteer, who just happened to have an ice cold beer in the trailer, *if* I wanted one.

Sunday, August 24 (as far as I could tell)

IF I WANTED ONE? Who was he kidding? Approximately 90 seconds...and *exactly* 12 ounces later, Susan and I were on our way, where another aid station (and as I would later find out, another beer) awaited us only five miles (did I really say *only?*) down the road.

A couple hours later, Susan and I left the Mickelson Trail to begin the 16.6-mile stretch that took us up and down (and up and down and seemingly up and up and up) Argyle Road. For an hour or so, Susan and I repeatedly asked the other if they wanted to quit. Susan, who is so much like me it's frightening, refused to stop. I guess you know where I stood on this as well. We also reached agreement on several other things, such as we knew it was in our best interests to quit but were too stubborn to act appropriately, and there couldn't possibly be two other participants in the race that were in as much pain as we were.

I told Susan the walking was starting to wear out my hip sockets, and I asked her if she would mind if I ran to the bottom of the next hill and waited for her. Seconds later I found yet another thing Susan and I had in common: *We were both literally unable to perform the physical act of running.* It seemed my legs had a mind of their own, and they would simply not cooperate with my brain and move in a forward motion. I honestly thought my legs were trying to tie themselves in a knot. *What is wrong with me?*

My running experiment was short-lived, and I now realized I was destined to walk the remaining 15 or so miles of the race; in other words, Susan and I still had over four hours to go until we crossed the finish line in Hot Springs. That is, if we made it that far.

Around 90 miles into the race, a male runner passed Susan and me, and close on his heels was a female runner who appeared to be following his lead. I noticed the woman was leaning severely to the right, and I asked Susan what she thought was going on. Susan answered she didn't know, but *I've* been doing it for the last couple of miles. I stopped and looked at my shadow on the white dirt road and saw that from the waist up *I was leaning at a 30-degree angle!* In fact, I'm pretty sure that if I stood next to the leaning woman that our bodies would be parallel. *What was happening to me?*

Before long I found myself veering to the right, at one point actually walking off the side of the road. As the side of the road was severely banked, at one point I fell off to the side and had great difficulty getting back up to the road. Fortunately, the aforementioned male runner saw my dilemma and offered to pull me out of the ditch. He said he was from Canada, and he was always pulling people out of the ditch. Once he pulled me back onto the road, he asked if I would write a book about him. (Interesting sidebar: The Canadian, Jeff Hurdman, e-mailed me after the race and told me he was pacing his wife Elizabeth [my parallel partner] the last 50 miles of Lean Horse, that she was legally blind, and that he remembered me talking about heroes in my pre-race speech and that she was his hero. I was fascinated by his admiration for his wife and eventually asked her if she would let me tell her story in my next book. Thankfully, she said yes.)

We reached the final aid station at the 96-mile mark. The volunteers said we were about to enjoy the best four miles of our lives. At first, I couldn't believe they were talking to *us*. Good Lord, couldn't they see the condition we were in?

I asked one of the volunteers when Gary had gone through this checkpoint. They told me Gary came by shortly after midnight...well over five hours ahead of Susan and me. Gary apparently recovered quite well in the 44 miles since we had last seen him! I mentioned to Susan that Jill, who was approximately eight miles behind us in the middle of the race, should be catching up with us soon.

After sitting for a couple minutes in one of the volunteers' chairs, I was ready to go. Actually, ready to get it over with might be more appropriate. At this point, I was in so much pain—presumably for walking so long—that I had to stop, bend over, and stretch my back every couple of hundred yards. Then every couple of hundred feet. Then every couple hundred of inches. (This wouldn't be quite as funny if you knew it was true!) I honestly thought about quitting at miles 96, 97, 98, AND 99! The thought of intentionally dropping out of the race at the 99-mile mark intrigued me, as I can't imagine it had ever been done (intentionally, anyway) in any 100-mile race before. But at 99 miles, Susan could tell it was going to be a looooong 63,360 inches *(that's a mile but also indicative of how slowly we were covering distance)* to the finish line, and she thought I might move a little better if I leaned on her to take some of the pressure off my legs. She was right, and we staggered our way over the last 5,280 feet (that's a mile, but also indicative of how *quickly* we were now covering distance).

About a yard short of the finish line, Susan let go of me, and she managed to officially complete the race. Me? I lost my balance, fell backward, and was subsequently encouraged by the volunteers to *cross the line!* Good Lord, couldn't they see that this wasn't deliberate? After all, it had taken us almost *16 hours* to cover the last 50 miles!

Jill's husband Ken was at the finish, and he offered me his chair, which I quickly accepted. Another volunteer asked me if I needed a ride back to my hotel. I said I did. He asked where I was staying, and I pointed to the hotel less than 50 yards from where I was sitting. He thought I was kidding. He thought wrong.

Ken mentioned that Jill wasn't too far behind us and should be finishing soon. Typically, I would have waited around to see her finish her first 100-miler. But today wasn't anywhere near typical. I just wanted to lie down and sleep my 30-degree lean off (Susan assured me sleep would be my remedy). Susan and I staggered back to the hotel, and I managed to get in a three-hour nap before it was time to shower and make my way back to the post-race brunch. Susan was right; after the nap, the 30-degree lean was gone. However, the pain between my thighs and waist was almost unbearable; my body was simply not accustomed to walking particularly long distances.

Jerry Dunn hosted the brunch and indulged everyone in a short yet efficient awards ceremony. Gary received a special belt buckle for finishing in less than 24 hours and later was awarded the championship in his age group. Susan, Jill and, I received our belt buckles for completing the race in less than 30 hours. More importantly, Jill had finished her first 100-mile race. I couldn't have been happier for or prouder of Gary and Jill. They were both rewarded for their efforts, for fighting the good fight and coming out on top.

Susan and I had fought the good fight as well, but in hindsight, I'm not sure if we exactly came out on top. Post-race, Susan was examined by an orthopedic doctor who discovered that Susan had ruptured her plantar fascia during the race. I've had issues with my left groin muscle area apparently staying with me for a while.

Scott and Susan at Lean Horse, August 2008

At least I learned something very valuable during my adventure in South Dakota: Running for a really long time can be exhilarating; walking for a really long time, however, can be mind-numbing.

Postscript: Gary finished the race in an amazing 19:02, which is the fourth fastest time in 100 miles by a 58-year-old in the United States. If the race had been held six weeks later, Gary, who would have been 59, would have bettered the fastest time for that age by 40 minutes! The finishing times for the rest of the characters in this story: Elizabeth, 24:20; Scott and Susan, 25:24; Jill, 25:37; and Teresa (who also finished her first 100-miler!), 25:39.

* * *

37

CHAPTER

UNCOMFORTABLY NUMB

I hear you're feeling down
I can ease your pain
Get you on your feet again

When I was young, the dentist gave me a shot of Novocain before filling my first cavity. The three or four hours that followed—*trying to eat soup with a numbed mouth and failing miserably is what I remember most*—was something I decided right then and there was most definitely *not* going to happen again.

Most of the soup dripped down my chin as I couldn't feel my lips… the little bit of scalding-hot soup that found its way into my numb mouth caused blisters that wouldn't be evident until the Novocain wore off. I accidently and unknowingly bit the inside of my mouth as I had no idea where my cheek left off and my teeth began.

I decided right then and there that under no circumstance did I ever want to be numb again. The dentist doesn't even ask me if I want to be numbed up anymore (although he does suggest a hit of nitrous oxide for the procedures he thinks might be particularly painful— but to be quite honest I'd rather endure a few seconds of pain than several hours of numbness).

At precisely the 21-mile marker of the 2001 Shamrock Marathon, I took a right-hand turn and felt something twinge in my right thigh. To this day, the feeling in my right thigh is akin to having had an injection of Novocain slightly above the kneecap. A good yet slightly older running friend of mine told me that at "our age" once a body part goes numb, it stays numb. I didn't take her word for it at first, but now— 13 years later—she just might be right. My right thigh is still numb. But after all this time, it doesn't bother me nearly as much as it did in 2001. Sure, it still bothers me, but like I said— not nearly as much.

In the fall of 2010, I had a series of three spinal injections to address a bulging disk problem between my L4 and L5 vertebra. The evening of the second injection (September 29, 2010 for you historians), I noticed the right sides of my right foot and right ankle were numb. I called the doctor the next day who said the numbness was in no way caused by the injection, although he did say that the nerves in the area of the numbness originated between the L4 and L5 vertebra. (Coincidence? Methinks not.) I also remembered what my good friend told me years earlier: Once it goes numb, it *stays* numb.

A little numbness never hurt anyone, right? *Wrong!* First of all, many days it feels like I'm running on a stump. My right foot slaps the ground, while my left foot barely makes any noise whatsoever on impact. My right foot doesn't elevate as much off the ground as my left foot. The right foot doesn't allow me to push off as strongly as the left foot. My whole running motion feels disjointed due to what I am *not* able to feel and sense on the right half of my lower body. I found myself in desperate need of some help

Over the next eight months, I tried several things to kick-start the feeling in my right foot and leg. (Did I mention the numbness has spread to the right side of my entire right leg? Then let me tell you: the numbness has spread to the right side of my entire right leg!)

- I tried another spinal injection in the right side of my L4 and L5.
- I tried massage therapy.
- I saw a neurosurgeon. He said everything looked fine with my MRI and in specific reference to my numbness said it is what it is (before he charged me $240 for this ever-so-enlightening office visit).
- I actually took it easy for a few months (which for me meant cutting my weekly mileage by over 20%...although my good friend suggested I take three weeks off).

Long story short: The right side of my right foot and right leg remains numb, and I was about to board an airplane taking me to South Africa to compete in arguably the most prestigious ultramarathon in the world, the Comrades Marathon (*forgive the oxymoron/contradiction in terminology/whatever you call referring to an 'ultramarathon' as a 'marathon'*). Ironically, Comrades took place on May 29, 2011—exactly eight months after I first detected the numbness, which made me remember that when I first noticed the problem, I was thinking at least I have eight months until my race in South Africa.

So now, instead of heading into one of the most important races of my life with the utmost confidence and enthusiasm, I was heading off to South Africa with a surprising (and hopefully unrealistic, but time will tell) amount of apprehension and anxiety.

Why?

Because the right foot and leg remained numb.

Uncomfortably numb.

* * *

NUMBINGLY UNCOMFORTABLE

Comrades Marathon, May 2011

Vic Clapham asked the League of Comrades for permission to stage a 56-mile race between Pietermaritzburg and Durban, South Africa as a living memorial to the spirit of the soldiers lost in the Great War (1914-1918). A veteran of the war himself, Clapham wanted to honor the pain, agonies, hardships, and deaths of his fellow comrades.

The first Comrades Marathon was held on Empire Day May 24, 1921 outside City Hall in Pietermaritzburg with 34 runners.

The good news is I survived. Literally.

In fact, I can't think of a more appropriate word for my 2011 Comrades Marathon experience.

Survived.

Susan Lance (my traveling companion) and I left Atlanta at noon on Wednesday. There was a two-hour flight to Washington D.C. followed by a three-hour layover, an eight-hour flight to Amsterdam, followed by another three-hour layover, and an eleven-hour flight to Johannesburg. Words can't describe how relieved we felt when I arrived at a local bed-and-breakfast at 11 p.m. on Thursday.

Before turning in for the night, I went to the hotel manager's office to ask for an electrical adapter. While the manager was nowhere to be found, his pistol was in plain sight in the middle of his desk... there for the taking *(I didn't—I hate guns)*. I was beginning to sense why there would be an eight-foot fence surrounding this quaint little bed-and-breakfast in downtown Johannesburg.

The next morning, we were on another plane to Durban, where we would be starting the Comrades Marathon in another three days. A gentleman on the plane who I could tell knew his way around Durban gave us two pieces of advice: (1) Don't talk to strangers *(Are you singing Rick Springfield's song in your head? I did— frequently—for the remainder of my time in South Africa.)*, and (2) *(this one for me only)* If you're approached by a prostitute, simply tell her you're gay *(lovely)*.

After checking into the hotel in Durban, Susan and I went for a run before eating breakfast, cleaning up, and heading to the race expo.

I made sure NOT to talk to strangers. Fortunately I wasn't approached by any prostitutes *(which I might add held true for the remaining five days we were in South Africa. I guess I'm blessed—or at the very least unsightly to South African women).*

Saturday morning I was interviewed by Catharina of Modern Athlete, South Africa's premier sports magazine. *(Her story is featured in the July 2011 issue. While she told me I would be featured on the cover, I found out later I was demoted to a small insert at the bottom of the cover, having been replaced by one of South Africa's "biggest losers", who coincidentally lost approximately as many pounds as I currently weigh. I'm beginning to understand why the prostitutes left me alone.)*

Susan and I made another trip to the expo where we had the pleasure of meeting—and having our photograph taken with— former Olympian Zola Budd. *(Once I returned to the U.S., I invited Zola to participate in my running club's race, the Peachtree City 25K in November. She accepted and ran a new women's course record as a prelude to her Comrades debut in 2012.)* We did a little shopping at the expo before heading back to the hotel so we could get a good night's rest before running Comrade's 54-mile route from Durban to Pietermaritzburg the next morning.

We were one block from the hotel. It was 5 p.m. The sun was shining. The streets were as crowded as Manhattan. A police presence was on virtually every street corner. Well, *almost* every street corner; just not the one where we happened to be.

A large black man approximately a head taller than I grabbed at the strap of my backpack. His partner, who was approximately my size (although I doubt he was ever featured in *Modern Athlete*), blocked me in on my left so that I couldn't get away. The crowd on the sidewalk had me blocked in on my right as well as behind me, so I had nowhere to go. Meanwhile, there was no way in hell I'm letting go of my backpack (inside are both of our cameras and, dammit, PHOTOS OF MY GRANDSON'S FIRST 27 MONTHS OF HIS LIFE on my iPad2!), so the larger man reveals a sharp and shiny six-inch knife, which he aimed directly at my heart.

Then came the moment I've always heard about. The life-flashing-before-your-eyes moment. What flashed before my eyes in that split second before the man with the knife was jolted by either Susan's loud "NOOOOO" or her wallop across his back, and he decided to rip the cell phone off of my belt instead of piercing my chest with his knife? I love my wife, and I'm going to miss her very much. I'm proud of my sons and hope they both do well in life. I am going to miss seeing the smiling face of my grandson—which melts my heart every time I see him—and I'll always remember him as the lovable two-year-old he is right now. And, oh yeah—I'm going to die once the knife penetrates my chest. All that in the matter of a literal split-second. Honest.

So now, instead of lying on a ridiculously-hard-to-pronounce street in Durban, South Africa with a knife in my heart, what runs through my mind in the next split-second?

That son-of-a-bitch stole something from me. And he's running like a scared rabbit. So is his partner.

So here's my thought process as I begin to run after them:

I'm running after these two yahoos with my backpack on my right shoulder; that will slow me down. I'm running after them in sandals; that will slow me down even more. What if there are more than two of them? There's still only one of me. I can't leave Susan behind; she may still be in harm's way. It's only a cell phone—even it is my primary link back home. What if I catch them? They still—at the very least—have a knife. I, alas, have nothing remotely resembling a weapon.

So after running 10 yards, I stop. I call them a few choice words. I notice my pulse has not quickened. Not. One. Single. Beat.

I checked my shirt to see if I'm bleeding. I figured in a moment like this adrenaline would mask out the pain of any knife wound. I discovered my shirt was still white. Susan told me she was glad I didn't run after them down the dark alley. She said how nice it was that a few citizens lent a hand (I totally missed that) and how the policemen drove up in a van to assist (I missed that, too) and asked if I heard her scream "NOOOOO" and how she slugged him across the back (which makes me oh-for-three...but I do know if it weren't for Susan's slug across yahoo number one's back, I'm pretty certain I wouldn't be writing this story right now).

We returned to the hotel, where the police arrived 90 minutes later to investigate. They asked for my cell phone information (insurance policy, etc.), which I didn't have. What did they expect? It's a business phone, it's the Saturday before Memorial Day, and I had no way to get the information and I'm what?...about a zillion miles away from home? The police said to fill out the Cell Phone Report when I had all the required information and mail it to their station. I asked if they now wanted to hear about the attack. They said they couldn't take that report until I filled it out. I shrugged and said fine. They said their captain would be in touch later in the evening. As I predicted at the exact moment they said it, they lied. There would be no captain later in the evening.

Scott and Zola Budd Pieters at the PTC 25K, November 2011

The police left without even asking my name.

I was still fuming mad when I turned the lights out around 9 p.m. The wake-up call was only six-and-a-half hours away. I slept very little—perhaps an hour at most—in that six-and-a-half hours.

I believe I ended up sleeping for an hour—just what I needed before tackling the hilly and uphill 54-mile route of the Comrades Marathon, the sole remaining race on my bucket list.

To be continued…

* * *

39
CHAPTER

BUCKET LIST

May 2011

When I first started running in the summer of 1978, my running mentor Tom Saine (who also happened to be my Masters thesis advisor at the University of Florida) spoke of two races as if they were the stuff legends were made of: the Boston Marathon *("You have to run a 2:50 marathon to qualify!")* and the Peachtree Road Race *("Over 6,000 runners!")*. I was intrigued, and they became the first two races-I've-got-to-do on my Bucket List. Soon the marathons of New York and Chicago would be added. Once I ran my first ultra (a 50-miler at Stone Mountain), I was intrigued once again with the mystique of the Comrades Marathon and the JFK 50-Miler, the first two ultras to make the Bucket List.

- I ran my first Peachtree in 1979, four weeks after I moved to Atlanta for my first job with JCPenney Catalog. I've run every Peachtree since. **Bucket List: Checkmark by Peachtree Road Race.**
- I ran my first Boston Marathon in 1987. In the years ahead I would run 11 more. **Bucket List: Checkmark by Boston Marathon.**
- I ran my first—and absolutely last (I don't take fondly to being treated like cattle)—New York Marathon in 1990. **Bucket List: Checkmark by New York Marathon.**
- I ran the Chicago Marathon in 1997 along with 19,000 other runners. It was incredibly congested. Today the field is twice as large; I have no desire to return. However…**Bucket List: Checkmark by Chicago Marathon.**
- A friend asked me to run the JFK 50-Miler with him in 2000 to celebrate his 50th birthday. Although I'm not particularly fond of running on trails, I was glad to get this one under my belt. **Bucket List: Checkmark by JFK 50-Miler.**

Then two impromptu races were added to my Bucket List *(some of this is old news, but these two bullet points bear repeating):*

- In 2002, my wife Cindy gave me a copy of Running on the Sun, a documentary of the 1999 Badwater Ultramarathon. I was once again intrigued and instinctively *(I just knew I was destined to run this race!)* and immediately added it to my Bucket List. Thirteen months later, I made my way across Death Valley and crossed Badwater's finish line on Mount Whitney. **Bucket List: Checkmark by Badwater Ultramarathon.**

- In 2003, my good friend Al decided he wanted to run the Western States Endurance Run, arguably *the* ultra to run in the United States. Although the race is a 100-mile trail run (you may recall I'm not particularly fond of trails), I attempted the race in 2004 (completing 62 miles before—literally—calling it a day) and finished the race in 2006. **Bucket List: Checkmark by Western States Endurance Run.**

Now back to business. What's left? Oh yeah, I still hadn't run the Comrades Marathon, arguably *the* ultra to run in the entire world. To be quite honest, I had been putting this race off for years. Why? Maybe because Comrades is in South Africa, which would require more than a 45-minute drive (Peachtree) or two-hour flight (Boston) to get there. Maybe because Comrades is approximately 90 kilometers of relentless hills through the South African countryside, not the easiest course to run. Maybe because Comrades is in South Africa, a country with a reputation of not being the safest place in the world (go figure).

Whatever the case, I had been putting Comrades off for years. When my friend Susan and I agreed to do it in 2010, there was no turning back. It was time to finish off my Bucket List, at least as far as races were concerned. I would still like to run 200,000 miles and 1,000 races in my lifetime; thankfully, I've learned to be patient. Good things do indeed come to those who wait.

Having read the previous chapter (getting robbed at knifepoint followed by only one hour of sleep the night before the race), you might imagine my mindset heading to the starting line: I just wanted to get the race over with and get the hell out of Durban. It was poetic injustice that I had to pass by last evening's scene of the crime to get to the starting line near Durban's City Hall. Once the starting cannon sounded at 5:30 a.m.—less than 12 hours since the incident—Susan and I were on our way toward the finish line in Pietermaritzburg, 54 miles away.

To say the Comrades Marathon is hilly is an understatement. Grossly so, in fact. There are five infamous hills on the course, all of them having names. To go into the race thinking there are *only* five hills is a mistake (which I happened to make). A few miles into the race, I started noticing signs which read "The Land of 1,000 Hills." The signs weren't kidding; it just so happens the other 995 hills don't have names, which, believe me, doesn't make them any easier. Susan and I ran up several substantial hills in the first few miles of the race, and I kept asking if any of them were the first of the five "named" hills. They weren't; we were merely running up several exit ramps until we made it to the main highway we would take to Pietermaritzburg. Yes, it was *that* hilly.

I wouldn't call them highlights, but here are several items of my recollection from the race:

- Once the sun rose in the sky, it became very warm very fast. Fortunately, the race-time temperature was 50 degrees Fahrenheit (which is 10 degrees Celsius, and I couldn't help but notice the locals were dressed as if it were 10 degrees Fahrenheit).
- Water and Energade was provided in sachets, enclosed plastic tubes which you had to bite/puncture before you could drink. They worked very well, as the spills or choking normally associated with paper cups were eliminated. Two problems with sachets, however: (1) Some are dropped on the ground unopened, and when you step on them, they explode, splashing liquid on other runners at times and sounding like gunfire

every time, and (2) the empty sachets dropped along the course become very slippery should you step on one (trust me on this).

- There wasn't a cloud in the sky, which caused the sun to slowly sap one's energy... or consciousness.
- There was plenty of crowd support. And lots of young kids wanting to slap hands with the runners (Susan and I were both happy to oblige).
- There were numerous (48, I believe) aid stations, all amply and enthusiastically supported by encouraging and competent volunteers.
- The crowd called to the runners by their first names (which were printed on the race bib). Not one person pronounced my name correctly (Scoot...Scout...Skut...).
- I had an unusual bout with leg cramps the final 10 miles. Susan battled nausea for much of the entire race.
- Susan and I were together the entire race (safety in numbers, right?) and walked most of the uphills and ran most of the downhills.
- I asked three people in the crowd to give me a beer toward the end of the race. All three complied, and all three beers tasted WONDERFUL! Less than half a mile from the finish line, I asked a fourth person for a beer, and I unknowingly slammed down an entire bottle of hard cider (it looked just like beer!), which caused the crowd to break out in a large roar...and me in a huge smile. (It's times like this that make you want to come back and do it again. But in this case, I'll pass.)

Susan and I triumphantly crossed the finish line—together—in a better-than-expected 10:35:01, earning us the coveted bronze medal. The medal is surprisingly small—about the size of a quarter. Later in the week, a local asked me what I was going to do with my medal. Jokingly, I said I had already used it in a parking meter. The local didn't find that funny. (I realize I have a lot of growing up to do. I realized it the other day in my fort.)

Will I return? Most definitely. Not.

Ironically, when I crossed the finish line not even 24 hours had passed since the incident. It hadn't been an entire day since I almost kicked the bucket.

Speaking of bucket...

Bucket List: Checkmark by Comrades Marathon.

KEYS TO SUCCESS

Of the Big Four that were on my bucket list, this is the one in which I truly capitalized on my ability to compete when I was on the edge of exhaustion. Getting less than 60 minutes of sleep the night before tackling a challenging, mountainous 54-plus mile course under a warm, brilliant South African sun is not the most advisable course of action one should take. Beyond that, I was dealing with some physical ailments which severely limited my ability to not only run long distances, but to run *any* distance without pain.

Having Susan with me every step of the way was a godsend, as she kept me focused, and at times, I believe I did the same for her: She was my Yin, and I was her Yang.

***

The next six chapters will reveal some things about running ultras which may not have been readily apparent in the book up until this point.

First, I'll get the ugly stuff out of the way and address the growing concern revolving around (drum roll, please) PREMATURE ACCELERATION. Not everyone has it, but I consider it my responsibility to make you aware of the symptoms so if you have it you can take the necessary precautions. You have been warned.

Then I'll address what takes place the day after running ultras of 100 miles or more, specifically as it applies to me, a streak runner.

Next, I'll discuss what liquids are available for an ultrarunner once they tire of the standard fare of water, soda, and electrolyte replacement drinks.

After that, what happens to a runner's speed once the miles and, more importantly, the years begin to take their toll.

Then some words of wisdom for the budding ultarunner. Not running gospel by any stretch of the imagination. Just what I've learned from experience over the past 34 years.

Finally, my perspective on why an ultramarathon could very well be in your future.

40

CHAPTER

STARTING WITH A VENGEANCE

(But Finishing With a Whimper)

This is tough—damn tough—to admit, but the first step toward recovery is admission. So let me begin by being up front and telling you: I suffer from premature acceleration (PA).

I realize I'm not the only one out there with this problem, but let me be the first to have the courage to come clean in a public forum. Twenty-five years of racing the first half of virtually every 5K and 10K I entered at breakneck speed, only to hold on for dear life in the second half, is as clean an admission of my problem as any.

But my problem is worse than that. Much worse. Not only does my problem rear its ugly head in marathons, it later manifested in many of my ultras as well. Three stand out.

1995 Strolling Jim 40-Mile (actually 41.2 miles) Run

My wife and I drove the course the day before the race to get an idea what it was like. It didn't appear too difficult, at least not from behind the wheel of a Chevy Astro van. Initially I thought I stood a chance of breaking five hours, so when Cindy met me at the 15-mile mark on her bicycle, I had averaged a robust 7:15 pace per (hilly!) mile. Great news, except for one thing: I had literally hit the wall. To make matters worse, I still had a full 26.2 miles (marathon distance) left. For those of you who have hit the wall at the 20-mile mark of a standard marathon, imagine having an entire (hilly!) marathon left at that point. It was nothing less than horrific.

2000 JFK 50-Mile (actually 50.2 miles) Run

The gentleman providing the preface instructions stated that the first three miles were on an asphalt road, but once you hit the Appalachian Trail (AT) in the fourth mile, you were facing 13 miles of single-lane trail, so it was best to be in the position you wanted to be in at that point. Since I wanted to be near the front (a side-effect of my chronic PA) when I hit the trail, I sprinted from the starting line. Mission accomplished. When I entered the trail, I was almost in the top 20! However, there was just one slight problem I had to contend with: I can't run trails. I hopped off the trail countless times to allow faster (trail) runners to pass, and when I left the AT, I was holding on for dear life. The next 26 miles of the course (there's that distance again!) followed a towpath along the Potomac River. Again, I was running marathon distance after hitting the wall yet again. Only this time, after these 26 miles, I still had eight miles left on treacherous, rolling blacktop country roads. I also must mention the roads are open to traffic, and there are no shoulders on the road. This one took *horrific* to the next level.

2004 Western States Endurance 100-Mile (actually 100.2 miles) Run

At the pre-race meeting, I was advised by another runner that the course was "runnable." My initial, sensible goal of finishing within the 30-hour time limit was now a distant memory, as I had bigger fish to fry; namely, breaking 24 hours. After all, the axiom everyone was preaching was that you add four or five hours to your fastest 100-miler on roads and that would be a good indicator of your Western States finishing time. So adding five hours to my 100-mile best of 18:23, I figured a sub-24 was in the bag. I started off wisely by walking briskly to the top of the Escarpment (just over 4 ½ miles into the race). Then *sensible* and *wise* turned into *irrational and what-the-hell-are-you-thinking,* as I took off like I was running the last couple of miles in a marathon. Hell, make that a 5K. Only this time, I still had over 95 miles left. By the time I reached the Last Chance checkpoint at 43 miles, my knees were in more pain than I ever thought possible. When I met up with my pacer at the Foresthill checkpoint at 62 miles, I had no other choice but to throw in the towel, seeing as my knees were holding a gun to my head.

Western States, June 2004

Over time, I've learned to live and cope with my PA. Part of that is because the years have taken their toll on my body and, maybe to a lesser degree, my psyche as well. "Starting with a vengeance" has been relegated to memory status. Unfortunately, "finishing with a whimper" is still very much alive and well.

* * *

41
CHAPTER

THE MORNING AFTER

For a streak runner like me, participating in races of 100 miles or longer allows me to kill two birds with one stone. That is to say, the final stages of running 100 miles or more ordinarily occurs after midnight, so any miles I run from that point on counts as a new day, thus continuing my streak of running every day. Once I complete the race—whether it be a 100-miler or longer or a 24-hour event—I am free to enjoy the balance of that second day for what amounts to be a day off for me. It really feels great if I'm able to complete the race in the wee hours of the second day, because following a short nap (remember, 5 ½ hours of sleep for me constitutes a full night's sleep), I have the rest of the day to mow the lawn, wash the car, clean the…oh, never mind.

Back to what I was saying earlier, let's say I were to start a 100-mile race at 6:00 a.m. on a Saturday morning and complete the race at 2:00 a.m. Sunday morning. The rest of Sunday would feel like an off day for me, even though I have already met the requirements of continuing my streak by putting in a few miles between midnight and 2:00 a.m. on Sunday (at the conclusion of a 100-mile race, this could mean a distance somewhere between 8 and 12 miles).

However, there is always the run the next day: the dreaded *morning after*.

I reviewed my running logs to take a walk (crawl?) down memory lane and remember my first 10 mornings after:

September 19, 1988: A three-mile run the morning (actually it was the following afternoon at 4:30 p.m.) after running 101 miles in the 24-Hour Championship in Atlanta.

Comment: *Of all of my 10 morning-after runs, this one had the longest elapsed time from the finish of the race to the start of my morning-after run: 35 hours and 54 minutes.*

September 16, 2002: A three-mile run the morning (again, actually 2:00 p.m. the following afternoon) after running 129 miles in the 24-Hour Championship in Ohio.

Comment: *I was on Cloud Nine after the race as I had won the National Masters Championship. I felt really good after the race and only ran three miles the next day to reward myself. However, I could have easily run 30 miles: I felt that good! (Note: This was the exception; I would not have this feeling ever again.)*

July 24, 2003: A three-mile run the morning after completing the 135-mile Badwater Ultramarathon in California.

Comment: *I finished Badwater at 10:32 p.m. on a Wednesday night. At 9:00 a.m. Thursday morning, Paula May, my crew chief, woke me up by banging on my hotel room door. As I opened the door, she handed me two bottles of water and said, "'Drink these and put on your shoes; we're going running." One of my more memorable morning-after runs, as Paula and three other members of my crew accompanied me. By running a mere 11 hours and 13 minutes after crossing the finish line on Mount Whitney, it was my shortest recovery time. I have to wonder if anyone who has finished Badwater was running again that soon.*

September 14, 2003: A five-and-a-half-mile run the morning after completing the 100-Mile Championship in Ohio (in a personal best of 18:23).

Comment: *I obviously felt pretty good after the race, as I ran 73-plus miles in the seven days following the race. Of course I hadn't turned 50 yet.*

November 8, 2004: A three-mile run the morning after running 111 miles in a 24-hour event in California.

September 12, 2005: An eight-and-a-half mile run the morning after completing the 100-Mile Championship in Ohio.

Comment: *Again, I felt pretty good after the race and ran 75-plus miles in the seven days following the race. To this day, eight-and-a-half miles remain my longest morning-after run.*

November 14, 2005: A three-mile run the morning after running 114 miles in a 24-hour event in California.

Comment: *One of my shorter recovery times—17 hours and 25 minutes. I had to complete my morning-after run at 3:25 a.m. to catch an early flight back to Atlanta.*

June 26, 2006: A three-and-a-half mile run the morning after completing the Western States Endurance Run in California.

Comment: *Another short recovery—17 hours and 33 minutes. A 4:50 a.m. morning-after run to catch an early flight to Atlanta. The morning AFTER the morning-after run, I was stopped by a Peachtree City policeman who thought I was intoxicated: I was hobbling (and wobbling) on the side of the road at 4:30 a.m. in the morning wearing a polo shirt, khaki shorts, (running) sandals, and socks. So in the policeman's defense, it was impossible NOT to think I was intoxicated.*

April 7, 2008: A four-mile run the morning after completing a 100-mile event in North Carolina.

August 25, 2008: A three-mile run the morning after completing a 100-mile event in South Dakota.

Comment: *My earliest morning-after run ever: 2:25 a.m. in Rapid City (again, an early flight to Atlanta). This run was so ugly that if the Peachtree City policeman had seen me, he would have locked me up, no questions asked. Actually, I was hurting so badly for days after finishing Lean Horse, I ran for two weeks in Peachtree City constantly looking over my shoulder in case a police car was headed my way.*

Josh and Scott crossing Death Valley, July 2003

Oddly enough my two toughest morning-after runs followed races of less than 100 miles.

The first? After finishing the JFK 50-Mile Run in 2000 (my first foray into trail running), my thighs and feet were trashed. The morning after, I literally hobbled three miles in 33 minutes before my return flight to Atlanta. When I got home, I thought that the pain in my legs had surely subsided so I put on my running shoes and proceeded to *attempt* to run (but actually hobbled) another three miles. Again, in 33 minutes. And I was dead wrong about the pain in my legs having subsided.

The second was the morning after dropping out of the 2004 Western States Endurance Run (my first real foray into *100-mile* trail running), as my knees were battered to a pulp and every step reminded me of how painful it must be to get hit in the kneecap with a hammer. After returning to the Placer High School track to watch the final finishers of the race, Al Barker (who had also dropped out of the race) joined me for my morning-after run. We tried to run on the streets of Auburn but found every undulation in the asphalt caused excruciating pain in our legs. So we finished our run on the rubberized track and somehow had the resolve to complete 12 laps while watching local legend Tim Twietmeyer help the volunteers clean up after the race—a mere eight hours after he completed the difficult 100 miles from Squaw Valley to Auburn in less than 24 hours.

Ouch.

* * *

42
CHAPTER

THE MAGIC POTION
THAT IS...BEER

Do you ever get tired of the same old fluids that are served up by race directors with absolutely no imagination or no clue what it's like to drink Gatorade, POWERADE, and water race after race after race? Let me tell you, after a while it just gets plain *old!* As I grow older, I'm more likely to run a 50K than a 5K...more likely to run for 24 hours than 24 minutes...more likely, well...to drink *BEER* than drink water while I'm running.

Sound strange? Keep reading.

I think it first dawned on me in 2003 when I was experimenting with fluids in preparation for Badwater later in the year. I had my usual lineup of fluids (I was experimenting with how *much* to drink, not *what* to drink): water, Gatorade, Diet Coke, and Diet Mountain Dew. After six hours or so, I was absolutely sickened with the thought of drinking anything sweet or anything with no flavor. Surely there was something else out there that could take the place of these fluids; something that would kill the sweet. Unfortunately, I didn't make the discovery until 2004.

At an eight-hour run in August of that year, I put a couple of Coors Lights (my beer of choice) in my cooler to enjoy after the event. However, after running for about six hours, I was looking, once again, for something to kill the sweet. I saw a can of Coors Light peering through the now melting ice, and right then it dawned on me: Something to kill the sweet! Why not? What's the worst that could happen? Disqualification? Intoxication? Either way, it was better than the nausea that was taking over. Besides, how much harm could one little sip of beer do? None, I found out. In fact, further "research" showed that as many as *12* little sips didn't hurt. In fact, I owe the successful completion of the event to my new discovery...my new long distance magic potion: beer.

Later that year, I found myself running in the 24-Hour Championships in San Diego. Naturally, I had plenty of Coors Light (along with my usual lineup of fluids, which now included the mystical Red Bull as well) in my cooler. Somewhere during the wee hours of the event (around 2:00 a.m., if I recall correctly), a man who I met at Badwater in 2003, Bill Lockton, approached me and asked me what he could do to combat his nausea. I told him of my newfound discovery, and he was instantly game—anything to kill the sweet. I showed him my cooler, told him to sit in my chair (the course was a one-mile loop, so runners had access to their support stations every mile), and I would catch him on my next lap to see how he was doing.

After my next lap, I found that Bill was doing just fine. In fact, Bill continued to do fine for my next lap...and the next...and the next. Finally on my fifth time around since Bill had popped open that first can of beer, I found my chair empty—which is how I found three cans of beer. *Empty!* Apparently, Bill had taken quite a liking to my choice of beverage.

However, after spending the next five or six laps looking for Bill on the course, I discovered that he had dropped out of the race at exactly the point on the course where I had last seen him. My chair. Apparently, my magic potion isn't for everyone. Then again, the most I've ever consumed during the course of an event was two beers.

Until July of 2005.

At the world-famous Peachtree Road Race that year, after running it to the best of my ability for 26 years in a row, I decided that I would take it easy for a change. In fact, I called it a "beer run." It wasn't difficult to round up others for my event. Paula May, Eric Huguelet, Susan Lance, Billie Sloss (Paula's sister), and her boyfriend Bob— they all wanted to participate. We each wore our official race number as well as handmade bibs with captions such as "will run for beer" and "only here for the beer." Our goal: to consume as much beer as possible without spending a dime during the course of the race. We all lined up in Alex Huguelet's (Paula and Eric's daughter) time group corral and took off as one in search of the magic potion.

It only took a mile until I spotted a portable bar on the left side of the road. After zig-zagging through several dozen runners, I found my way to the side and bellied up (literally) to the bar. I was surprised to find all six of my beermates had found their way to the bar as well. Actually, I was more surprised we didn't knock over any other runners while we were veering off the straightaway that is Peachtree Street. The bartender offered us an entire pitcher, but since no one was willing to carry it, we each (except for Alex, Mom!) took one 16-ounce plastic cup of the golden elixir and continued with our event.

Beer Run Peachtree Road Race 2005

Over the next 5-plus miles, we managed to find beer four more times along the course. Where? Well, not at any of the official aid stations along the course but from the coolers of fans watching the race and doing what most people do at 7:45 a.m. on the 4th of July if they're not running: drinking beer. I noticed our pace for beer miles was approximately 9:15 per mile, while our pace for non-beer miles was around 8:20. After 60 ounces (granted, I did drink a lot of foam—all that running really shakes up a beer), I was surprised to discover that (a) the pain in my legs that I had experienced for the last four months was gone, and (b) I crossed the finish line in under 55 minutes (55 minutes is the unofficial time to beat to earn a T-shirt...according to legend, anyway).

While I didn't set any personal bests at Peachtree, I did manage to catch a buzz well before 8:00 a.m. After a typical Peachtree (where I run hard), the buzz doesn't normally occur until about 8:20. So, I guess I did set a personal best after all.

However, this personal best lasted for a total of two months. At the Labor Day 5K in Macon, I managed to beat my previous best by a good 15 minutes, as the race started at 7:15 a.m., I finished at 7:34 a.m., and the beer started flowing immediately afterward. Good times. And Paula, Billie, Bob, and Al Barker were all there to share in them.

Whether it is during or immediately after a race, you can't go wrong with an ice-cold beer.

I would be remiss if I didn't mention one last discovery I've made in this discussion of the finer points of running and beer.

After running the 100-Mile Championships in Ohio in September of 2005—during the competition I was sipping on a Coors Light throughout the wee hours of the morning. In fact, Susan and I were caught by an official of the event and asked "is that a *beer* you're drinking?" I guess my reply of "absolutely" caught him off guard, as we were allowed to finish the race. However, I digress.

After the race, we (Susan, Al, Gary Griffin, and his wife Peg who served as our one-woman support crew) went back to the hotel for a shower and a nap. Later in the evening, we went to dinner, where I drank two large Coors Lights on draft. Quickly. (I was pretty dehydrated.) When we returned to the hotel, I discovered I still had two Coors Lights left in the cooler. Better yet, Peg (a self-proclaimed beer snob) had three bottles of her Labatt's Blue left. So, faced with the dilemma of it getting to be late in the day, an early wake-up call scheduled for the next morning, and the possibility of wasting five perfectly good beers, what did Peg and I decide to do? Drink the beer! Once they were gone (45 minutes later), Peg suggested I buy some more.

This is where my latest discovery comes into play. I've discovered that (a) if you run for an extraordinarily long amount of time and (b) become dehydrated while doing so, you can (c) drink as much beer as possible (i.e., without drowning yourself) and not become inebriated.

Try it for yourself if you don't believe me. (By the way, milk works to kill the sweet as well, which, if you drink too much of it, you most certainly will not become inebriated. Lactose intolerant? Stick with the beer.)

***

43
CHAPTER

TO SACRIFICE SPEED

In mid-2002, when I set my sights on completing the 2003 Badwater Ultramarathon, I knew that by converting my training program entirely to ultramarathoning, I would be sacrificing not only a great bit of what little free time I had, but also any semblance of *speed* I had as well. About three years after reaching Badwater's finish line at the portals of Mount Whitney and realizing I was right on both counts, I had to ask myself: Was it worth it?

I had experienced two wake-up calls recently. The first was when I looked back over my last 27 marathons (dating back to October 2002) and noticed that I had written in my running log that I had paced another runner(s) in 24 of them. The reference to pacing wasn't like the days of yore (in the 90s) when I was pacing fellow runners to Boston Marathon qualifying times in the 3:05-3:30 range. Theses were more like long training runs with paces ranging from eight to nine minutes per mile; it just so happens that one (or more) of my training partners ran the marathon with me.

The second wake-up call was when a fellow runner who had just qualified for Boston (without my pacing experience) asked me if I was going to run Boston with her in 2006. I told her (a) I didn't think I had a qualifying time, and (b) I wasn't even sure what my qualifying time was. Given my love of the Boston Marathon, you would have thought I was kidding in point b. I wasn't. I did look it up, however, and found that I needed a 3:35 or better to qualify. As for point a, I actually did have a qualifier (Atlanta, November 2004), but that is irrelevant to this story.

Following these two wake-up calls, I decided I would run marathons on four consecutive weekends (beginning with Callaway Gardens Marathon on January 29, 2006) with a goal of qualifying for Boston in all of them. A secondary goal was to break 3:30 each time, and a third goal was to run a faster time each successive week.

I realize that 10 years prior, being unable to qualify for Boston never crossed my mind. It was automatic, so much that I took it for granted. At that time, I'm fairly sure I could have run qualifiers on four consecutive *days*. But as the saying goes, that was then, and this is now, and in a world of what have you done for me lately, it was certainly time to see what—if anything—I had left.

Callaway Gardens Marathon, January 29. I ran a cautious 3:29, so I met my first two goals (qualifying first and breaking 3:30 second). . Finishing 6th overall and winning my age group was a pleasant surprise.

Flashback: Callaway Gardens Marathon, 1999. I paced Nancy Stewart to a 3:10, which qualified her for Boston for the first time, even though in the last three miles of the race, Nancy had to walk occasionally for a total of about seven or eight minutes. Three months later, Nancy was a member of the women's team champion Atlanta Track Club at the 1999 Boston Marathon.

Tybee Island Marathon, February 4. I ran a fairly even pace toward a finishing time of 3:24, achieving all three of my goals (qualifying, breaking 3:30, faster than previous week).

Flashback: Tybee Island Marathon, 1999. I ran my only sub-three hour Tybee in 2:59, winning the men's Masters Championship.

Flashback: Tybee Island Marathon, 2002. I ran a 3:08, drove back to Peachtree City after the race, and then drove to Callaway Gardens the next morning to run another marathon. I met future Badwater crew member —and good friend—Gary Griffin around the four-mile mark at Callaway, and we ran together the last 22 miles, finishing in 3:22.

Mercedes Marathon, February 12. I ran a solid pace in extremely cold, windy conditions on a hilly course (forcing me to walk for almost a minute around the 20-mile mark) and finished in 3:26. I met my first two goals, although I failed to lower my time from the previous week.

Flashback: Vulcan Marathon (the forerunner of the Mercedes), 1994. My (then 9-year-old) son Josh paced me on his bicycle. I ran a comfortable 3:08 and had to push Josh up two hills toward the end of the race—a total of about 1 ½ miles. To this day, it remains my fondest marathon memory and was the very first time I won an award in a marathon. Correction: It was the very first time we won an award in a marathon.

Flashback: Vulcan Marathon, 1999. I ran a 3:05 and successfully defended the men's Masters Championship I had won in 1998 (3:02).

Five Points of Life Marathon, February 19. I ran the best of the four marathons in my favorite city on earth—Gainesville, Florida—finishing in 3:18. Despite finishing 20th overall, I was relegated to a 3rd-place finish in my (apparently pretty competitive) age group. I met all three goals and was pleased to run my fastest time of the four marathons in front of the home crowd in Gainesville.

Flashback: Florida Relays Marathon, 1979. I ran my first marathon in Gainesville, Florida. My graduate school professor and mentor, Tom Saine, met me at the 18-mile mark to pace me to the finish. When we met, my pace was just under eight minutes per mile. I held on to run the last eight miles at just under 10 minutes per mile, finishing in 3:44. Considering I had only been racing for four months, I was satisfied with the time.

In summary, I realized my conversion to training strictly for marathons and ultramarathons would have its consequences, primarily the sacrifice of what little speed I had left. I also realized there were other factors at work which support my conversion to the long, slow stuff:

- My age (at that time 51), which has caused me to realize the theorem that runners lose 1 percent of their speed per year after age 40 may be an understatement. (In my case, a *gross* understatement.)

Western States, June 2006

- 27-plus years of running every day had taken its toll on my body, especially the human shock absorbers non-runners refer to as knees.

- 101,000-plus lifetime miles, which had not only taken its toll on my body, but also in the sacrifice of countless hours of sleep needed to complete them. Sweet, precious sleep. (I live by the old adage: I'll sleep when I'm dead).

You may ask if I have any regrets.

The week after the Five Points of Life Marathon, I ran the Silver Comet Ultrarun 50K and finished 4th overall in a time of 3:57—my fastest 50K in over seven years and a Georgia state age group record (which still exists, by the way).

Referring back to the very first paragraph, which asked, was it worth it?

I wouldn't have it any other way.

***

GRIZZLED WISDOM

Some of you may have been looking for running advice in these pages. Please know that it's never been a practice of mine to dole out unsolicited advice: To each his own is the best advice I have to offer. Perhaps you can find some things I've tried that might work for you. Perhaps not. I have learned that you are the best judge of what works best for you: Your best coach is YOU!

I will, however, leave you with 15 pearls of wisdom I've managed to pick up over the years. Please don't expect to read the generic advice (do speed work, rest, drink, etc.) you're likely to find in virtually every training book ever written; you won't find it here. It always amazes me how the simple, basic advice virtually every training book offers is somehow stretched into 200 pages or more.

So, speaking purely from experience, here goes:

1. When it comes to running a marathon or an ultra, don't put all your eggs in one basket. Face it, some days you're just not going to have your A game. It's one thing to gut out a 5K or 10K when you're not at your best; a marathon or an ultra is a different story. So on those days that you're not at your best, just take it easy and enjoy the ride, and remember that tomorrow is another day.

2. Be very wary of running inaugural races, particularly marathons. I've been to many that—for a variety of reasons—weren't around to celebrate their second annual event. It's best to select races that have proven themselves; let someone else be the guinea pig for anything that promotes itself as an "inaugural event." Later, let others tell you all about it.

3. Remember, when you're outside after running one mile, the temperature will feel 20 degrees higher than it actually is. Dress—and run—accordingly.

4. Find running shoes that are comfortable and work for you, and then look for them when they become year-end closeouts or discontinued models. Then, buy as many pairs as your budget allows. As for those who would tell you that running shoes have a shelf life, and it's not wise to stock up on shoes...well, those people are the ones who make a living selling running shoes. You be the judge.

5. On a training run, you should be able to hold a conversation and smile. If you can't do both, you're overdoing it.

6. When it comes to running a marathon or longer, there is absolutely no training substitute for mileage. None.

7. However, training runs on hills is a viable substitute for speed work.

A SPECIAL RACE

Scott travelled to South Africa this year with his friend and running partner Susan Lance to run the Comrades for the first time. They ran it together, finishing in 10:35 and enjoyed every minute. Interviewed just before the race, they said they loved the atmosphere in Durban and felt like celebrities, but what amazed them most was the amount of people running an ultra-marathon. "In the USA, the ultra community is really small. You can run an ultra pretty much anywhere in the country and know almost everyone in the field – it's like a little reunion every time. Here you have thousands of people running! I've heard running the Comrades is one of the greatest things in the world to do and a member of our club said it was the best thing he's ever done. I don't know what to expect in terms of crowd support or how bad the hills are, but I just want to finish and enjoy the sights and the experience," said Scott.

So why do the Comrades now, after 33 years of running? Scott said he always knew about the Comrades and wanted to do it since forever, but he saved it for a special occasion. His 50th and most probably last ultra-marathon. "The Comrades may not be the longest or the hardest ultra in the world, but it has a reputation in the USA for being the most prestigious. I've done much harder races, like the Western States 100 miler and the Badwater Marathon, but this was the last thing on my bucket list. I wish I ran it in the late 90s when I was running really well and fast, because then I would have aimed for a seven or eight-hour finish, but I just want to finish it now. All the other goals, like reaching 200 000 miles and getting the longest streak will be nice, but the Comrades I had to do."

After the race, Scott sent an e-mail from the USA where he simply said the race was tough, but amazing. He loved meeting Zola Pieterse at the expo, and the Castle Light tasted really good afterwards. Seems like most runners' feelings towards Comrades are pretty much universal.

A STREAK OF WHAT?

For more information on the Darkside Running Club, or if you want to join the club, visit their website at www.darksiderunningclub.com.

// All the other goals, like reaching 200 000 miles and getting the longest streak will be nice, but the Comrades I had to do. //

Comrades

8. If you have trouble finding time to get in your daily run, do it first thing in the morning. If you hate getting out of bed earlier than normal, never underestimate the power of caffeine.

9. In races of marathon distance or less, 9 out of 10 runners tend to be competitive, and they are out to do anything in their power to beat you. In races longer than a marathon, 9 out of 10 runners tend to value camaraderie and seeing others succeed and in most cases will do anything in their power to make sure both of you make it to the finish line.

10. In marathons, the wall you may hit will be physiological. In ultras, the wall you hit (and you will hit it!) will be psychological.

11. You will get the best running advice from ultramarathon veterans.

12. If you are capable of running a marathon, you are capable of completing an ultra.

13. In ultras of 50 miles or longer, once you've had your fill of electrolyte replacement drinks, water and soda, try beer. It's anti-sweet' flavor will hit the spot and alleviate some of the nausea. (Note: Milk is a viable substitute as well.)

14. Good running books, movies, and magazines are a great motivator. *(Hopefully you found this book to be a good example!)*

15. Never take your ability to run for granted. Never. Consider your ability to run as a gift. Because it most certainly is.

* * *

45 CHAPTER

IS THERE AN ULTRA IN YOUR FUTURE?

If You've Run a Marathon,
Then You're Ready for the Next Step (or Two)!

"If you can run a marathon, then you can run an ultra."

Every runner who has endured the time and effort required to complete a race of 26.2 miles has heard this at one time or another. If not, it's only a matter of time before they do. *(See—you just heard it from me, so I was right!)*

And it's true…so very true. By definition, a race of any distance over 26.2 miles is classified as an ultra. The most common and recommended next step is 50 kilometers, which is a shade over 31 miles. (Although some have been known to jump from 26.2 to 50 miles or farther; in fact some have been known to run ultras before they've ever completed a marathon. Crazy, right? Not really. Read on.)

Perhaps I can shed a little light on the allure of the ultra.

- A true marathon of 26.2 miles is considered, for the most part, a race. Anything over that distance is considered an endurance run. To finish an ultra with the same body and mind that you started with is one of the many measures of success in an ultra. Taking it a step further: *Simply finishing* is the ultimate measure of success in an ultra.

- It is very acceptable—and highly recommended—to eat and drink as much as you need/want/crave during an ultra. Unlike a marathon, you should feel no guilt if you stop running at any time to replenish. Stopping to rest is permissible as well. Or to answer the call of nature. Often, in many cases.

- Speaking of running, should you walk during an ultra, remember that this is the *norm*, not the *exception*. Again, no guilt necessary should you have to stop running or feel a need to walk for any reason. In fact, in the latter stages of some ultras, the simple act of walking is a challenge.

- Talking to other competitors is highly encouraged. Actually, anything you can do to keep your mind occupied while you cover 30-, 40-, 50-plus miles is highly suggested. Note: In most ultras, the camaraderie is undeniable, and in all honesty, a more appropriate word than *competitor* might be *ally*, if not *future friend for life*.

- Bathroom breaks really don't interfere with your overall time, especially when you calculate your pit-stops-to-miles ratio is only 1 to 15 (OK, those of you who knew me in my hey-day knew my ratio was more like 1 to 4, but I made up for them by trying to eat and run at the same time).
- The cardinal rule of ultrarunning: WALK THE UPHILLS! Where else do you find an athletic event with a recommended strategy such as this (besides perhaps mountain climbing)?
- The competition in an utra is always thinner than in any race of 26.2 miles or less. Of course, *competition* is probably not the correct word. With very few exceptions, participants in an ultra are really not competing but simply trying to get to the finish. By any means necessary.
- Once you complete an ultra, you are ordinarily not as physically exhausted as you would be after running an all-out race of a shorter distance. Speaking from experience, a 5K race took more out of me than a 50K (Note: A pace for a 50K is about 28% slower than a pace for a 5K. If you run a 5K at an 8:00 minute/mile pace, expect to run a 50K slightly slower than a 10:00 pace).[5]
- Success in an ultramarathon is more mind over matter than anything else. Slow- or fast-twitch muscles, carbo-loading, interval and fartlek training, racing flats, negative splits—forget all that. Just lace up your shoes and make sure you have enough to think about for several hours.
- When tackling an ultra, remember one word:

PATIENCE

---

5   Addendum to note: Be advised that this is merely a rule of thumb and is most definitely NOT supported by scientific research. It is merely an educated estimate on my part.

Get used to the idea that you're going to be out there pounding the pavement or the dirt for quite a while. And while you're out there, please make sure to stop and smell the roses. You'll be glad you did.

Where else can you find an athletic event you can be successful at while eating—drinking—walking—talking—even answering nature's call? Where else can you meet the finest people in the world whose dreams and goals mirror yours—the ones all your friends refer to as insane? Where else can you meet like-minded individuals whose focus, dedication, and determination reminds you of your own focus, dedication, and determination? Where else can you get the most amazing feeling of accomplishment and personal achievement?

You know where.

In the fantastic, mesmerizing world of ultrarunning.

By the way, one thing I feel is my duty to warn you about: In an ultra, you are liable to say things you wouldn't ordinarily say around other people (i.e., non-runners) or in other situations (i.e., a non-running situation). Should you speak them, be advised there is a very real possibility that what you say may follow you around for years to come. If you don't believe me, ask Al Barker: People still come up to him all the time and tell him to put them down for a turd.

***

46
CHAPTER

POSTSCRIPT

*I mentioned earlier I was targeting
the 2012 Honolulu Marathon as my 200th marathon.
I wouldn't want to leave you in suspense…*

Aloha Also Means Goodbye

The Honolulu Marathon, December 2012

March 3, 1979. Cindy, my bride of less than two years, kissed me for good luck as I ventured out into the streets of Gainesville, Florida to tackle my very first marathon.

December 9, 2012. Cindy, my wife of over 35 years, gave me a congratulatory kiss moments after I crossed the finish line in Honolulu, Hawaii as I finished my 200th marathon.

It's been a great run, literally and figuratively. I've been fortunate to have run the fabled Boston Marathon 12 times. I've run through the Brandenburg Gate on my way to finishing the Berlin Marathon. I've run my all-time favorite marathon, the Atlanta Marathon (the Thanksgiving Day version; sadly, it no longer exists) 27 times. I feel blessed to have completed every marathon I've ever started. I ran 10 Shamrock Marathons (Virginia Beach, Virginia), as much a reason to visit my parents as a reason to run a marathon. I was Master's Champion at the Vulcan Marathon (Birmingham, Alabama). Twice. I've lost track of how many inaugural marathons I've run (some of them didn't survive, while others have flourished). I ran New York City and Chicago when the field was only (only!) 20,000 runners.

I set my sights on the 2012 Honolulu Marathon as my 200th marathon as early as 2010. In late 2011, I realized I would have to run an aggressive schedule of marathons in 2012 in order to complete #200 on December 9. To begin the year, I ran 11 marathons in a 13-week window. I optimistically registered for the Honolulu

Marathon early in the year and was lucky enough to get an early-bird registration of only $40. The trip to Honolulu was going to be a surprise 35th wedding anniversary present (which she would find out about on June 18) for Cindy and me. Virtually everyone I knew was aware of the impending trip; in fact, I wrote about it in my running club's quarterly newsletter, a monthly online column I write for a running magazine and on my running club's Facebook site. In all instances, I would mention "It's a surprise wedding anniversary trip for Cindy, so don't mention it." No one did.

But Scott, you said it was going to be a surprise! What if Cindy read about it and found out?

I appreciate your concern, but if there's one thing I've come to realize, it's that Cindy doesn't read much of what I write. Granted, she did read my first book...two-and-a-half years after it was published. But I knew there was no way she would read anything I wrote in 2012 *in* 2012. I was absolutely right. When Cindy learned about the trip on our anniversary, it came as a complete surprise, although in my circle of friends, it had been common knowledge for well over six months.

You may be wondering why I chose Honolulu for #200? My dad, an officer in the U.S. Navy, was stationed in Pearl Harbor from 1967 to 1970, and in all honesty, it was the best assignment my dad—and our family—ever had. I learned to play golf in Hawaii (thank you Navy-Marine Golf Course). I was in the inaugural class of Moanalua Intermediate School in Hawaii (go Mustangs!). Our family lived in the greatest military housing in Hawaii (Radford Terrace). *Hawaii 5-0* (the Jack Lord version) and *Tora! Tora! Tora!* were filmed in Hawaii while we were stationed there. I learned to walk barefoot—*everywhere*—and eat Li Hing Mui (salty dried plums soaked in salt, sugar, and licorice—pretty frightening, huh?) in Hawaii. I kissed a girl for the very first time in Hawaii.

So more than 42 years later, I returned to the scene of the best assignment our family ever had. The Thursday before the race, Cindy and I endured a 10-hour flight (thankfully, *direct* from Atlanta to Honolulu) and upon landing on the island of Oahu, Cindy immediately looked for a restroom in the terminal. I told her to look for a door with *wahine* (woman in Hawaiian) on it. Oddly, I hadn't spoken or even remotely thought of that word in 42 years.

We then rented our Ford Mustang (a red convertible!) and drove in Honolulu rush hour traffic (wow—it wasn't anything like that 42 years ago) to our hotel. The next morning (Friday), we went to the Honolulu Marathon Expo, which was like any other with one major difference: virtually everyone was Japanese. I was a definite and dare I say *distinct* minority. Cindy decided to enter the 10K race walk to be held in conjunction with the marathon. Her entry fee? $70! (So much for the money-saving early-bird marathon registration!) I figured it was worth it: Cindy would enjoy a walking tour of Waikiki, and since both our races shared the same finish line, she would be there to see me as I completed marathon #200.

We went to the pre-race luau that night where—for the "bargain" early-bird fee of $54 each—had a meal eerily reminiscent of the lunches I ate at Moanalua Intermediate many years ago. The entertainment? The good news: It was exactly what the audience wanted. The bad news: The audience was predominately Japanese, and their idea and my idea of entertainment are worlds apart. (The host? Remember the lounge lizard entertainer Bill Murray portrayed on the old *Saturday Night Live* episodes? His brother.)

After the luau, we stayed on the beach to watch the Pearl Harbor Memorial Parade (it happened to be December 7, which I haven't mentioned yet). The highlight of the parade was seeing the Pearl Harbor survivors—all of them heroes and all of them beaming with pride. The lowlight? A Japanese woman in her 40s asking me what the parade was for. Me: To honor Pearl Harbor. Her: What happened at Pearl Harbor. Me: It was attacked on this day 71 years ago. Her: Attacked? By whom? (At least her grammar was good.) Me: *The Japanese!* (I couldn't help it; I stayed PC as long as I could.)

Saturday we took a drive to the north shore and encountered considerable traffic on the two-lane road as there was a surfing competition going on at the infamous Banzai Pipeline. We had a great lunch at the artsy-hippie village of Haleiwa, vowing to return later during our vacation when we had more time (translation: When I didn't have to get back to the hotel to rest up for the marathon). Once we got back to the room, I laid out my running gear and noticed the screen of my chronograph was blank; the battery had apparently died. Cindy and I made a quick trip to a drug store at the Ala Moana Mall where I bought a battery and borrowed a watch tool (from the counter clerk) and a pair of reading glasses (right off the rack) and replaced the battery. The chronograph was as good as new, and after setting a 3:00 a.m. wake-up call (the race would start at 5:00 a.m. the next morning), I was fast asleep by 9:00 p.m. Cindy wasn't far behind.

Race morning, I walked to the starting line (a mere 1/3 mile from our hotel) where I lined up in the middle of the three-to-four-hour corral. A fantastic fireworks display began minutes before the start of the race; in fact, the fireworks were still lighting up the sky (and waking up the locals and any tourists who weren't in town to run, which fortunately for the local Tourism Board couldn't have been very many) when the marathon began. As I watched the fireworks, I felt a lump in my throat, partially because I knew how much Cindy enjoyed fireworks (and they *really were* amazing) and she was missing them as her race walk didn't start until 5:25 and partially because I knew it was signaling the start of my very last marathon. Yes, #200 was going to be my finale. My swan song. My farewell. *Sayonora* (for my Japanese readers). *Aloha*.

I started my chronograph as I crossed the starting line and spent the next hour or so dodging other runners, and by other runners, I mean a good many of the Japanese runners who were stopping here, there, and literally *everywhere* to take photographs of the Christmas lights of Waikiki Beach, the historic landmarks of Honolulu and last but not least *of each other*. The aid stations posed another problem: In the dark, the white paper cups discarded on the road looked a lot like the white traffic reflectors, so I made every humanly effort I could muster to avoid stepping on anything white. All I wanted from this marathon was to finish; time was irrelevant. I couldn't afford to twist an ankle, trip and fall, or entangle myself with another runner—anything that would jeopardize me finding that pot of gold at the end of my final 26.2-mile long rainbow.

Once daylight arrived (two hours into the race), I found the course much easier to navigate. I could see the reflectors in the road. The crowd had thinned out. The temperature had only risen seven or eight degrees (keep in mind, however, that the temperature at the start of the race was 70 degrees so by now things were getting pretty toasty). With every nine (10? 11?) minutes, another mile could be checked off.

Then the unthinkable happened. I saw a life-size Scooby-Doo (who happens to star in my grandson Krischan's FAVORITE cartoon), and I knew I just *had* to have a photo of the two of us. So on the only out-and-back section of the entire course, I cut through the crowd running, in the opposite direction *(Ruh Roh)*, took my cell phone out of my waistband (I would later use it to call Cindy when I had one mile left in the marathon), and asked an obliging elderly Japanese gentleman if he would take a photo of my pal Scooby and me (if you can't beat 'em, join 'em). This two-minute drama made me realize two things: (1) I am no longer in any way, shape, or form the serious marathoner I used to be, and (2) I am now more a grandfather than I am a runner. Not that there's anything wrong with either of those revelations.

Almost four-and-a-half hours after the firework display signaling the start of the marathon, I had one mile left and called Cindy. She would be on the right side of the road just before the finish line… which is exactly where I later found her as I was duking it out with a Japanese man dressed in a white swan costume, complete with a two-foot long neck with a tiny swan head on top.

As I approached the finish line, I wondered why I wasn't getting a lump in my throat or sensing that special feeling of pride and accomplishment I normally have when I'm about to finish a marathon. The only thing I felt was anxious; anxious to get it over with.

After completing lifetime marathon #200 (the time is totally irrelevant; better to focus on the 100% marathon completion rate!), I met up with Cindy who gave me a congratulatory hug and kiss and asked me how it felt to finish my final marathon. I told her two things: I was relieved to be at the end of my 34-year journey and embarrassed I had been duking it out with a guy dressed as a swan for the final eight miles of it. Cindy said I would be *more* embarrassed if I had seen some of the other runners who finished in front of me.

Sometimes fate has a funny way of telling you when your time is up.

Less than 30 minutes after finishing the Honolulu Marathon, the face on my chronograph was blank once again.

Like I said, sometimes fate has a funny way of telling you when your time is up.

Marathons are no longer fun. I can no longer run marathons without pain. Sure, in the old days I didn't mind some good old-fashioned *self-inflicted* pain—the kind of pain you can only get from pushing yourself to your anaerobic threshold. But the kind of pain I had been experiencing in marathons wasn't that kind of pain. It was the kind of pain that was telling me I shouldn't be running 26.2 miles any more. Truth be known, I knew it over a year ago, but I've always been good at lying to myself as well as being a numbers guy, and I found 200 to be a nice round number. And from what I can tell, my body and (believe it or not) my mind had been telling me that 200 would signal the end of the marathon road. And I'm good with that.

For the rest of the week, we enjoyed the sights and sounds of Oahu. Pearl Harbor. Punchbowl Cemetery. Diamondhead. We celebrated my 58th birthday the day after the marathon. We returned to Haleiwa (we had more time to spend this time) and the Banzai Pipeline (when there was no surfing competition). We drove to the northeast side of the island and watched the windsurfers at Kane'ohe Bay. We took a trip to the Navy-Marine Golf Course, Moanalua Intermediate, and

Cindy and Scott's Wedding Day, June 1977

Radford Terrace—for old times' sake. We took a dolphin-watching/snorkeling cruise along the southwestern shores of Oahu. We ate Li Hing Mui seeds *(yes, we)*. We celebrated 35 years of marriage. We also celebrated the end of my 34-year marathon career.

March 3, 1979. Cindy, my bride of less than two years, kissed me for good luck as I ventured out into the streets of Gainesville, Florida to tackle my very first marathon.

December 9, 2012. Cindy, my wife of over 35 years, gave me a congratulatory kiss moments after I crossed the finish line in Honolulu, Hawaii as I finished my 200th marathon.

It was only fitting that Cindy, who has been with me every step of the way, was there for the first and last steps of my marathon career.

Sometimes fate has *just the right way* of telling you when your time is up.

***

47
CHAPTER

AFTERWORD

I hope you found this book useful.

Useful in the sense that it inspired or motivated you to reach for the stars…to pursue your goals…to go the extra mile(s).

For you beginners, useful in the sense that it will lead you down the path to running ultramarathons.

For you veterans, useful in the vein that it will take you on the roads and trails you've dreamt about.

I like to think my involvement in the sport of running for the past 34 years has made a difference. I consider myself fortunate. Some of you have told me I have, and for that I am grateful.

My actions—as a runner, volunteer, coach, race director—have spoken well for me over the years. I can only hope my written words will do the same.

As for my running, I'm still doing it every day with one major difference from the days of yore:

The forever pace I mentioned earlier has now become my training pace. It will only be a matter of time before it becomes my race pace.

Whatever the future brings, please know that I've had a good run. A good, long run...

On that note I'm going to say goodbye for now.

I'm exhausted.

* * *

48 CHAPTER

ACKNOWLEDGMENTS

This book would not have been possible without the support, encouragement, and companionship of my training partners who have pushed me farther than I thought possible over the past 35 years. You all know who you are, and if any of you really, really want to know, I can tell each one of you how many miles we've run, walked, and occasionally crawled together. I appreciate all of you more than you will ever know. You have all proven that the loneliness of the long-distance runner doesn't necessarily have to be.

For those of you behind the scenes in the ultrarunning world—the race directors, the medical staff, the lap counters, the aid station attendants—thank you for your support. Without all of you, I would have never been able to complete my running bucket list or tell the tales contained in my running logs.

Stephanie Robinson—once again, it was a great joy having you assist me with the more technical aspects of compiling this book. I hope you'll stick around for the next one.

To my wife Cindy, thanks for putting up with my early bedtimes, my 3:30 a.m. alarms (even though you've always managed to sleep right through them), my running "vacations" as well as my post-running vacation recoveries (some of which proved to be very, very ugly).

Finally, to those of you who supported me in my Big Four: Al Barker, Susan Lance, Paula May, Eric Huguelet, Gary Griffin, Danielle and Bill Goodgion, Gordon Cherr, and my son Josh. I could never have done it without all of you.

* * *

CREDITS

Cover design:	Sabine Groten
Copyediting:	Elizabeth Evans
Layout:	Claudia Sakyi
Typesetting:	www.satzstudio-hilger.de
Chapter graphics:	©Thinkstock/iStock/EpicStockMedia
Cover photo:	Scott Ludwig
Photos:	All photos are from the author's personal collection. The cover photo shows the author in his natural habitat: Exhaustion.